The Conquest
of the
American
West

by the same author

The Second World War
Stories of Famous Sieges
Thomas Morris (editor)
Stonewall Jackson
The Paper Dragon
The Boer War
The Thin Red Line
The Stonewall Brigade
The Iron Brigade
The United States Cavalry
The United States Marine Corps
Shaka's Heirs
Over the Sea to Skye
A Short History of South Africa

The Conquest
of the
American
West

JOHN SELBY

London   George Allen & Unwin Ltd
Ruskin House   Museum Street

First published in 1975

© George Allen & Unwin Ltd. 1975

ISBN 0 04 973008 8

Printed in Great Britain
in 11 point Baskerville type
by the Devonshire Press Ltd.
Barton Road, Torquay, S. Devon

Foreword

'The West', wrote a distinguished Englishman, Lord Bryce, in 1888, 'is the most American part of America.' 'What Europe is to Asia,' he went on, 'what England is to the rest of Europe, what America is to England, that the Western States and Territories are to the Atlantic States.'

So it was in 1888, and so it is today. Through the three hundred years needed to settle the North American continent, those traits that differentiate Americans from their British ancestors have appeared in exaggerated form along the frontiers; there mobility (both spatial and social), wastefulness, materialism, boastfulness, an aggressive nationalism, a fervent belief in democracy and the equality of peoples (excepting, alas, the Red Indians and such minority groups as Mexican Americans and Chinese) have been enshrined in the national character. Where better to study the American variation of genus *homo* than in the successive Wests? Understand the frontiersman and one can understand all Americans by a mere process of dilution.

Through much of the eighteenth century and most of the nineteenth this was realised by the hordes of visitors from Britain who found in the United States a perennial subject of interest in their homeland. They came by the hundreds, pencils in hand, eager to explain to their countrymen why England's unruly progeny had drifted so far from their Mother Country's laudable behavioural patterns, and they found in the West the best source for their inquiries. In magazine article after magazine article, in book after book, they reported their observations: the American frontiersmen, they wrote (and hence all Americans in lesser degree) were a lawless crew, restless, overflowing with energy, crassly materialistic, brashly nationalistic, always on the move, and so disdainful of proper social values that the class distinctions needed to maintain an orderly society were woefully lacking among them. The pioneer, many reported, had sunk far toward barbarism, and was carrying the majority of his fellow-Americans along the road to near-savagery.

Fortunately this picture of the frontiersman, exaggerated though it was, proved to be vastly appealing to British readers. Books that stressed the western scene and glorified violence—books by Thomas Ashe, Basil Hall, Frederick Marryat, Harriet Martineau, Frances Trollope, and dozens more—captured the popular imagination. Through them the American West became a living symbol of the unshackled freedom from society's restraints that has ever been the goal of the romantic on both sides of the Atlantic. Nor has that interest in the 'Wild West' flagged with the passing years. Today paperback thrillers glorifying the cowboy and bad man provide an escape-hatch into a more glamorous world for hundreds of British readers; shoot-'em-up 'Westerns' crowd superior films from television screens or cinema palaces. Today an English 'Society of Westerners' (the term 'Society' is the sole concession to British traditionalism; similar organisations in the United States are known as 'Corrals') allows buffs to meet regularly to argue the quick-draw prowess of 'Wild Bill' Hickock or the defects in Reno's strategy on the Little Big Horn.

This fascination with things Western can create surprising situations—as I once discovered to my sorrow. Some years ago, when lecturing to an extra-mural class at the University of Birmingham made up of the usual assortment of school teachers, retired librarians, and a handful of tradesmen and businessmen, I made the mistake of assuming that no one in the room had the slightest knowledge of things Western. Why not, then, embroider the truth to enliven the subject, even if some of my statements could not be documented? Thus on one occasion when contrasting means of law enforcement on various frontiers I ventured to tell a few tales of the shooting prowess of cattle-town marshals and particularly of Wyatt Earp's feats with a six-shooter. A hand went up. 'The surprising thing is', volunteered one of my audience, 'that Earp could draw that quickly when he was using an unusual type of gun, a Colt Buntline Special .45 with a twenty-one inch barrel.' I retired then and there. When a Birmingham businessman knew far more than I did about frontier bad men, my usefulness as an instructor was over. Perhaps my informant was unusual in his fascination with the American West, but he only exaggerated a national interest. A vast number of Englishmen today thirst for readable information on that land where romance and violence walk hand in hand.

That reading is there, but all too many of the books and films catering to the popular taste sacrifice authenticity for romantic invention. For those who seek a sturdier fare, based on solid research but just as readable as the most outlandish thriller, the publication of this book will provide an opportunity for hours of informative pleasure. For Major John Selby has succeeded in blending historical authenticity with enough blood and thunder to satisfy the most avid 'Western' fan.

He has accomplished this miracle by giving free rein to his own enthusiasms. He has described the expansion of America strictly in his own way. Events that might bulk large in more academic histories (the occupation of the Great Plains 407 million acres by millions of pioneers during the last three decades of the nineteenth century, for example) receive only capsule treatment, just enough to provide continuity without dulling reader interest. His concern is with the colourful and dramatic: with the succession of wars—against the French, Spanish, British, Mexicans, and red Indians—that made expansion possible. These are described in stirring detail; so are some of the more glamorous explorations; Major Selby dwells lovingly on the exploits of Daniel Boone, Meriwether Lewis, and John C. Frémont. A few of the overland treks are meticulously described; that of the Mormons he finds particularly interesting, and with reason. When recounting these tales, and particularly when describing the wars along the borderlands, he relies heavily on documentary sources, sprinkling his narrative with anecdotes and thrilling episodes that bring the past to life.

Here, then, is a book on the American West geared to the demonstrated taste of British readers. Those who like their history in the raw, spiced with bloodshed and flavoured with descriptions that reveal the true character of that most American part of America, will find in the pages that follow a narrative that remarkably blends interest and accuracy, and that sheds light on a drama of conquest unrivalled in the world's history. Read and enjoy.

The Huntington Library,
San Marino, California   Ray Allen Billington

Acknowledgements

I wish to thank Professor Bremner and Dr Cole of Columbus University, Ohio for hospitality, help and advice; also Colonel and Mrs Baldry for hospitality and introductions during my stay at Fort Leavenworth; also Mrs J. Myler of the Texas Research Library at the Alamo, San Antonio for her help. I am indebted to Mr Henry Eide for explaining to me so patiently his descriptive photographic studies of the Oregon and Santa Fé Trails; also to Judge Arthur J. Stanley for allowing me to have photographed some of the old maps of North America in his fine collection at his home at Fort Leavenworth. I wish to thank my son Charles Selby and his wife Darlene for escorting me round the Huntington Library, the Southwest Museum and other places in California, and for providing valuable information on the Mother Lode Country; and also Dr Ray A. Billington, Senior Research Associate of the Huntington Library, Art Gallery and Botanical Gardens of San Marino and author of *Westward Expansion* and *The Far Western Frontier* not only for writing such a splendid foreword but for reading the draft chapters of my book and making valuable comments on them.

Contents

Foreword by Dr Ray A. Billington   *page* 7

Acknowledgements   11

1   The Winning of the Ohio   I   17

2   The Winning of the Ohio   II   36

3   Across the Mississippi   62

4   The Mountain Men   91

5   Over the Rockies with the Mormons   106

6   The Occupation of Texas: The Alamo   123

7   The Conquest of California   146

8   With the Miners to the West   178

9   The Subjugation of the Plains Indians   I: The
    Fetterman Massacre   199

10 The Subjugation of the Plains Indians   II: Custer's
    Last Stand and Wounded Knee   221

11 Conclusion   241

Appendixes   247

Bibliography   251

Index   261

Illustrations

facing page

I   Map of the British Dominions in America, 1763   32
Map of Mexico, California and Texas c. 1850   32

II   George Washington as a young man, by Charles
Willson Peale   33
Daniel Boone by Chester Harding   33

III   General Anthony Wayne by John Trumbull   64
President Thomas Jefferson   64

IV   Meriwether Lewis by Charles Willson Peale   65
William Clark by Charles Willson Peale   65

V   Fort Laramie by A. J. Miller   96

VI   Kit Carson   97
Colonel Custer   97

VII   Panning for Gold   128

VIII   Red Cloud   129
Sitting Bull   129

Maps

1	Early settlements	*page* 18
2	Colonies on the Ohio 1748–63	20
3	Washington's route to the Ohio	22
4	Forts in the Ohio region	37
5	Settlement of Upper Tennessee, Kentucky and Illinois	41
6	Louisiana Purchase: route of Lewis and Clark	71
7	Removal of the Eastern Indians	79
8	The country of the Mountain Men	95
9	The Mormons	111
10	Texas	129
11	The West	152/3
12	Mining areas	185
13	Mother Lode	189
14	Colorado	195
15	The Bozeman Trail	211
16	The Northern Plains	225
17	The three battlefields of Little Big Horn 1876	234
18	The United States	243

Chapter 1

The Winning of the Ohio I

In the years preceding the American Revolution pioneers left the settled seaboard lowlands of the English colonies and began to people the valleys of the Appalachians. They used the trees they felled for their buildings and cultivated as best they could the ground they had cleared. Although relying primarily on themselves and their family, neighbours came together for house-warmings, weddings, competitions and the like, and also to build central forts to protect a community against Indian attack. Pelts normally replaced money as a medium of exchange; a beaver, otter, dressed buckskin or large bearskin being reckoned equal to two foxes, four coons or eight mink. Iron and salt and other commodities which could not be had in the wilds were obtained in exchange for furs sent down to the coast on pack-horses.

Having peopled the mountain area, the next stage was to cross over and settle the wilds beyond. The upper Ohio valley consisted of forest land in the north and the bluegrass region of Kentucky between the Ohio and Cumberland rivers farther south. At some date uncertain historically, the aboriginal Indian tribes had disappeared, and their successors, the Iroquoian-speaking Erie, had later been driven out by the Iroquois confederacy[1] of the Mohawk, Oneida, Onendaga, Cayuga, Seneca and Tuscarora. These nations, whose main territory lay across upper New York westwards from Lake Champlain, became allies of the colonists in 1744. They were traditional enemies of the Iroquoian-speaking Huron further

---

[1] The Six Nations or Five Nations until the Tuscarora joined.

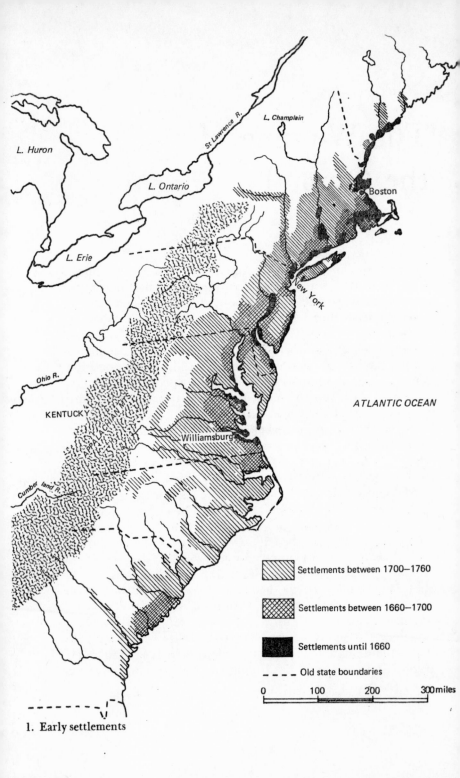

L. Huron

St Lawrence R.

L. Champlain

L. Ontario

L. Erie

Boston

New York

Ohio R.

ATLANTIC OCEAN

KENTUCKY

APPALACHIAN MTS

Williamsburg

Cumberland R.

Settlements between 1700–1760

Settlements between 1660–1700

Settlements until 1660

Old state boundaries

0   100   200   300 miles

1. Early settlements

west who had for long been allied to the French. In the first half of the eighteenth century Algonquian-speaking Delaware and Shawnee had drifted into the Ohio region along with some Seneca, and the former were allowed to remain after they subjected themselves to Half King Tanachariston who was the local Seneca chief and main representative among the Ohio Indians of the Six Nations' ruling body, the Onendaga Council. The English called him Half King because of his dependence on the Council. An enemy of the French, he was ally, adviser, informant, scout and comrade-in-arms of the English.

Some white traders had followed the Delaware and Shawnee from the eastern settlements into the wilderness. They were mostly Pennsylvanians, who reckoned the region part of Penn's woods. They provided the Indians with manufactured goods in exchange for furs, and made a good profit thereby. They were the first whites other than the early explorers to penetrate the region. Inevitably they clashed with the French whose posts stretched round the landward side of the English colonies, from the St Lawrence along the Great Lakes, through Illinois to the Mississippi, and thence to New Orleans. As the Indians tended to side with whoever provided the best goods, a bitter struggle for domination of the Indian trade began. This was intensified when besides the lone traders, merchant companies came to be formed in the English colonies to open up trade and establish settlements in the interior. Among the settlement schemes was one by a group of Scots merchants to establish the colony of Charlotina between the Wabash and Illinois rivers; some New York speculators planned to plant a settlement called New Wales between the Wabash and Ohio; and a New Jersey company sought to convert the lands by the forks of the Ohio into the colony of Pittsylvania. Benjamin Franklin was also active. He planned to create one Pennsylvanian colony north of the middle Ohio, stretching half-way to Lake Erie, and a second by the Ohio Forks in competition with other colonies. The Greenbrier Company sought grants east of the Greenbrier River, and the Ohio Company, the most practical of all, claimed a large area for settlement between the Upper Ohio and the Great Kanawha. Finally in 1763, the Mississippi Company, with George Washington as its principal promoter, purchased a number of grants which had been allotted to soldiers of the colony's militia as war bounties and attempted to establish the Mississippi Company athwart the lower Ohio (see map. 2). The Ohio Company which was formed as early as 1747 had the object of winning the Indian trade and establishing settlers on 500,000 acres of territory

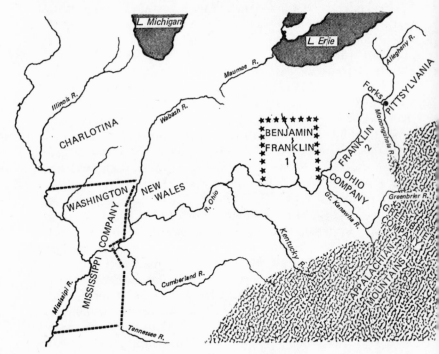

2. Colonies on the Ohio, 1748–63

granted by George II on the understanding that it would be settled within ten years. Among its directors were members of the Virginian Legislature and others including Lawrence and Augustine Washington, older half-brothers of George Washington. In 1750 Lieutenant-Governor Robert Dinwiddie of Virginia became a partner.

In 1749 the French sent a military force to try to win back Indian allegiance and assert French sovereignty in the region. This force ordered the English out of the area, and subsequently made prisoners of traders caught there. Under the orders of Marquis Duquesne, the new Governor of Canada, the French also began to build a string of forts to consolidate their hold. These included Presque Isle on Lake Erie, Le Boeuf twenty-five miles south on French Creek, and Venango thirty miles south again at the junction of French Creek and the Allegheny. They also later erected a fort at the junction of the Allegheny and the Monongahela where the Virginians tried to establish a post (see map 3).

The Pennsylvanian Legislature, dominated by Quaker merchants, had already refused their Governor money to erect a fort on the Ohio, and this resolute French action dissuaded Pennsylvanians from trying to trade and settle in the Ohio valley for the time being, and left the field open to the more persistent Virginians. The Ohio Company obtained a grant from the Mingoes[2] to create a post and establish a settlement in the neighbourhood of Logstown, and in the pursuance of this a Company agent, William Trent, was sent to build a warehouse at the mouth of Redstone Creek on the Monongahela and a Company fort near the Forks of the Ohio. Trent was also given a commission as a captain and authorised to enlist 100 of his fellow traders and frontiersmen and form them into a company of infantry to protect the workmen building the fort until troops could be brought. In 1752 and 1753 the Company had a rough road cut from Wills Creek, where they established a store, north-west to Trent's warehouse at Redstone Creek; and Christopher Gist, a frontiersman employed by the Company, set up a plantation of one family beside his own with some Indians near the Youghiogheny River twenty miles east of the warehouse at the mouth of Redstone Creek. Another place of call for the Company in the Ohio area was Frazier's, a post on Turtle Creek five miles from the Forks, where John Frazier, an Indian trader, had a blacksmith's shop in which he repaired guns and tools for the Indians. His shop had originally been at Venango,

[2] A Seneca tribe.

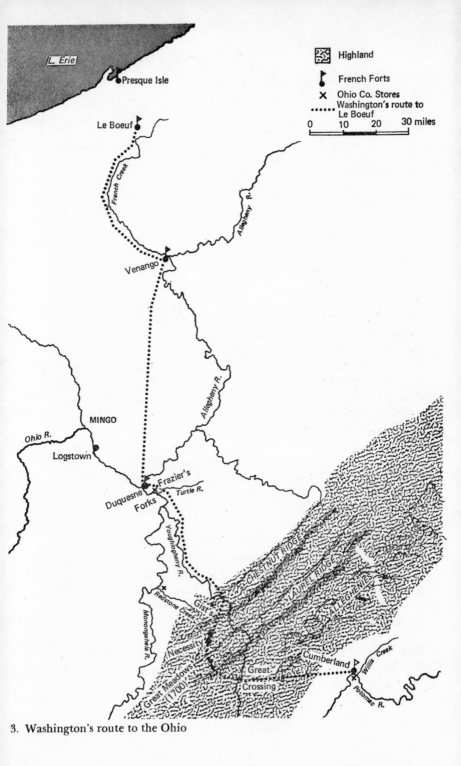

3. Washington's route to the Ohio

at the junction of French Creek and the Allegheny, until he was driven south by the advancing French.

When news reached Virginia that the French were moving south and occupying forcibly the valley of the Ohio to which the Colony believed it had a rightful claim, Robert Dinwiddie, who was doubly involved as Lieutenant-Governor of Virginia and a partner in the Ohio Company, decided to send an official letter of complaint to the Commandant of the French forces on the Ohio; and he entrusted this to George Washington, twenty-one years old and a newly commissioned major of the Virginia Militia. Dinwiddie's letter began:

'The lands upon the River Ohio in the western parts of the colony of Virginia are so notoriously known to be the property of the Crown of Great Britain that it is a matter of equal surprise and concern to me to hear that a body of French forces are erecting fortresses and making settlements upon the river within His Majesty's Dominions. The many and repeated complaints I have received of these acts of hostility lay me under the necessity of sending in the name of the King my master the bearer here of George Washington Esq., one of the Adjutants General of the Forces of this Dominion, to complain to you of the encroachments thus made, and of the injuries done to the subjects of Great Britain in open violation of the Laws of Nations, and the treaties subsisting between the two Crowns . . .'

George Washington assembled at Wills Creek a party consisting of an interpreter, agent Christopher Gist, and four assistants, two of whom were seasoned Indian traders. Across the Potomac from the post at Wills Creek, which was soon to be styled Fort Cumberland, was the new Company storehouse. This consisted of a strong two-storey building of timber and logs, large enough for quarters for the agents. The party set out on 15 November on horseback, with pack-animals bearing their baggage and essentials. They struck west and set about ascending the Alleghenies, reaching an elevation of 3,000 feet before descending and arriving at the Great Crossing of the Youghiogheny between thirty and forty miles west of Wills Creek—as a practised surveyor, Washington made a careful note of heights and distances. From Great Crossing they struck north-west and climbed over the 2,400-foot high Laurel Ridge to reach a plateau approximately 1,700 feet above sea level lying between Laurel Ridge and the next chain of mountains known as Chestnut Ridge. Gist announced that this area was called Great Meadows, and it interested Washington because although boggy in places, it had fewer laural thickets than the country they had so far crossed, and was more suitable for settlement. On Sunday, 18 November, having travelled some seventy miles from Wills Creek, they reached Gist's settlement. Near Gist's they crossed to the east bank of the Youghiogheny. After which they followed the river northward to its junction with the Monongahela, and then on to the mouth of Turtle Creek where was situated Frazier the gunsmith's store. Fortunately the trader was at home, for he had much to tell them. Friendly natives headed by Half King and other Sachems had recently visited him, he said, and left a string of wampum and a message for the Governor of Virginia to the effect that the Indians allied to the French had taken up the hatchet against the English; but General de Marin commanding the French having died, the greater part of the French forces had temporarily withdrawn northward to winter quarters. From Frazier's they passed east of the Ohio Forks where the turbulent Allegheny meets the slow-flowing waters of the Monongahela and Youghiogheny. There, or nearby, Governor Dinwiddie planned to erect a fort to hold back the French advance. Trent was planning to build it north of the Ohio on the route to Logstown; but Washington was soon convinced, having seen both sites, that the land between the forks offered the better position.[3] The men and the baggage crossed the Allegheny River in canoes, while the horses were persuaded to swim the chilly stream. This crossing put them on the right or north bank of the Ohio, down which they could ride to their first objective, the Indian longhouse and huts known as Logstown where Washington hoped to meet Half King.

[3] It was later chosen as the site for the French Fort Duquesne, which became the English Fort Pitt (Pittsburgh).

Half King, whose tribal name was Tanachariston, was then about fifty-three years old. A loyal friend of the English, he expressed at this meeting with Washington resentment at the treatment he had recently received at the hands of General de Marin. When Washington inquired about the best routes to the nearest French fort and asked whether he could provide an escort, the chief not only agreed to do so, but also said he would accompany the party to make his own complaint to the French. He said he would tell the new Commandant what he had said to de Marin, namely, 'This is our land, not yours. If you had come in a peaceable manner like our brothers the English, we should not be against your trading with us as they do; but to come, fathers, and build houses upon our land and to take it by force is what we cannot submit to.'

According to Half King, General de Marin had replied contemptuously, saying, 'I am not afraid of flies or mosquitoes, and Indians are such as those. I tell you, down that river I will go and will build upon it according to my command. If the river was blocked up, I have forces sufficient to burst it open and tread under my feet all that stand in opposition together with their alliances, for my force is as the sand of the seashore. Therefore, here is your wampun! I fling it at you!'

After some delay while the Sachems[4] deliberated on the size of the escort they could provide, the party, together with Half King, finally left with a very small escort on 30 November. After a relatively uneventful march of some fifty miles they approached Venango on 4 December and saw to their chagrin that the fleur-de-lis was already flying above the trading post. The commander was Captain Joncaire, the son of a Seneca squaw by a French officer and one of the shrewdest of the Frenchmen in dealing with Indians. He received Washington's party with the utmost courtesy, but refused to accept the Governor Dinwiddie's letter of complaint and referred them to his superior at Le Boeuf in the north. While at Venango Joncaire used his wiles on Half King who had earlier announced he would deliver back the wampum belt of friendship and warn the French to leave the land. Joncaire

[4] Chiefs.

acted as if the Indians with Washington were the closest of allies and warmest of friends. He gave them presents and plied them with brandy; and he made them so drunk that not only was there no question of telling the French to quit, but Washington found it extremely difficult to persuade them to leave Venango and accompany him to Le Boeuf.

At Le Boeuf Washington was received by Captain St Pierre[5] to whom he presented his letter, asking for an early answer. While the French officers were perusing it, Washington and his companions had time to examine the fort and stockade, to note the nature of the armaments, and to count the number of war canoes in the creek. When he had read the letter, St Pierre suggested that Washington should go to Quebec to present it to the Governor of Canada, but Washington flatly declined, saying his orders were to deliver the letter to the commander on the frontier the French had occupied. St Pierre then agreed to draft a reply, and Washington, having urged Half King to seek an audience to return the treaty belt and make his speech of complaint, planned to leave next day with the French reply. However, the French at Le Boeuf adopted the same attitude towards the Indians as those at Venango. When Half King came back to Washington he had a lame tale to tell. He had undertaken to deliver back the wampum, but St Pierre had been unwilling to accept it. The Frenchman protested that he had great friendship for the Indians over whom Half King held sway. The French wished to trade with the tribes, he said, and as proof of this, would send goods immediately to Logstown. Washington had already heard some French were going downstream. Coupled with what had previously been said about seizing English traders on the Ohio, St Pierre's talk of forwarding goods to Logstown made him suspect that the French were moving south to pick up English traders. In any case his hosts were ready to speed their parting guests. That very evening, a written answer was received to Governor Dinwiddie's letter. Along with the paper was an assurance that canoes laden with provisions would be at Washington's disposal next morning.

But Washington still had the problem of persuading the

[5] Sieur Legardeur de St Pierre de Repentigny.

Indians to accompany him on the return journey. Every blandishment was being offered to keep them from leaving. Particularly great consideration was shown to Half King. There were hints of much pleasure for him and his companions if they remained. It was not cleverly done. The artifice was plain; but defeating it was another matter. Washington said afterwards: 'I can't say that ever in my life I suffered so much anxiety as I did in this affair. I saw that every strategem which the most fruitful brain could invent was practised to win Half King to their interest, and that leaving him behind would give them the opportunity they aimed at.' Washington realised that this was a critical affair on which the continued support of the Six Nations to the English cause might depend. He went straight to Half King and with all the strength of argument at his command tried to prevail on the chief to depart with him. Eventually he succeeded. The Indians reluctantly agreed to accompany the Virginians on their journey to Logstown.

Winter had now set in, and on almost every day they had to endure rain or snow. Eager to get the French reply back as soon as possible, Washington and Gist left the rest of the party with the worn-out horses that could not complete the journey and went forward alone on foot to Frazier's to acquire new mounts. After narrowly escaping being murdered by their sole Indian guide, they next got marooned on an island in the Allegheny River, having failed to cross right over on a raft. After spending a miserably cold night, they woke to find that the frost had frozen the river solid from the shore of their island to the bank that was their goal. Crossing without any sort of trouble, they then walked ten miles and arrived at the hospitable door of John Frazier's cabin. The remaining days of the mission were tedious, but not dangerous. With fresh horses, they made their way back in something like comfort, and arrived at Williamsburg, Virginia precisely one month after they had left Le Boeuf—season considered, a splendid achievement.

Captain St Pierre's reply proved to be a courteous though firm refusal to recognise the English claim. As it was now clear that the French were starting to move down the Ohio valley again, Governor Dinwiddie began energetically organising a force to set up fortresses in the region so that the French advance might be stemmed. At first he tried to raise the Virginia Militia for the task, and after this proved a failure, set about forming a special force of Volunteers, enticing them to enlist with the offer of 200,000 transmontane acres to be divided among them. The bounty was in addition to the daily pay of fifteen pounds of tobacco allowed an infantryman. A colonel's commission and the command of the force was given to Joshua Fry, a Militia officer with frontier experience, and Washington applied for and received the post of Second-in-Command, with a commission in the Virginia Militia as Lieutenant-Colonel. Before the expedition started in 1754 some bad news arrived from the frontier. In view of Washington's comments William Trent had decided to build the Company fort at the Forks instead of on the north bank of the Ohio; but before it was done news came of the advance of a large French force. Only Edward Ward, a brother-in-law of Trent and some forty soldiers were at the Forks at the time, but with the help of Half King and his men a stockade of sorts was set up. It had hardly been completed when a large number of French in canoes arrived on the scene. When the commander told Ward he had an hour to decide whether to surrender or face bombardment, Half King, remembering what Joncaire had done the previous winter, persuaded Ward to say he was not of a rank that gave him authority to answer such a demand, and he asked permission to forward it to Trent. The French would have none of this. Ward must surrender instantly. If he did so he and his men could leave unharmed with all their tools and belongings. Otherwise, the stockade would be stormed. As Ward estimated the French had about 1,000 men while he had only forty-one and a few Indians, he decided he would have to accept these terms. He and Half King, and all the whites and Indians, thus marched out, the chief, still defiant, shouting out as he passed the French that *he* had ordered the fort to be built and laid the first log. The French subsequently erected their own much stronger fort on the site of Ward's, and named it Fort Duquesne.

Meanwhile, Washington at the head of the advanced half of Fry's command had marched slowly with baggage and swivel-guns from Wills Creek, had crossed the Allegheny Mountains, the Youghiogheny River, and Laurel Ridge, and reached the plateau of Great Meadows where he went into camp. Next day Christopher Gist rode in and, after greeting his companion of the mission to Fort Le Boeuf, described how the day before a force of some fifty French had raided his settlement, killed his cow and would have broken up all his belongings; had not the Indians with him persuaded them to forbear. He believed the French had come up the Monongahela, and had left their canoes by the Company store on Redstone Creek.

If the Frenchmen were so far from their landing place, thought Washington, there must be a good chance of cutting them off, and this he immediately planned to do. He was encouraged to proceed when soon afterwards he met up with his ally Half King and some forty Indian followers. Scouts were sent out who located the unsuspecting French, after which the English and Indians advanced silently through the woods to fall on them. Caught by surprise, the enemy sprang to arms, shots were exchanged, and casualties inflicted; but the French were so outnumbered that they could not do much. When an officer was captured, most of them gave ground and made off; and then came running back with uplifted hands. They had seen Indians in the rear, and knowing what would happen at their hands, preferred to surrender to the English. Behind, in fact, came half a dozen Indians braining and scalping the wounded. Half King demanded that the unwounded also be delivered to him, saying he must be avenged on the French who had killed, boiled and eaten his father; but Washington interposed and, with some difficulty, kept Half King from snatching the prisoners. By this time firing had ceased, and when the twenty-one unwounded French survivors had laid down their weapons, they were marched off under guard bound for Virginia. On the ground were ten dead and a wounded man who had somehow escaped the hatchet. Another French soldier had been seen to make off, and one Englishman was dead and three were wounded.

Before advancing against the main French force Washington planned to increase the number of his Indian allies, and he sent off messengers to ask a friendly Sachem settled near Logstown to move up the Monongahela and rendezvous with him at the Company store at the mouth of Redstone Creek. He next marched north and assembled his command—reinforced by an independent company of regulars and now numbering some 300—by Gist's settlement. From Gist's he sent off a body to cut a wagon-road to the Company store on Redstone Creek. But when he heard that a very large French force was moving south against him, seeking revenge for the recent ambush, he abandoned his plan to consolidate at Redstone Creek, called back the road builders and marched south, assembling his whole force at his previous camp in the centre of Great Meadows. This had already been slightly fortified, but Washington now proceeded to turn it into something like a fort. 'The whole and the parts were not a design of engineering art but of frontier necessity',[6] he wrote, 'so I gave it the name, Fort Necessity.'

Soon after Washington and his men were installed, a force of 500 Frenchmen with as many Indians arrived on the scene, surrounded the compound and opened fire on its defenders. Before the encirclement had been completed, Washington's Indian allies, including Half King, mistrusting his chances of success, slipped silently away. Although Washington had managed to improve the fortification of his camp during the respite before the French approach, his chances of holding out against such odds were slight, and after a token resistance, as soon as the French made peace feelers he agreed to parley. The terms finally arrived at were generous. Two officer hostages had to be left with the French as a guarantee that the twenty-one prisoners sent to Virginia after the earlier engagement would be returned. With this proviso, Washington was allowed to march his force out of the fort unmolested, and take them back intact to Virginia. However, in the first fight on the upper Ohio at the beginning of the Seven Years War[7] the French were undoubtedly the victors.

6 Freeman, Vol. I, p. 402.
7 Known as the French and Indian War in America.

They were victors again next year, 1755, in the same area, when General Braddock at the head of 1,000 regulars, 450 Virginia militiament under Washington and 50 Indian scouts blazed a trail from Baltimore to Fort Cumberland and from there slowly on towards Fort Duquesne at the Forks of the Ohio, with the object of capturing the fortress. A force of some 600 French and 200 Indians moved out from Fort Duquesne to halt the British advance, and in the battle that resulted the French had the distinct advantage. Seizing a hill on one side of the British column, and a ravine on the other, they poured in a deadly fire from under cover and routed the massed British force and mortally wounded its leader. But there was one advantage gained from this unsuccessful attempt to take Fort Duquesne. The wagon-road that Braddock had cut so laboriously over the mountains became later one of the main arteries followed by settlers moving into the Ohio area.

Eventually the war was won by Britain in America as well as in the other theatres. Quebec fell to Wolfe in 1759. One year earlier, in the fall of 1758, an army under General Forbes cut its way across Pennsylvania to Fort Duquesne which, having being evacuated by the French, was reconstructed and renamed Fort Pitt. The wagon-road made by Forbes was also put to good use by settlers crossing over the mountains on their way to the West. Along with Braddock's Road and The Wilderness Trail[8] (later an Inter-State Highway) which used the Cumberland Gap farther south, Forbes's Road provided a main route used for the settlement and development of the region south of the the Great Lakes (see map 4).

After the war Major Rogers was sent with a few troops to enforce the capitulation of the French posts. In the course of his duties he met the Ottawa Chief, Pontiac, who questioned what he was doing, but who seemed satisfied when told the French had surrendered the whole area and its forts to the British. However, neither Pontiac nor the other Indian chiefs were, in fact, content that their territories should have been transferred by one white nation to another without a word of consultation with them. Moreover, the French traders who still lived among the Indians inflamed resentment against

[8] See page 40.

the British; and Chief Pontiac, who emerged as a leader of skill, was able to form a great confederation of Indian tribes to attack many of the British posts simultaneously. He achieved this by sending messengers far and wide to the various chiefs, northward as far as the heads of Lakes Michigan and Huron, southward to the very mouth of the Mississippi. By the spring of 1763 he was ready to strike.

The forts at this time were only lightly garrisoned by men of the Sixtieth, The Royal American Regiment, a corps largely composed of foreigners. Lonely and friendless, the officers often took Indian girls for companions, a practice which, whatever judgement be passed, at least proved the salvation of the British at Detroit. Detroit and the other main forts are shown on map 4. In the east Fort Cumberland on Willis Creek and Fort Bird at the mouth of Redstone Creek were not affected; but Fort Bedford east of the Alleghenies and Fort Ligonier between Laurel Ridge and Chestnut Ridge on Forbes's Road to Fort Pitt were attacked, as were Presque Isle on Lake Erie, Le Boeuf on French Creek, Venango at the junction of French Creek and the Allegheny, and Fort Pitt [9] itself. Farther west, Sandusky on the southern shore of Lake Erie, Michilimackinac on the strait between Huron and Michigan, and St Joseph on the south-east corner of Michigan, were also attacked.

On 7 May 1763 Pontiac and sixty other chiefs entered Fort Detroit ostensibly for a friendly conference with the commandant, Captain Gladwyn, but every man had a weapon under his blanket ready for a treacherous attack. Gladwyn, warned by his Indian girl, was on his guard and able to frustrate the plot, but foolishly let the chiefs go instead of keeping them as hostages, and three days later the fort was beset by some 600 Indians. Gladwyn had 120 soldiers and 40-odd traders and half-breeds, by no means all to be trusted implicitly, but he gave them arms and held out vigorously. Meanwhile, came tidings of wholesale disaster. On 16 May Sandusky fell and the entire garrison was killed or taken prisoner; on 25 May the same fate befell St Joseph; and on

[9] Fort Duquesne on map 4.

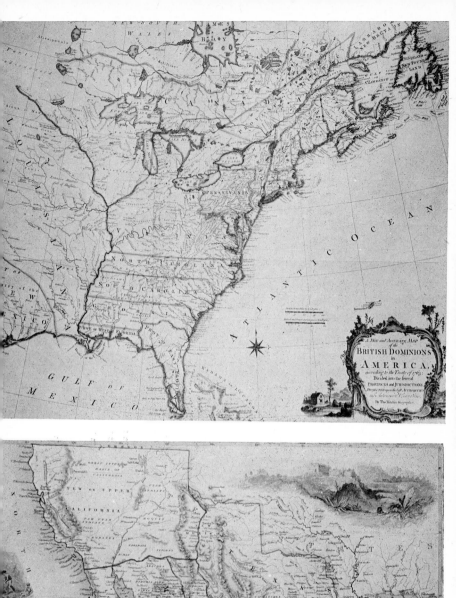

A NEW and ACCURATE MAP
of the
BRITISH DOMINIONS
in
AMERICA,
according to the Treaty of 1763;
Divided into the several
PROVINCES and JURISDICTIONS.
Projected upon the best Authorities
and Astronomical Observations.
By Tho.ˢ Kitchin Geographer.

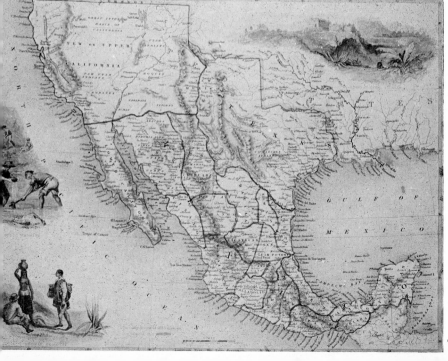

II George Washington as a young man, by Charles Willson Peale (*Washington — Custis Lee Portrait Collection: Washington and Lee University*)

Daniel Boone by Chester Harding (*Massachusetts Historical Society*)

Previous plate

I The British Dominions in America, 1763 (*Ingvard Eide, Montana: collection Judge Arthur J. Stanley*)

Mexico, California and Texas, c. 1850 (*Ingvard Eide, Montana: collection Judge Arthur J. Stanley*)

28 May a relieving force of 100 men with stores and ammunition from Niagara was cut to pieces within a day's march of Detroit. The fall of Presque Isle, Le Boeuf, Venango and Michilimackinac followed in the last days of May and the first days of June, some few, but very few, of their garrisons escaping. By the middle of June there was not a British soldier in the region of the Lakes except at Detroit; and on the route from Pennsylvania, though the posts held out, the country between was laid waste so that the settlers had to seek refuge in the forts. When the first violence of the storm had spent itself, these settlers scurried off to Pennsylvania, and it was impossible to persuade any of them to stay and help defend the posts against further attack, although for example, Fort Ligonier was left with a garrison of only twelve soldiers.

It was the same when the Governor of Canada attempted to raise a force to quell the rebellion. Quaker Pennsylvania refused to provide a man, and a force of 500 regulars had to be got together to do the job. This, placed under the command of Colonel Bouquet, a Swiss, reached Fort Bedford on 25 July. From there he followed Forbes's Road and made for Fort Pitt. After reinforcing Fort Ligonier, where he left his oxen and wagons, he continued the march on 4 August with 350 packhorses and a few driven cattle. Early on the morning of 5 August while short of Bushy Run, a creek fifteen miles from Fort Pitt, his advanced troops brushed with hostile Indians, whereupon he recalled them, and formed the whole of his force in a protective ring round the packhorses. The Indians came at the British from all sides, charging again and again with great gallantry; but steady volleys from the defenders drove them back. For seven hours the fight raged; not until nightfall was there a respite. Numerous outposts were then pushed into the forest to guard against a surprise night-attack, and in the centre a ring of flourbags was made into a shelter for the wounded. Throughout the night occasional whoops told of the presence of the enemy and at dawn the Indian attack was renewed. At ten o'clock the British line had become so thinned that Bouquet brought his front and rear companies back under cover of the flimsy defences in the centre of his position. He also contracted his flank companies, but left part of them out in position. The Indians, thinking the day was theirs, charged in through the gaps, whereupon they were met with fire from three sides, and were quickly shot to pieces. Then the British went in with the bayonet and drove them off. In a short time every sign of a living Indian had vanished. Around the British lay the corpses of some sixty dead warriors; but Bouquet's own loss was little less severe. It amounted to eight officers and ninety-six men, or fully a fourth of his force killed and wounded in two days' fighting.

Bouquet's victory eased the pressure in the area about Fort Pitt; but there was still much to be done to restore the situation around the Lakes and farther west. The Six Nations of the Iroquois had, with the exception of the Seneca, kept firm to the British alliance, and although the Seneca had wrought no little havoc on western New York they too were soon to be reattached to the British cause. However, Detroit was still blockaded and the Delaware and Shawnee were on the rampage between the Ohio and Lake Erie. The Governor of Canada appealed to the Colonies to supply soldiers to help subdue the Indians; but the response was not good. Rhode Island, always churlish, sent no answer whatever, New Hampshire was profuse in excuses, Massachusetts and Connecticut were hesitant, and only New York and New Jersey promised to send 1,000 men between them, stipulating that two-thirds should remain on their frontiers. Virginia had already sent a force to protect her outlying settlements, but Pennsylvania refused to vote her contingent of 1,000 men, and even denounced the expedition conducted voluntarily by some of her citizens as seditious and murderous. Finally, nothing less than the march of a body of Pennsylvania armed frontiersmen upon Philadelphia was necessary to awe the Quaker Assembly into helping to defend its people. All this took so much time that the expeditions could not be mounted until the spring of 1764. A column made up of regulars and levies from New York and New Jersey under Major Bradstreet was the first to move. It reoccupied Sandusky and Michilimackinac, and relieved Detroit, but made little effort to subdue the Indians settled around the Lakes. The second column under Colonel

Bouquet, hero of Bushy Run, met with difficulties at first when 200 of its 1,000 Pennsylvanians deserted; but he was able to pick up a welcome reinforcement of Virginian backwoodsmen, and then reached and subdued the Delaware and Shawnee settlements without firing a shot. From that time[10] although there was later to be more trouble from the Miami and Wabash the power of Pontiac's conspiracy was broken; and the French having been defeated and the local hostile Indians held in check the upper Ohio basin became available for occupation by settlers from the thirteen Colonies.

[10] Settlement was held up by a proclamation of George III in 1763 stating that no settlers were to cross the Appalachian divide, and the purchase of lands was outlawed. It did not really get under way until after the American Revolution.

Chapter 2

The Winning of
the Ohio II

The exploration and peopling of Kentucky came about as a result of the journeyings of stalwart pioneers like Daniel Boone. Boone was born in 1734 in the Quaker State of Pennsylvania, the starting place of many who were to push across the mountains. Brought up in North Carolina, he went on several hunting expeditions in the mountains before venturing beyond; but in 1769 he joined a party that spent two years roaming the bluegrass region of Kentucky, living off bison, elk and smaller deer. At one time he was captured by Indians, but although a companion taken with him was killed in captivity Boone managed to escape. He returned to North Carolina, but set off back again to Kentucky two years later accompanied by his wife and children and sixty others, driving their cattle and horses. While passing through a defile in the Cumberland Mountains the party was attacked by Indians, and six men including Boone's eldest son were killed. Following this, they turned back, recrossed the Powell River and Powell Mountains and established a settlement on the banks of the River Clinch.[1] At the time there were several parties on the move in the region beyond the mountains. Three young men named McAfee were navigating the Ohio and exploring the north of Kentucky; and a group headed by John Floyd were descending the great Kanawha in canoes. Although menaced by Shawnee, Floyd's men managed to explore part of the eastern borders of Kentucky before moving

[1] The Powell and Clinch along with the Holston, Nolichucky and Watauga are headwater tributaries of the Tennessee.

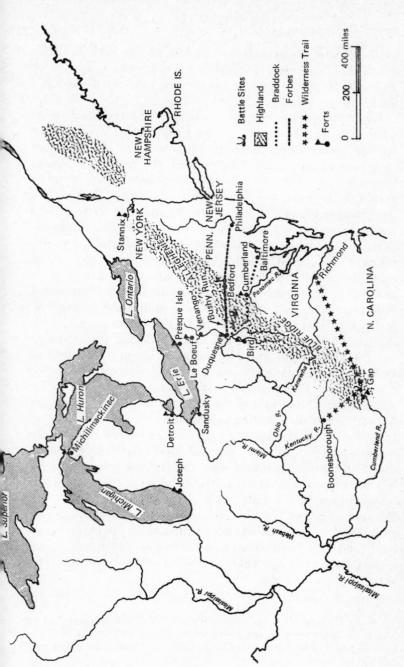

4. Forts in the Ohio region

south to join Boone and his settlers on the Clinch. They found them gathered in a wooden fort preparing to face an attack by Shawnee, and were welcomed as a useful reinforcement.

Meanwhile, other parties of settlers had established themselves in upper Tennessee on the banks of the Watauga and Holston rivers. These believed at first that law and order and their protection against Indians were the responsibilities of Virginia, but following a rough survey found their area lay within the bounds of North Carolina. As North Carolina had been unable to enforce law and order in home territory, the upper Tennessee settlers decided to try to manage their own affairs. They adopted written articles of agreement under which their region should be governed, and elected an assembly of thirteen representatives who chose five of their number to be commissioners and conduct the governmental business of the little colony. The commissioners were empowered to deal with Indians and in 1772 made a treaty with the Cherokee whereby all the land bordering the Watauga was leased for eight years in consideration of a donation of some 6,000 dollars worth of blankets, muskets and other commodities. This proved a satisfactory arrangement as for several years the people of the Holston Settlement[2] were left unmolested by their Indian neighbours.

By the eve of the Revolution pioneers mainly from Pennsylvania and Virginia had planted themselves firmly beyond the mountains. A collision with the Indians was imminent, but there was almost as much likelihood of the Pennsylvanians being drawn into a fight with the Virginians as with the Shawnee. The two colonies claimed westward from the ocean an indefinite tract limited only by their ability to explore and hold; and this brought endless confusion and much bitter feeling, so that an intercolonial war was only averted because of the common danger.

Virginia took the lead in the struggle with the Indians. In

[2] Also called the Watauga Commonwealth. Another group of Upper Tennessee settlers set up the independent colony of Franklin in 1784 but this reverted to North Carolina in 1787—as the Holston settlement had already done.

1774 its Governor, Lord Dunmore, having garrisoned the frontier forts, raised 3,000 men to carry out a punitive expedition. The plan was for two columns under Lord Dunmore and General Lewis respectively to march separately to the spot where the Great Kanawha meets the Ohio in order to form a firm base from which to conduct operations, but in the event the project was never fully carried out. Dunmore entrenched his men before reaching the proposed meeting place and contented himself with sending out small detachments to harass the Indians. Lewis, meanwhile, having left some men to garrison frontier posts marched down beside the Great Kanawha and camped on the cape of land between that river and the Ohio that had been the rendezvous for both columns.

Just before daylight on the morning following the arrival of his column two of Lewis's hunters left the camp to try for game to supplement the rations, and in the darkness brushed with a party of Shawnee. One hunter was killed in the skirmish, but the other managed to get back and raise the alarm. After some delay, due to doubt as to the number of Indians involved, a force of 500 men under Colonel Field was dispatched to deal with the Indians. The battle that followed consisted of a series of combats between individuals sheltering behind stumps, rocks or tree trunks; and although the colonial backwoodsmen were superior in firepower, the Indians proved better at protecting themselves. One device the latter used was to taunt the Americans and try to make them expose themselves. In this way Colonel Field met his end. He was behind a big tree and was shot by two enemy on his right while trying to get an Indian in front who was mocking and jeering at him. The Americans, however, were not daunted by the fall of their leader and continued to fight on bravely. Meanwhile, the Indians were being exhorted throughout the battle by their famous old chief, Cornstalk. About noon he attempted to get his people to envelop the American position and attack their camp, but this was frustrated by violent volleys being fired at the braves attempting the flanking movement. The Americans countered by advancing along the banks of the Kanawha with the object of taking the

Indians in the flank in their turn; but this move was not successful either. Then, at about one o'clock in the afternoon, the Indians fell back and occupied a new position fortified with log ramparts, and this was virtually the end, for although skirmishing went on until sunset, during the night the Indians slipped away, skilfully carrying all their wounded across the Ohio to safety. The Battle of the Great Kanawha may be said to have been one of the most important in the early Indian wars, for although the Americans suffered more casualties, the Indians sued for peace after the battle. The result was that Kentucky was relieved of Indian pressure and for several years prospective settlers were able to move in unmolested.

The first significant settlement in Kentucky was the achievement of Richard Henderson assisted by the versatile Daniel Boone. Henderson, who was a speculator from North Carolina, had for some time been planning a proprietary colony beyond the mountains. He had had business connections with Boone and in 1775 sought his help in the venture. Henderson asked permission of the local Cherokee to purchase land lying between the Kentucky and Cumberland rivers, and this was granted after a meeting of 1,200 men of the tribe. As soon as it was evident that the Indians would consent to a treaty, Henderson sent Boone ahead with thiry men to blaze a trail from Holston to the Kentucky River. This was the first regular track cut through the wilds and came to be known as the Wilderness Trail. Just before they reached the river, Boone's men were attacked by Indians, who killed two of them and wounded another. Undeterred, the remainder pressed on, and when they arrived, started to build near the river's bank the fort of Boonesborough. This eventually consisted of a series of log cabins with an open space for cattle in the middle enclosed by a stockade having two-storeyed, loopholed blockhouses in each corner. Boone sent back a message warning Henderson of the Indian danger and urged him to come as soon as possible; but as Boone had not been able to complete a path for wheeled transport, Henderson had to change to pack animals at the halfway stage and was slow to reach his colleague. Other groups were also arriving in the area, and

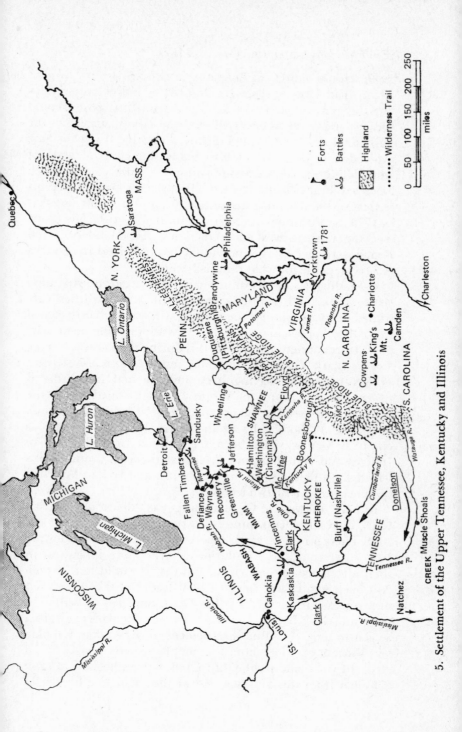

5. Settlement of the Upper Tennessee, Kentucky and Illinois

three stations similar to Boonesborough were set up. Around all of them large tracts were granted to individual settlers, but the general plan was to rally on fortified posts should Indians attack. Henderson allotted the task of surveying the individual tracts to Daniel Boone and after this was done proceeded to deed to colonists many thousands of acres of land. However, he set about ruling his little colony which he called Transylvania in such a proprietary manner that his settlers revolted against his authority, and the result was that in 1778 the Virginian authorities annulled his title. Nevertheless, the venture was not a total loss, for Henderson and Boone were given large individual grants of land in the area as a recompense for what they had achieved.

Even during the Revolutionary War western expansion went on, for most frontiersmen, regardless of hostilities, continued to try to conquer the wooded wilderness that stretched from the Appalachians to the Mississippi. One man who played a prominent part doing this during the war was George Rogers Clark. Clark, having done much to foster settlement in Kentucky, and having been instrumental in getting it recognised as a county of Virginia, next planned to use the territory as a base for the occupation of Illinois. This region, stretching on both sides of the River Wabash, was not as empty as Kentucky had been, for it was occupied by warlike Indians and contained old French settlements around posts which since their victory in the French and Indian War had been manned by British troops.

In 1777, the year of General Burgoyne's defeat at Saratoga, Clark dispatched two hunters north-westward to spy out the land. These on their return reported the French were showing little interest in the Revolutionary War, were lukewarm in their allegiance to the British, and that it would not be difficult for a small force under a bold leader to take possession of the area. Encouraged by this, Clark returned to Williamsburg and laid before Governor Patrick Henry of Virginia a plan to seize the Illinois settlements of Kaskaskia, Cahokia and Vincennes. The matter was not placed before the Colonial Assembly or made public, but Clark was authorised to raise 250 men from the counties west of Blue Ridge. The official instructions merely ordered the reinforcement of Kentucky, but Clark also carried secret orders empowering him to enter the Illinois region. To start with he had difficulty in raising the necessary men, for besides the jealousy between Virginians and Pennsylvanians many were opposed to the idea because they believed the drain on their strength was more serious than the value of the land warranted. However, eventually by perseverance Clark managed to assemble four companies of frontiersmen for the operation.

The expedition began at Pittsburg, and from there the Ohio was descended in clumsy flatboats rowed or drifted cautiously down river for some four hundred miles between unbroken reaches of Indian-haunted forest. When the Ohio rapids were reached Clark halted his party and got them to build a fort[3] on an island in the river to protect future trade, and he next selected some of the few families who were accompanying him to remain behind and man it. Before tackling the rapids Clark disclosed that the true goal of the expedition was Illinois. In general this news was received with enthusiasm, but a few Holston men were so upset that they fled into the woods and had to be pursued and brought back. Clark's boats eventually shot the rapids just at the time of an eclipse of the sun, a phenomenon they all considered a good omen. Then double-manning the oars, they rowed day and night until they reached a small island off the mouth of the Tennessee River where they disembarked and set about making final preparations for the invasion.

Soon after they landed on the north bank of the Ohio at the start of their approach march they met up with some hunters who had recently visited Kaskaskia fifty miles up the Mississippi, and these willingly agreed to lead them there. For several days they marched through the wilds until they reached the River Kaskaskia at a spot a few miles from the town on the far bank. Their first action before crossing the river was to seize a nearby farm and take the family prisoner. Their captives told them that the people of Kaskaskia had

[3] Later a settlement was established on the river bank and named Louisville after the French king. Louis XVI in 1778 made an alliance with the Americans.

been alarmed at the rumour of a possible American attack, but now their suspicions were lulled; and they also said that the Commandant was loyal to the British and likely to resist. After getting hold of some boats Clark ferried his men across the stream under cover of darkness. Then on nearing Kaskaskia he ordered the bulk of his force to surround the town and went forward with a few chosen companions to reconnoitre the fort. There were dancing and revelry going on inside; the officers of the post were giving a ball, and it was obvious that the garrison was quite unprepared to meet an attack. Realising his opportunity, Clark rejoined those surrounding the town, and after calling a council-of-war, drew up a plan to take the place. First, detachments were dispatched to secure every street, and runners were sent round the town to order the people to stay indoors on pain of death. Then, at the head of a hundred picked men, Clark stormed the fort, and taking the garrison completely by surprise won the post without a shot being fired. Clark treated the captured township generously. He sent the Commandant as a prisoner to Virginia and sold off his slaves, but took no further punitive action, and instead, by gentle persuasion managed to get the people to give their allegiance to the new American republic.

Next day a small detachment marched on Cahokia, on the Mississippi, fifty miles to the north. Here the people, having been told of what had happened at Kaskaskia, were also persuaded to join the American cause.

There now remained only Vincennes to be taken; and here the Catholic priest of Kaskaskia lent a hand. He became a willing ally after the Americans spared his church, and volunteered to go to Vincennes to try to win over its people. He started at once and after only a few weeks returned to say that he had been completely successful. The entire population had gathered in the church and had been so moved by his appeal that they had taken the oath of allegiance. Now the American flag was flying over the fort. As it was considered impracticable to split the small American force up again to garrison Vincennes, Captain Helm was sent over on his own to take command and deal as best he could with the townsfolk.

Clark now found himself in a position of utmost difficulty.

With a handful of backwoodsmen, many anxious to return home, he had to protect and control a region as large as a European country; and he had to keep loyal a population alien in race, creed and language, while he held his own against the British and local Indians. He was hundreds of miles from the nearest post containing American troops and farther still from the Virginian seat of government. But being a man of resource he was not deterred. He had already had some success in dealing with the French and now decided to try to appease the Spanish leaders of the scattered villages across the Mississippi, and to placate the chiefs of the local Indian tribes. The Spaniards had never been friendly, either with the British or the Americans; but the forceful Clark managed to establish something like cordial relations with them.

With the Indians it was more difficult. Many local chiefs with detachments of their warriors had already begun to assemble at the American camp to hear the intentions of the invaders, and one group attempted to force their way into Clark's house and carry him off. Clark, however, was fully on his guard and managed to thwart them, and to seize his intended captors and put them in irons. The prisoners protested that they had only been trying to discover what was happening, and begged to be released. Clark refused to free them even when chiefs from other tribes came up to intercede, but next morning he summoned all the Indians to a grand council with the prisoners present. The preliminary ceremonies were all carefully carried out in accordance with Indian custom. Then Clark, standing up in the midst of the rings of squatting warriors, with his riflemen clustered behind him, produced a war-belt. Pointing to it he challenged them to see which side could make it the most bloody, threatening them that if need be he could call from the thirteen American States numerous warriors to drive them from their lands. He also explained the nature of the quarrel between the Americans and the British, likening it to a rising of one of their tribes against the Iroquois. At the end of his speech he presented again the belt of war, but proferred also a belt of peace, asking them to choose one or the other. Impressed by his words, they eagerly took the peace belt. He declined to smoke the calumet, however, and told them he would not start the ceremonies of the peace treaty with them until the following day. He likewise refused to release all the prisoners, and insisted that two of them should be put to death. They even agreed to this, and two of the youngest came forward, sat down before him, and covered their heads with blankets to receive the tomahawk. Then he granted them full peace, forgave the young men, and the next day, after the full council, held a feast. The friendship of these Indians was won. Clark ever after had great influence over them; they admired his oratory, his address as a treaty-maker, and the skill with which he had led his troops.

The news of the occupation of the French settlements by Clark and his men caused the British commander at Detroit to organise an expedition against the Americans. On 7 October 1778 he marched on Vincennes with a column of troops and allied Indians numbering, in all, five hundred men. The arrival of the British caused both the French and Indians to desert the American cause, and Helm was obliged to surrender. The original British plan had been to move on from Vincennes and retake Cahokia and Kaskaskia; but as the countryside was submerged by autumn floods, it was decided to suspend active operations until the spring. Most of the troops were thus sent back to Detroit, and only about ninety men were left to garrison the fort at Vincennes.

News of the British decision to suspend operations was brought to Vincennes by a trader who had been released from prison. Clark decided to forestall the enemy and attack at once in spite of the floods. He started out on 7 February 1778 along with 170 men. The route was 240 miles long, and the floods made the journey extremely hazardous. Particularly difficult was the crossing of the two channels of the Little Wabash and the 5-mile-wide flooded area between them. This passage was only accomplished through the inspiring leadership of Clark. In the worst area he built scaffolds on islands in the waters, ferried men and baggage over to these refuges, and then repeated the process to other islands on the route. When the main Wabash river was at last reached, they came upon a boat containing five Frenchmen from Vincennes. These confirmed that there was only a small garrison and that the British commander had no suspicion of a likely attack. At dawn next day Clark began to ferry his men over the Wabash. He had hoped to reach Vincennes by nightfall; but on the far side there was no dry land for miles, only a few hillocks rising here and there above the flood. Another slog had thus to be faced, and the men waded forward slowly with water up to their armpits, some dragging canoes carrying those too weak to march through the water. They had a lucky encounter while still a few miles from Vincennes with a canoe, paddled by some Indian squaws, containing half a quarter of buffalo and some corn, tallow and kettles: all the ingredients for a hearty meal. Then, having refreshed themselves, they continued for a short distance until they reached a copse from which they could see the fort and township of Vincennes two miles away.

A man found near the copse was sent to the townspeople with a message which told them that only the fort was going to be attacked by the Americans, and if they stayed indoors they would not be harmed. Then, at dusk, Clark marched through the town and attacked. Surprised, the garrison resisted staunchly throughout the night, though casualties were light on both sides. Early in the forenoon next day Clark summoned the fort to surrender, but its commander refused to capitulate and countered-proposed a three days' truce. In the afternoon Clark repeated his demand, and this time the commander agreed that the whole garrison, seventy in all, would surrender as prisoners-of-war. Clark was forced to parole most of them owing to shortage of guards, but managed to send the commander and twenty others back to Virginia. By a lucky chance reinforcements had just arrived from Kentucky so it was possible to place small garrisons in all three towns. Peace was then established with most of the local tribes and during the remainder of the Revolutionary War neither the British nor the Indians were able to weaken the hold over the region that Clark had gained. It was not until 1779 that Clark left. Raised to the rank of brigadier he was moved south to the Ohio rapids. There with a small force he established an outpost that guarded both Illinois and Kentucky from attack.

In 1780 a more direct contribution by frontiersmen to the Revolutionary War was made in South Carolina. At the time General Cornwallis was carrying out operations in the south with a mixed force of British, Hessians and loyalists, along with some bands of Creek and Cherokee. So far everything had gone well for him. Charleston had been captured with its 6,000 defenders, and General Gates, the victor at Saratoga, had been defeated at Camden. Now, as his army moved northward, Major Ferguson, in command of the American militia, roamed in advance, scouring the country to raise more loyalists, and at the same time attempting to scatter any rebel bands encountered. By September, Ferguson had advanced to the foot of the Great Smoky Mountains on the western border of the Carolinas, and here he learnt that some of the men of the upper Tennessee settlements had been intimidating British supporters and harbouring rebel refugees. By a prisoner he sent them a warning to cease hostilities, and he threatened that if they did not do so he would march across the mountains, seize and hang their leaders, and set fire to their homes. On hearing of Ferguson's threats, the upper Tennessee men rose in arms. A thousand of them, led by William Campbell, Isaac Shelby, John Sevier and others, with Joseph McDowell at the head of the refugees, moved over the mountains to confront the British leader. Armed with flintlock rifles, tomahawks and scalping knives, with the trappings of their horses stained red and yellow, their fringed hunting shirts girded by bead belts, and their coonskin caps stuck with a bucktail, they must have looked a motley crowd. But they proved good fighters.

Just before they crossed Blue Ridge at Gillespie's Gap two members of Sevier's band deserted and fled to warn Ferguson of the force moving against him, whereupon the British leader, realising he was likely to be attacked by a superior force while on his own, sent calls for help to a nearby column under Colonel Cruger and a message to Cornwallis explaining his predicament. After this, Ferguson first pulled back as if to join the main body at Charlotte, and then changed his mind and turned south and took up a position on King's Mountain. King's Mountain extends from South Carolina into North Carolina. It is a stony ridge with steep sides clad with trees. Ferguson manned the whole northern half of the ridge and apparently felt quite confident when installed, for he declared: 'I am on King's Mountain. I am king of that mountain and God Almighty will not drive me from it.'[4]

Meanwhile the Tennessee men hurried after their quarry. They lost the trail by Cowpens short of the crossing of Broad River and went into camp; but a spy reported Ferguson's movements to some local rebels under Edward Lacey, and Lacey rode in and put them wise. When they heard where Ferguson was, they decided to attack him in position, confident that with the reinforcement of the rebels they outnumbered him. At sunrise on 7 October they left their camp, and after marching several miles splashed through the Cherokee Ford over Broad River. Throughout the forenoon it rained steadily, but they pushed on without halting, merely wrapping the skirts of their hunting shirts round their rifles to keep them dry. About three o'clock in the afternoon they learnt of Ferguson's exact position from two captured loyalists, and soon afterwards reached King's Mountain and took up position round its base, almost completely surrounding the area where Ferguson's men were installed. Then they dismounted, formed two lines, primed their weapons and prepared to attack.

Ferguson, with 100 men from King William's American Regiment, the Queen's Rangers and New Jersey volunteers and 1,000 well-trained militia[5] prepared to receive them, forming into battle array behind ledges of slaty rock along the summit. Ferguson was wearing a light-coloured hunting shirt which was to make him an easy target. He carried his sword in his left hand because he had not regained the full use of his right after being wounded at Brandywine Creek. Round his neck hung a silver whistle which he used to rally his men. He planned to repulse his adversaries by volley firing coupled

[4] Draper, p. 211.
[5] All were American loyalists. Ferguson was the only Britisher.

with bayonet charges, methods he had previously found successful against the Americans.

The battle began by Campbell's men storming up the hill, yelling, and firing their rifles. The men on the summit replied with a heavy volley, and then, cheering lustily, charged and drove them down again. But no sooner had they done so, and returned to the top, than Shelby's men came swarming up from the other side. Ferguson rode on horseback from point to point encouraging his men with blasts from his whistle, and bayonet charges pushed back Shelby's men, and Campbell's men again, and then other groups as well. But in every charge many fell and severe losses coupled with the risk of ammunition running out so discouraged the men on the hill that some started to raise the white flag of surrender. Noticing this, Ferguson rode over and cut down two such flags. Then he rallied a regiment and led it in a further charge. He had not gone twenty yards, however, before he fell from his horse pierced by seven enemy balls, 'literally shot to pieces'.[6] After the loss of their leader the whole line round the summit began to give way, and although Captain de Peyster, who took over command, managed to stage a rally round the baggage, it was not long before he was forced to surrender. Three hundred loyalists had been killed or wounded, and half as many Tennessee men; but the worst features of the battle was the aftermath. Because the British Colonel Tarleton had earlier hanged captured rebels, the Tennessee men now clamoured for what they called 'Tarleton's Quarter'. Some continued firing after the surrender, and even when this butchery ended the surviving prisoners faced further ordeals. The wounded on the field of battle were left largely unattended and from among those who marched off as prisoners nine were hanged from a giant oak, watched compulsorily by their fellows. Many died in captivity. A few, including three officers, managed to escape. By November, of the 600 captured only 150 remained in rebel hands to be marched under guard and confined at Hillsborough in North Carolina.

[6] Letter from de Peyster to Cornwallis, 11 October 1780.

Meanwhile, other frontiersmen were continuing to further the cause of westward expansion regardless of the war. James Robertson, prominent leader for ten years in upper Tennessee, had not taken part in the battle at King's Mountain, for before it was fought he had set out to form a settlement on the great bend of the Cumberland River. Early in the spring of 1779 Robertson had left with eight companions, and after a long and tedious journey reached a suitable spot near the Salt Lick on the Bluff. A few days after their arrival they were joined by another batch of hunter-settlers who had come out under the leadership of Kasper Mansker; then, as soon as the corn was planted, and cabins put up, most of them returned to their old homes to bring out their families, leaving, as they said, only a few behind 'to keep the buffaloes out of the corn'. It was thought that the chosen region belonged to Virginia, so Robertson went on to Illinois to see George Rogers Clark, who was Virginia's agent for territory beyond the mountains, with the intention of purchasing cabin-rights from him, which under Virginia law gave each man for a small sum a thousand acres provided he built a cabin and raised a crop. However, it was eventually learnt that the Cumberland area was within the territory of North Carolina so Robertson might have spared himself a trip.

In October there was an inrush of settlers. Robertson brought a large party overland, and his partner, John Donelson, took another big group by a roundabout route, going down the Tennessee, up the Ohio and then back up the Cumberland. This latter expedition, which began on 27 February 1789, was of epic proportions. The first part of the voyage was uneventful, but after ten days the flagship *Adventure* stuck of a shoal, and it was not until the following day that the water rose sufficiently for her to float off. Next, another boat sank in the sand on the point of an island. This caused a considerable delay as the rest of the flotilla had to put on shore first to empty the boat, then to bail her out, and finally to replace the cargo.

When they came to an Indian village on the south bank while approaching the Chickamauga area, they at first found the red men friendly and willing to accept their presents.

But with the arrival on the scene of a number of canoes containing warriors, the atmosphere changed; and the Donelson party thought it advisable to leave as quickly as they could. The armed Indians disembarked and followed along the shore for a time, but were soon left behind.

With the flotilla was a boat containing about thirty men, women and children, some of whom were infected with smallpox. This vessel was kept well in the rear, and a horn was sounded at night to give notice when the main body was going into camp. As this forlorn boat-load came along, Indians ashore, seeing it defenceless, paddled out and butchered all aboard. The victims' cries were distinctly heard by the rear boats of the main flotilla; but these could not turn and help because of the strong downstream current. A dreadful retribution, however, fell on the Indians. They were infected with the disease and for months afterwards virulent smallpox raged among the local tribes of Creek and Cherokee.

When the boats entered the narrows in the Chickamauga-Chattanooga area, they were attacked by Indians who fired down from the cliffs and wounded four people including a young girl, but having successfully run this gauntlet the flotilla was not again molested. The great Muscle Shoals were run over in about three hours without incident, but the passage through these turbulent waters was a terrifying experience for those unused to river work.

On 20 March they reached the Ohio. Here some turned aside to tackle the four-hundred mile journey down the Mississippi to Natchez,[7] and others went on to the Illinois settlements, but the vast majority pointed their prows upstream along the Ohio. On 24 March they entered the Cumberland, but it was not until 24 April that they reached the Big Salt Lick at Great Bend and found Robertson awaiting them.

The central station was on the Bluff. Here Robertson had built a little stockaded hamlet and called it Nashborough (Nashville). With the arrival of Donelson's band there were nearly five hundred people in the new settlement, half of them

[7] These settlements around Natchez were the nucleus of the State of Mississippi which joined the Union as a separate State in 1817.

men in the prime of life. True to their customs and traditions, and to their capacity for self-rule, the settlers determined to organise a government under which 'law and order might be imposed among themselves, and protection afforded against outside attack'. Thus on 1 May 1789 representatives met together at Nashborough and entered into articles of agreement for a compact of government which was modelled on the constitution of earlier Holston with some features taken from Henderson's Transylvania. Thus a little self-governing state was set up on the banks of the Cumberland.

For several years the Cumberland settlements were harassed by Indians. In 1781 and 1782 a number of settlers were killed and the rest were so hard pressed defending themselves that they were not able to raise corn. After this a number left for the Kentucky settlement, others went to Illinois or Natchez, and some returned to their old homes among the Alleghenies. By 1783 there was talk of abandoning the Cumberland district altogether. However, Robertson's influence prevented this happening. By word and example, he finally persuaded the settlers to stay. Also, on 18 October 1781 General Cornwallis had surrendered to Washington at Yorktown, and in the spring of 1783 came news of peace with Great Britain. With peace came a large influx of new settlers, and Cumberland County began at last to thrive. By the end of 1783 the old stations around Nashborough had been rebuilt, and many new ones founded, after that the area never looked back.

The settlers beyond the mountains exercised the functions of civil government locally but, except for short periods, as for example in the upper Tennessee and Cumberland settlements, they usually sent representatives to sit in the legislatures of Virginia or North Carolina. The claims of these two States thus had behind them a substantial record of possession. Nothing of the sort, however, could be said for the claims of the other States, for actual possession was not part of them. Meanwhile, the States that did not claim lands beyond the mountains were strenuous in belittling the claims of those who did, and insisted that the title to the western territory should be vested in the Union. Not even the danger of a

British attack could keep this question in abeyance, and while the Revolutionary War was at its height there was a bitter wrangle over the subject. Maryland was the first to take action in the direction of nationalising the western lands, and was the most determined in pressing the matter to a successful issue. She also showed the greatest hesitation in joining the federation at all while the matter was allowed to rest unsettled; and insisted that the titles of the claimant States were void, that there was no need to ask them to cede what they did not possess, and that the West should be declared outright to be part of the federal domain. Maryland dreaded the growth of Virginia in wealth, power, and population, and also feared lest her own population might be drained into these vacant lands, thereby at once diminishing her own, and building up her neighbour's importance.

Each State, in fact, at that time, looked upon its neighbours as commercial rivals. New York's claims were the least defensible of all. On the other hand, New York led the way in 1780 by abandoning all her claims to western lands in favour of the Union. Congress, using this as an argument by which to encourage similar action from the other States, then issued an earnest appeal to them to follow New York's example without regard to the value of their titles, so that the Federal Union might be put on a firm basis. Congress also announced that the policy would be to divide this new territory into districts of suitable size which would be admitted as States as soon as they became settled. This last proposition was important, as it outlined the future policy which was to admit the new communities as States, with all the rights of the old States, instead of treating them as subordinate and dependent, after the manner of the European colonial systems. When this had been agreed Maryland decided to join the federation, but for some time no progress was made in the negotiations with the other States. Early in 1784, however, Virginia ceded to Congress her rights to territory on the Ohio, except for a small area retained as a military reserve for the use of her soldiers. A year later Massachusetts followed suit, and ceded to Congress her title of all lands lying west of the present boundary of New York State. Finally, in 1786, a similar cession was made by Connecticut, conditional upon being allowed to reserve for her own profit about five thousand square miles in what is now northern Ohio—a tract later known as the Western Reserve. Thus the project for which Maryland had contended was at last realised.

Once having gained possession of 'the land over the mountains' Congress set about organising its distribution.[8] This was systematically conceived. A corps of surveyors was appointed and the country was divided into ranges of townships six miles square. Fortunately there was available a valuable pool of settlers, many of them war veterans, so the area soon began to fill up and take shape. The Indians, however, remained a menace, and in 1790 two expeditions were organised to try to subdue them. The first started from Vincennes and marched upriver along the Wabash. It met with little resistance and after burning a few villages of bark huts and destroying corn returned to Vincennes. The second started from Fort Washington and moved up to the headwaters of the Miami. Here the settlements were found to have been evacuated, so the wigwams and log huts were put to the torch and the crops destroyed. Next, a party was sent out to probe ahead and discover where the Indians had gone. This brushed with a large force of Miami and was ignominiously put to flight, after which the whole expedition tamely returned to Fort Washington.

These two expeditions achieved almost nothing, for during the following months the harassment of settlers was if anything worse than before. Thus in 1791 a larger force was raised to try to cow the Indians once and for all. This was placed under the command of General St Clair, a Revolutionary War leader and the Governor designate of the north-west. St Clair's force, which was raised at Pittsburg, consisted of two regular regiments and some untrained levies and militia. It was shipped down the Ohio to Fort Washington, but after disembarking moved to a new fort called Hamilton, twenty-five miles to the north, where St Clair set up his headquarters. Following wearisome delays mainly due to inefficient quartermasters a start was made for the Miami settlements on 4

[8] Federal Land Ordinance 1785 and N.W. Ordinance 1787.

October 1791. On 13 October there was a halt to build another
fort named Jefferson, and then the army stumbled northward
again through the wilderness. It was soon clear that there
were Indians about, for scouts and stragglers in the woods
exchanged shots with braves and now and then lost a man
killed or captured. St Clair had been warned by Washington
before starting to be always on his guard, for the President[9]
had never forgotten the part played by surprise in Braddock's
defeat in 1755. In any case, as St Clair's army's passage through
the woods was known to the enemy, he should have made
caution his watchword and sent several scouting parties
ahead. In the event, although he had twenty Chickasaw with
him, he used very few scouts. In fact, he did not seem to
realise that he might be attacked, and while still some distance from the settlements was unwise enough to weaken his
force by sending one of his two regular regiments after some
militia who had deserted. The crunch came on 3 November
when he had put his reduced force of 1,400 men into camp
by a creek near the headwaters of the Miami. There was snow
on the ground and the puddles were skinned with ice. On both
sides and in the rear the ground was low and marshy, and
all around the wintry woods lay in frozen silence. Most of the
troops were crammed together on the narrow rise beside the
creek, but the militia were placed as an outpost on the flank.
Parties of Indians were seen during the afternoon, and they
skulked around the lines at night, but few sentinels were
posted and no special precautions were taken to guard against
surprise.

Next morning the force was under arms at dawn. St Clair
had intended to throw up an entrenchment and then make a
forced march against the Miami settlements. But he was
forestalled. Just as the men were being dismissed from stand-
to, the Indians attacked the militia in the outpost. The heavy
firing, the whoops and yells of the braves, but above all the
suddenness of it all, threw them into confusion, and after a
brief resistance they broke and fled toward the main camp
like a frightened herd. The Indians then moved in from all
sides, and although the soldiers fired incessantly not many

[9] George Washington, first President of the USA 1789–93–97.

bullets met their mark, for the elusive warriors in the smoke were painted black and red and this served as an horrific camouflage. Creeping even closer the Indians made a special set at the canoneers and started to pick them off one by one. Then they tried to seize one of the guns. This brought them into the open, and a bayonet charge led by St Clair himself drove them back. Further bayonet charges dispersed others who had left the cover of the woods; and each charge for the moment appeared successful, but all the time soldiers were falling and finally there came a poor response to the call to rally. Next, the unwounded started slipping off beside the wounded to seek the shelter among the baggage in the middle of the camp; and finally, such long streams began leaving the front lines that St Clair decided he would have to retreat. After ordering the guns to be spiked, he mounted one of the few horses left unhurt, and gathering some staunch men, he gave them the task of cutting a path through the Indians blocking the way home. Moved by his exhortations the men charged with a will, and the puzzled Indians opened out and not only allowed the van to pass but most of those behind as well. However, the retreat so well begun soon developed into a rout. Some began to run and then an uncontrollable stampede occurred, horses, soldiers and camp followers, all mixed up. Impervious to orders, those on horses and the stronger on foot forced themselves to the front, leaving the weaker to receive the pursuing Indians' vengence. Near Fort Jefferson the regular regiment detached before the battle was encountered. Order was then restored, and after the wounded had been left at the fort, the rest were able to make their way to Fort Washington in a more seemly manner.

St Clair's expedition had been a disaster signal. His casualties were huge compared with those of the Indians and the latter had seized from his camp guns, axes, powder, clothing and blankets, in fact everything their hearts desired. Their war spirit too had received an uplift and from then on the bands of warriors who marched against the frontier became more numerous, more formidable and bolder than ever.

After the failure of St Clair's operation, Congress decided to try to come to terms with the Indians and envoys were sent to the settlements to seek an understanding. The first two men dispatched were killed before they reached their destination, but others sent after them managed to contact the chiefs of the Wabash and Illinois, and in 1792 concluded a treaty with these two tribes. Nothing, however, could be achieved with the Miami, and as their raids continued, a further operation of war was set in motion against them. The force involved was placed under the command of General Anthony Wayne who was more competent and forceful than St Clair. 'Mad' Wayne, as he was called because of his impetuosity, had learnt his trade in the Revolutionary War. When a force he was commanding was surprised at Brandywine and subsequently routed by bayonet charges he learnt two lessons he never forgot. From then on he was always wary of a surprise attack and he never failed to train his men to use the bayonet. He was also experienced in Indian warfare, having carried out a successful operation against the Creeks in Georgia. Even before the punitive expedition following St Clair's defeat had been decided on he was training a force on the Ohio in a camp between Pittsburg and Wheeling for use if required, and by the spring of 1792 had 2,500 soldiers fit to fight the Indians. In May 1793 Wayne brought his army down the Ohio to Fort Washington and established his camp nearby. Here he awaited the negotiations being conducted to try and find a peaceful solution to the quarrel with the Miami. On 1 October 1793 when talks finally failed he was given permission to start his operation.

Wayne first marched his men eighty miles north and built a strong fortified camp which he named Greeneville in honour of his old comrade-in-arms of the Revolutionary War, General Nathanael Greene. Next, he led a strong detachment to the site of St Clair's defeat and built a post which he called Fort Recovery. In the spring of 1794, as soon as the ground was dry, Wayne prepared to advance from Fort Recovery towards the hostile Indians' settlements on the Maumee River and force a battle. At this stage he was joined by some mounted men from Kentucky under Captain William Clark, the brother of George Rogers Clark[10] who led the successful expedition into Illinois. One of Clark's first tasks was to escort with a few dragoons and infantrymen a column of packhorses from Fort Washington to Fort Greeneville. When he had covered nearly eighteen of the seventy miles of journey, he was attacked by Indians who drove off some of his packhorses. Appreciating the situation though at the rear at the time, Clark sent troopers after the Indians and these scattered the enemy and recovered the packhorses. Another packhorse column sent on from Greeneville in June was not so fortunate. Although it reached Fort Recovery it was attacked while encamped under the walls. The escort fled in to the fort losing nineteen killed and as many wounded and 200 packhorses were taken by the enemy. The Indians flushed with victory next tried to storm Fort Recovery, but were beaten off with heavy loss. They surrounded the fort and continued firing at it for two days, but during the second night, having decided the fort was too strong for them, they picked up their dead by the light of torches and drew off back to their settlements.

Three weeks after the successful defence of Fort Recovery, Wayne was joined by another force of mounted men from Kentucky under General Scott, and on 27 July he set off northward from the Miami River toward the Indian towns on the Maumee. It is said that the Indians who watched this march from hiding places in the woods brought word to their British allies that Wayne's army moved twice as fast as St Clair's had done, had many scouts out, marched with troops in open order ready for battle, and built strongly fortified camps at night. On reaching the Maumee, Wayne built a strong log fort in the cultivated field of a deserted Indian settlement which he called Defiance and here his troops enjoyed fresh vegetables and ears of corn. From Fort Defiance Wayne sent a final offer of peace to the Indians, inviting them to dispatch deputies to meet him, and when he received no reply, he marched on again until he reached the Maumee rapids not far from the British fort west of Lake Erie, where he erected a rough breastwork and went into camp. Next, he carried out a reconnaissance ahead, and discovered the

[10] Clark later crossed the continent with Lewis.

enemy[11] in position waiting for him in a forest known as Fallen Timbers where, following a whirlwind, dead trees were plied across one another in rows.

Wayne's attacking force of some 3,000 men approached the Indian position along the north bank of the Maumee. Clark's mounted men were out in front, the regular cavalry were on the right next to the river and Scott's troopers were on the left. The Indians were drawn up in line at right angles to the river. When the Americans approached they rose from cover, drove back Clark's men and dropped down under cover again. The American infantry were by this time in two long lines in open order. Wayne ordered the front line to attack, rouse the Indians from cover, and then fire a volley and go in with the bayonet. Meanwhile, Scott's men were told to try to turn the enemy's right and the regular cavalry were ordered to attack the left. It would be difficult to find more unfavourable ground for cavalry, but the regular dragoons rode in on the Indians with a will, their broadswords swinging and their horses dodging in and out among the trees and jumping the fallen logs. Both captains were shot down, and a dozen saddles were emptied, but they thoroughly routed their opponents. Meanwhile the infantry had met with equal success. The Indians, having delivered one volley, rose from their hiding places and fled. Many were shot down, and the rest were driven off at the point of the bayonet. So complete was the American initial success that only the first line of infantry had to be employed. The battle, in fact, was over and won before Scott's mounted volunteers on the Indian right could complete their flanking movement. Thirty-three of Wayne's men were killed and a hundred wounded, while the Indians lost two or three times as many. It was the most complete and important victory ever gained over the North-West Indians during the forty years of warfare to which it put an end, and it was the only considerable pitched battle in which the Indians lost more than their foes. After the battle, villages were burned and crops cut down, up to the walls of the British fort. The houses and buildings of the British agents

[11] About 2,000, consisting of Miami, Shawnee and Iroquois braves along with 70 white Canadian Rangers.

and traders suffered with the rest, but Wayne did not dare to try to storm the fort which was well built and heavily armed, and on completing his work of destruction he marched his army back to Fort Defiance. After halting for a fortnight in order to reprovision his men from Fort Recovery, he next undertook a punitive expedition against Miami settlements in the area where the American force had been defeated four years previously in 1790. Then, having spent six weeks burning towns and destroying crops, a new fort was built back on the headwaters of the Maumee which was christened Fort Wayne.

The Battle of Fallen Timbers caused the Indians to realise that although the British would encourage them in their struggle to stem the tide of American expansion and supply then with arms and equipment, they would not proceed to war themselves. Accordingly, almost all the leaders recognised it was time to make peace. In November the Wyandots from Sandusky sent ambassadors. Wayne spoke to them with his customary frankness, saying that if they did not make peace he would surely destroy them all in the near future. They went away and considered the matter, and soon resolved on peace; and not long afterwards several other tribes decided likewise. This was followed in the summer of 1795 by the signing of the formal treaty of Greeneville in which Wayne on behalf of Congress made a formal peace with the North-West tribes. At the ceremony was a full delegation from every hostile tribe and no less than 1,130 Indians were present at the treaty grounds. All solemnly covenanted to keep the peace and surrender the area which is now southern Ohio and south-eastern Indiana, and the United States acknowledged the Indian title to the remaining territory and agreed to pay to the tribes annuities totalling 9,500 dollars. It was the first time the border had been quiet for a generation and for fifteen years this quiet was to remain unbroken. Kentucky had come into existence as a State in 1792 and Tennessee in 1796. Now as a result of the new stability Ohio emerged in 1803, and Indiana in 1816, Illinois in 1818, Michigan in 1837 and Wisconsin in 1848.

Chapter 3

Across the Mississippi

In 1794 another conflict between the United States and Britain seemed imminent. In her war against the French Republic Britain applied the traditional doctrine that enemy property on the high seas was good prize even if in a neutral vessel and seized a number of small American vessels carrying provisions to the French West Indies. News of these captures brought consternation to the American trading community, and there was talk of war. Wiser counsels, however, prevailed, and Chief Justice John Jay was dispatched to London to seek justice for the United States. Also at this time Canada had proposed that the area between the Great Lakes and the Ohio, together with a strip of New York and Vermont, should be made into a satellite Indian state giving a further object of Jay's visit in countering this and obtaining the evacuation of British forts in the territory concerned.

The mission proved largely successful. Under Jay's Treaty signed in London on 19 November 1794 a limited American trade was allowed with the British West Indies, the idea of an Indian satellite state was quashed, and a promise was obtained to evacuate the British posts. There followed the movement of many tribes into Canada, and the establishment of an agreed general line of the border between Canada and the United States following the modern 49th Parallel.

A development from Jay's Treaty also gave in the following year the unexpected temporary dividend of a settlement with Spain that included the right of transit at New Orleans. The Spanish Government had feared that Jay's Treaty might contain the rudiments of a secret Anglo-American alliance. When America's envoy Thomas Pinckney arrived in Madrid the Spanish authorities were eager to come to terms themselves.

In the Treaty of San Lorenzo on 27 October 1795, which followed Pinckney's deliberations, permission was given to the Americans to navigate the lower Mississippi, transit rights at New Orleans were conceded, and Spain evacuated posts on the east bank of the Mississippi north of the border between Florida and the United States.

Washington retired from the office of President in 1797. He was succeeded by John Adams, who in his turn made way for Thomas Jefferson in 1801. Meanwhile, the war in Europe had upset the arrangement with Spain outlined above. After Napoleon's victory at Marengo in June 1800 had broken up the Second Coalition against him, Spain agreed to exchange her vast and largely unoccupied territory of Louisiana west of the Mississippi for the Duchy of Tuscany. Late in 1802 the Spanish Intendant withdrew America's transit rights at New Orleans and prepared to hand over the colony to a French expeditionary force already on the way. America's new-won rights at New Orleans and on the Mississippi appeared to be about to be lost, and her subsequent expansion westward blocked by a colony of a powerful and ambitious France in place of one of an easy-going Spain. In face of this serious situation, the diplomats Robert R. Livingston[1] and James Monroe were entrusted with the task of negotiating for the transfer of New Orleans and the delta of the Mississippi from France to the United States. Livingston was a member of a distinguished New York family, a member of the committee which drafted the declaration of Independence and a Chancellor of the State of New York. He had refused a post in Jefferson's cabinet before he was asked to go to France. To help him, Jefferson sent over James Monroe who later became President of the United States. Of the two main French negotiators, Foreign Minister Talleyrand and Director of the Treasury Barbe-Marlouis, the former was the more formidable. As a political exile Talleyrand had sought refuge in America and lived there for two years. He had returned to Europe with a dislike for the American people, who had not been impressed by his elegant irony, but he was never-

[1] Livingston was the American minister in Paris.

theless a more ardent advocate of American colonisation than Napoleon.

It seemed vital to obtain some concession at this time. The States of Kentucky, Tennessee and Mississippi would not be likely to remain within the Union if Congress could not secure for them navigation rights on the River Mississippi which they had enjoyed under easy-going Spain, who had shown herself unwilling or unable to interfere with the activities of American frontiersmen. When it was learned that Spain had been forced to transfer Louisiana the settlers were horror-struck. Spain could be bluffed or bullied, but an eager France determined to re-establish her American empire presented a very different problem. Even as the settlers discussed their fate New Orleans officials were posting a proclamation ending the right of upriver exporters to deposit their produce at the town and thence export them. Actually, France had nothing to do with this order, which was a belated Spanish attempt to put a stop to smuggling, but the frontiersmen who knew nothing of this were convinced that here was an example of the treatment they could expect from the new masters of the Mississippi.

What the negotiators in Paris did not know was that in spite of pressure from Talleyrand, Napoleon was fast recoiling from the idea of acquiring new colonies in America. At the outbreak of the French Revolution nearly two thirds of the American commercial interests of France had been centred on San Domingo (Haiti). Since then there had been revolts and disorders which were difficult to control. Half a million Negro slaves were freed during the French Revolution, and afterwards the Negro leader Toussaint de l'Ouverture had attempted to set up an independent black State. A French expedition was dispatched, and Toussaint surrendered and was executed. But the combination of the black army and yellow fever had decimated the French force, and it had become clear that the domination of San Domingo and the full restoration of French rule would be difficult to achieve. In 1802 there was peace in Europe. So long as there was a chance of rebuilding his colonial empire, Napoleon was anxious to avoid renewed hostilities with England. With the

III General Anthony Wayne by John Trumbull (*Library of Congress*)

President Thomas Jefferson, engraved by J. B. Forrest from the painting by G. Stuart (*Library of Congress*)

IV Meriwether Lewis by Charles Willson Peale (*Independence National Historical Park Collection, Philadelphia*)

William Clark by Charles Willson Peale (*Independence National Historical Park Collection, Philadelphia*)

difficulties in San Domingo in mind, his thoughts turned to securing the hegemony of Europe where England would be his principal opponent. If he began another war with England, he knew his American possessions might very well fall as prey to the British navy, and he felt that if he could not hold on to them he had better abandon the nebulous Louisiana empire. Even if the British were not able to seize Louisiana, granted the character of the American pioneer, Napoleon would ultimately lose the territory to America. There seemed no possibility of France being strong enough to stem the rising tide of American expansion for long. Why not then sell not just New Orleans, but vast Louisiana as well? He could demand a good price, and the money would be useful to provide an armada of flat-bottomed boats for the invasion of England.

Plans for this invasion may well have been in his mind when Napoleon summoned Talleyrand immediately after High Mass on Easter Day, 1803 and announced that he was going to sell Louisiana to the Americans. He had already informed his brothers Joseph and Lucien of his intentions. He became very angry when Lucien had pointed out that the French constitution forbade alienation of national territory without a vote, and that as the terms of the treaty with Spain by which France had acquired Louisiana had not been fully implemented, Louisiana could not legally be sold. According to this treaty, which Lucien had helped to negotiate, Spain had agreed to give back Louisiana, which she had received from France in 1762 at the end of the Seven Years War, and in return would receive a large slice of territory in Italy. This Napoleon had done nothing about, although he had immediately set to work to link Louisiana to the French islands of the West Indies by supplying those articles hitherto purchased from the United States. Where an earlier generation of French colonial officials had sought to connect Louisiana and Canada by a chain of forts, he would bind Louisiana to the West Indies by trade. The unfortunate experiences in San Domingo altered the whole picture. Napoleon's enthusiasm for colonies so carefully nurtured by Talleyrand had turned first to indifference then to disgust. Talleyrand's remonstrances and Lucien's arguments were brushed aside, and he insisted that Louisiana should be sold if the American negotiators were willing to pay a good price. As for Spain, she was in no position to make her complaints heard.

On Easter Monday when Livingston was summoned to the Ministry of Foreign Affairs he once again trotted out the old familiar arguments: the United States cared nothing for Louisiana and wanted only West Florida and New Orleans; the area was one of barren sands and sunken marshes with a small town built of wood of about seven thousand souls; the territory was important to the United States because it contained the mouth of some of their rivers; it would be a mere drain on the resources of France. Talleyrand had heard it all before. He listened politely, but when Livingston finally paused for breath, he broke in with his momentous question: 'What will you give for the whole?' For a moment Livingston who was slightly deaf did not understand. When he finally grasped what he was being offered, he was careful not to appear too eager. He would be glad to explore the possibilities, he said, but the matter demanded reflection, and he would have to consult his colleague, Mr Monroe.

Negotiations got under way at once, and within a week the main outlines were settled, though Monroe himself was so ill that he remained on a sofa throughout the discussions. Both parties understood that they must reach a decision quickly. Napoleon's brothers were known to be bitterly opposed to the sale, and it was a question of how far their family loyalty could be stretched. If the negotiations dragged on, the secret was bound to leak out and Napoleon might find himself compelled to disown the whole scheme. Under these conditions Livingston did well to stop haggling and agree to the French demand of fifteen million dollars. The documents were signed on 2 May 1803, and the treaties were antedated to 30 April, the day the agreement was reached.

Elated though they were at having bought an empire, the American diplomats must have had serious misgivings as to how their treaty would be received at home. They had been authorised to obtain New Orleans and as much of Florida as thay could secure east of the Mississippi, but what they

had actually done was to buy New Orleans and a vast unde-
fined territory west of the Mississippi. When they asked for
a clearer definition of the boundaries they met with no
satisfaction. 'I can give you no direction,' said Talleyrand,
'you have made a noble bargain for yourselves, and I suppose
you will make the most of it.' The United States had bought
what had originally belonged to France, no more and no
less. During the forty years of Spanish administration the
boundaries had not changed. So sketchy were the maps that
Livingston understood that western Florida was included in
the purchase. Talleyrand did not disabuse him. He was quite
sure in his own mind that Florida still belonged to Spain,
but it would do no harm if the Americans and Spaniards
developed a little quarrel of their own over frontiers. In all
these discussions he was no doubt acting under orders of
Napoleon who always drafted his treaties in such deliberately
ambiguous language that he could interpret them as he
chose.

Monroe later stated that the cession of Louisiana was an
act of great and enlightened policy rather than an affair of
commerce. But he was wrong. There was nothing enlightened
about Napoleon's decision. He acted from a variety of motives,
but altruism was not one of them. As it turned out the
acquisition of the new territory, though it was destined to
make the United States a great power, was to have a curiously
different result from what Napoleon expected. Instead of
becoming a great naval power as he had believed she would,
the United States concentrated on the development of its vast
new domains and left England in undisputed possession of
the seas. But Napoleon had still another object in mind. He
wanted to strengthen the United States temporarily so that
she might act as a counterweight against England, and yet
he hoped to prevent the rise of too powerful a state in the
western hemisphere. The experience of history indicated that
a republican form of government, which Napoleon detested,
could only thrive in a small state. Thus by doubling the size
of the United States he calculated that he was sowing the
seeds of its eventual dissolution. Sooner or later the unwieldy
republic would split apart. President Jefferson accepted the

possibility of fission,[2] but was not disturbed by it, for he
believed that whether the United States remained one confederacy, or split into Atlantic and Mississippi confederacies,
it would not affect the happiness of either part. The only
thing that mattered to Jefferson was that Europe should be
excluded from the New World. In his inaugural address in
1801 he had spoken of there being room enough in America
for its descendants to the thousandth generation. Now he was
proposing to double its area on the plea of security. It was a
strange fate indeed that required the author of the Declaration of Independence to buy a colony by an act which made
a nonsense of the constitution. Even more strange was the
theory, new to international law, that security meant freedom
from contiguity, not of an enemy, but of a former ally. No
doubt it would have been better for Jefferson to have secured
the passage of an amendment to the constitution authorising
the acquisition of territory, but there was not time for such
niceties. Livingston and Monroe advised him to close the
transaction as soon as possible in case Napoleon should change
his mind.

The treaty was submitted to both Houses at a special
session of Congress. It was ratified by the Senate on 20 October
1803 by a vote of twenty-four to seven. In the debate in the
House of Representatives on the appropriation of the necessary funds, a few members objected to the admission of a
foreign people to the Union. Others argued that the price
was exorbitant, and that the boundaries had been purposely
concealed by France; but the opposition was half-hearted, and
the fifteen million dollars were appropriated by a vote of ninety
to twenty-five. Those who objected were the New Englanders
who realised that with the addition of this new territory the
balance of power would inevitably turn against them.

There still remained one problem—that of the attitude of
the French and Spanish inhabitants, who were being handed
over from one nation to another without any consideration
of their own wishes. For some reason, inexplicable to Jefferson,
the Louisianians believed that French or Spanish rule, despite
its political absolutism, was more congenial to their easy-going

   [2] This nearly came about in 1861.

way of life than the authority of republican Americans. Jefferson forestalled any danger of an anti-American demonstration by dispatching troops, and the French prefect cooperated by organising a fête in New Orleans on the day of transfer. The celebrations began at three o'clock in the afternoon of 20 December 1803 and lasted until nine the following morning. Toasts were drunk in wines appropriate to the three nations; madeira for the United States, malaga for Spain, and champagne for France. Dancing continued through the night. In this way unpleasantness was averted, and Jefferson may well have settled any question of conscience by reflecting that the government of Louisiana rested, if not on the consent of the governed, at least on their indifference. Jefferson was not therefore worried by the impropriety of not allowing Louisiana self-government. It is easy to accuse him of sacrificing principles to expediency, but today, many years after the event, any one who follows the meandering negotiations which led to the purchase of Louisiana will be more than ever convinced that Jefferson was a great statesman as well as a master politician. No one could have been more surprised than he was when he opened the dispatch from Livingston and Monroe informing him that they had bought an empire instead of a town, but he accepted the grave issues involved in the staggering deal without hesitation. He wanted to be remembered as the author of the Declaration of Independence, of the Statute of Virginia for religious freedom, and as the father of the University of Virginia; but posterity would do well to remember him also as the man who doubled the area of the United States. By doing so he created that vast reserve of land that has done so much to shape the course of American history. By nature and habit the American is restless. Undoubtedly it was his manifest destiny to inherit the earth from the Atlantic to the Pacific, but it was the quick action of Livingston and Monroe in accepting Napoleon's offer, combined with the magnificent inconsistency of Jefferson, that hurried the American into his inheritance.

Thanks to Jefferson and his skilful diplomats, the West beyond the Mississippi had been gained for the United States much more quickly than had ever been anticipated. The next step was to explore the territory newly added to the national domain, for nobody knew much about it. The first expedition was set in motion by Jefferson himself. Nominally its purpose was to find out the best places to establish trading stations with the Indian tribes, but in reality it was a voyage of exploration, planned to ascend the Missouri to its head, cross the continent to the Pacific, and report on the geography and flora and fauna. The two officers chosen to carry through the work were William Clark, brother of George Rogers Clark, and Meriwether Lewis, who had been President Jefferson's private secretary. Both had fought under General Wayne at Fallen Timbers. They started their trip with twenty-seven men who intended to complete the whole journey and sixteen who were going to stop off on the way at the Mandan villages. The main party included a half-breed interpreter, two French voyageurs, Clark's Negro servant, nine volunteers from Kentucky and fourteen regular soldiers. All the main body except the Negro were enlisted into the army before starting so that they might be kept under discipline.

The party set off from St Louis in May 1804 up the Missouri valley in three large boats, well supplied with arms, powder and lead, clothing, gifts for the Indians, and provisions. As they went upriver they passed several settlements, the most important being St Charles, where the people were all Creoles. The next town was peopled mainly by Americans, and another had as one of its occasional residents old Daniel Boone himself. As they gradually worked their way northwestward, buffalo and elk were met with in considerable numbers, also antelope, black-tail deer, prairie dogs, and coyotes, whose uncanny wailing after nightfall vied in intensity with the baying of the grey wolves. With the Indian tribes encountered the explorers held councils, distributing presents to the chiefs, and telling them of the transfer of the territory from Spain. The Indians professed satisfaction at the change, although not probably understanding its significance. Their acquiescence, however, temporarily satisfied Lewis and Clark who followed this up by trying to make each tribe swear to keep the peace with its neighbours. The tribes usually con-

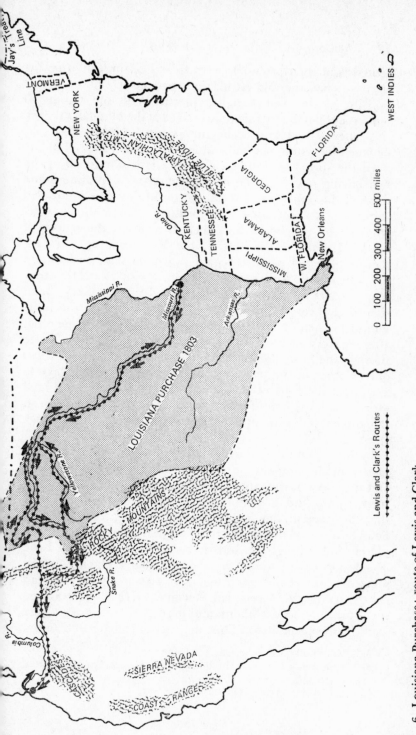

6. Louisiana Purchase: route of Lewis and Clark

sented, and then promptly went to war again, for in reality
they only had the vaguest idea of what the ceremonies of the
hoisting of the American flag meant. With the coming of
winter and having by this time arrived at the Mandan villages,
the party halted and went into camp, building log huts
enclosed by a stout stockade which they called Fort Mandan.

In the spring of 1805 Lewis and Clark started off again,
first having sent back ten of their party with specimens and
notes of the journey so far. Those continuing now numbered
thirty-two and included a Frenchman with a squaw wife[3]
whose baby was but a few weeks old. From the mouth of
Little Missouri to the head of the Missouri proper the explorers passed through a region swarming with buffalo and
elk. The buffalo were so plentiful and so easy to kill that they
soon became the mainstay of their food supply. They found
the grizzly bears very dangerous. Again and again the bears
attacked when neither molested or threatened. They ran
after hunters on horseback and chased them on foot. To go
through the bush alone proved most hazardous. Several times
one or other of the party was charged and forced to take to
a tree at the foot of which the bear sometimes mounted
guard for hours before going off. On one occasion a bear on
shore even plunged into the water and swam out to attack
a canoe.

In the autumn they reached the headwaters of the Missouri,
and from then on they had to pass through the mountains
and the way was difficult. They were helped to increase their
speed by the Indian wife of the Frenchman who had joined
them at Mandan. She had been captured originally from the
Shoshoni, one of the Rocky tribes, so was able to act as interpreter, and through her aid they made friends with a band
of Shoshoni[4] from whom they bought horses. Having cached
some of their gear they made their way westward through
the passes of the forest-clad Rockies. Here game was less
plentiful than on the plains, and harder to kill, so they were
soon on short-commons. They met many Indians and found

---

[3] Sacagawea : she was to become a heroine.
[4] Shoshone Indians include Shoshoni proper, Snakes, Bannocks, Utes,
and Comanches.

them in some ways different from those encountered on the plains. Both east and west of the Rockies the Indians owned horses, but those in the mountains had fewer guns and relied more on tomahawks and bows and arrows, the traditional weapons for hunting and war. For some of the mountain tribes it was the first time they had encountered white people, but when the mouth of the Columbia was reached, the coast Indians were found to be quite familiar with them, for this region had been visited thirteen years before by Captain Gray of Boston, and ships had been coming there continuously ever since. Also some of these tribes had been visited occasionally by traders from the British fur companies. They reached the Pacific coast just before cold weather set in, and having built Fort Clatsop near the mouth of the Columbia River, passed the winter there.

In March 1806 they began to retrace their steps. At first they were short of food, as game was hard to get and they could find few salmon in the streams because the fish had gone upriver, but again the worst section of the journey was passing through the passes beside the snow-covered mountain tops, and they were glad indeed when they emerged on to the plains and found their caches undisturbed. Early in July they separated for a time, Clark descending the Yellowstone and Lewis the Missouri. Clark's journey was uneventful, but Lewis's party had several affrays with Blackfoot Indians, in one of which a horse was lost. As, however, they killed two braves and seized four horses they had the better of this engagement. Later Lewis had the misfortune to be accidentally shot by one of his own party and suffered much from the wound. Near the mouth of the Yellowstone, Lewis and Clark reunited, and then the whole company floated down the Missouri together. Before they reached Fort Mandan they encountered two Americans, the first seen for a year and a half. They were the hunters Dickson and Hancock, who were setting off to trap along the headwaters of the Missouri on their own account, the first of many bands of hunters and trappers who were to roam across the Far West for the next three-quarters of a century. They had come from the Illinois country the year before to hunt and trap. They had been robbed, and one of them wounded in an encounter with Sioux, but were undauntedly pushing on towards the mountains. They returned with Lewis and Clark to Fort Mandan where Colter, a soldier of the party, eager for more adventure, turned back with them when they set off again. He proved to be the first to explore Yellowstone Park. Lewis, Clark and the rest drifted downstream past the Sioux settlements, and after an uneventful river voyage reached St Louis in September. From St Louis they forwarded an account of what they had done to President Jefferson. On their return to the East the two explorers became national heroes and were later rewarded for their achievements by receiving important appointments. Lewis became Governor of Louisiana, and Clark was made Governor of the area which eventually became Missouri.

While these first exploratory expeditions were taking place in the West, the area east of the Mississippi was steadily filling with population and becoming a more coherent part of the Union. In the north, settlers were firmly established along the entire northern bank of the Ohio in what are now the southern portions of Indiana and Illinois, Georgia had gained control of most of the Indian land within the State limits, all the country between Knoxville and Nashville had become part of Tennessee, and the only Indian lands in Kentucky were those held by the Chickasaw, who were friendly. Only Florida in the south remained in foreign hands. However, all was by no means quiet in the area where many tribes remained hostile and determined to halt American expansion. The first to attempt to do this were the Shawnee under Tecumseh and his brother Prophet, who in 1807 formed a confederacy to stop the American advance. The military commander of the Ohio area, General W. H. Harrison[5], tried to counter Tecumseh's move by buying on behalf of Congress territory from friendly tribes amounting to three million acres, for which he paid some ten thousand dollars. Tecumseh, however, repudiated this deal made by his neighbours, and

[5] President of the United States in 1841. He died of pneumonia one month after inauguration.

told Harrison that if he wanted the land he would have to fight for it.

Before hostilities began, Tecumseh left on a journey south to enlist the other tribes of his confederacy in the struggle, and he put the Shawnee capital beside Tippecanoe Creek[6] in the charge of his brother. Considering this too good an opportunity to miss, Harrison decided to attack immediately, and he mustered for the task a force of a thousand men, made up of regular and militia infantry, and mounted riflemen. He marched from Vincennes on 26 September 1811, and early in November, having reached the Shawnee settlement, encamped on high ground above the marshes bordering Tippecanoe Creek. Prophet, on learning of the American approach, chose a hundred warriors of repute and ordered them to attack the camp and kill General Harrison, saying that if he was not in his tent he would be easily recognisable on his grey charger. On 7 November in the hour before dawn the Indian assault band crawled up unnoticed towards the camp whose fires still flamed sufficiently to outline the tents around the baggage in the centre. Just before daylight, when General Harrison was pulling on his boots preparatory to ordering his drummer to beat reveillé, there was a shot from a guard followed by the dying shriek of an Indian.[7] Next, wildly whooping, the rest of the band fell on the camp, some managing to penetrate the tents, and to tomahawk and scalp their occupants before they sprang to arms. By a stroke of good fortune Harrison's grey had broken its tie rope and a bay horse had been brought for his use. This probably saved his life, as the Indians concentrated on officers riding light-coloured mounts, and Harrison was able to ride round and rally his men unmolested. The American resistance proved so effective that before dawn broke the Indian onset, although reinforced from the settlement, had begun to slacken. On noticing this, Harrison ordered a counter-attack by his regulars with bayonets fixed, timed to synchronise with volleys of covering fire from his militia. Then, when the Indians

[6] On the Wabash, 150 miles north of Vincennes.
[7] This was lucky for the Americans, as it gave the alarm. Most Indians would have died silently.

began to show signs of breaking, the mounted men were sent in. With sabres swinging these rode down any Indians who did not manage to reach the safety of the marshes at the foot of the hill. Both sides lost heavily, the Americans having sixty killed and the Indians almost as many. But the Americans could claim a victory, for not only did the Indians flee the battlefield, they also evacuated their settlement.

At the outbreak of the War of 1812 Tecumseh was allied to the British and met with more success. This was in some degree due to the incompetence of the American leader, Brigadier-General William Hull, and the contrasting efficiency of the British commander, Major-General Isaac Brock. Hostilities began with a British attack on American-held Detroit. While the British in Fort Malden opened cannon fire across the river, their Indian allies cut in between an American relief column and troops sent out from Detroit by General Hull, and caused both bodies to beat a hasty retreat. Next the Indians surrounded the stronghold, and appeared so menacing that Hull raised the white flag. The fall of Detroit on 16 August 1812 was followed by the successful storming of other northern American frontier forts; and the result was that many of the northern tribes who had not decided whom to follow joined the British side. Tecumseh next went off on a journey to rouse the southern tribes; and when he returned there had been assembled from previously doubtful tribes in the north some three thousand men.[8] Nevertheless, the fortunes of war were about to turn against him, for the forceful General Harrison of Tippecanoe fame had replaced General Hull, and the British General Brock had been killed in battle and succeeded by the incompetent Colonel Proctor. Without the support of a British commander with whom he had co-operated so well, Tecumseh was not able to repeat his early successes.

General Harrison had been ordered to redeem the disgraceful loss of Detroit without delay, and he set about his task most methodically. First he built Fort Meigs on the Maumee River near the site of the Battle of Fallen Timbers,

[8] His own Shawnee, and bands of Sauk and Fox, Winnebago, Wyandot, Chippewa and Sioux.

and then he prepared to march on the lost town. He had hardly completed the new fort, however, before he was besieged by a large force under Colonel Proctor and Tecumseh. The first American move proved disastrous. Eight hundred Kentucky reinforcements made a sally and were surrounded and cut to pieces by Tecumseh's braves. Only a hundred escaped back to the fort. Five hundred were killed and over a hundred made prisoner. The latter were made to run the gauntlet by their Indian captors, and twenty-five were tomahawked before Tecumseh galloped up and stopped the massacre. However, in spite of this success of his Indian allies, Colonel Proctor did not feel capable of pressing the siege of Fort Meigs; and from then on the war started to go better for the Americans. Commander Perry built up a powerful fleet on Lake Erie, and General Harrison sent two contingents to fill out crews for the ships. In September 1812 Perry won a naval victory which enabled him to cut the British supply line across the lake. Next Perry ferried a part of the American army over the water, and General Harrison was able to take Fort Malden.

After these American successes Colonel Proctor's men and Tecumseh's braves were forced to fall back deep into Canada, and it was not until they reached Thames River, eighty-five miles north-east of Fort Malden, that they turned and took up a defensive position to try and stem the tide of American advance. General Harrison had an army of 2,000 regulars and volunteer infantry, 1,500 mounted riflemen, and some Indian allies. He faced a British and Indian force nearly as large in a position that had been well selected. On the British right was swampy ground manned by her Indian allies, and on their left was woodland held by British regulars in open order. Harrison, after some changes of plan, sent in his mounted men against the British soldiers among the trees, having decided that it was the best place for his backwoodsmen. By a combination of spirited charges, a lot of wild whooping and dismounted action and some volley firing, the horsemen drove the British from the field in this quarter. The British in the centre were also driven back fairly easily, but Tecumseh's braves in the marsh on the British right proved more difficult to dislodge. They were only thrown out after a series of spirited bayonet charges, and at the expense of severe casualties. During this assault Tecumseh was killed, his body being carried off lest it fall into the hands of the Americans. Although Thames River was a sharp little encounter, only about thirty were killed on each side. However, the Americans took a number of prisoners, and the death of Tecumseh weakened Indian resistance from then on in the north.

In the south, meanwhile, the Creek bands roused by Tecumseh were still on the warpath, fighting back hard against the American advance. In this area the principal leader was Chief Red Eagle, who proved as difficult to subdue as Tecumseh had been. The Louisiana purchase had opened the floodgates to American emigration, and settlers had begun to encroach on the lands of the Creek nation in Alabama, south Georgia, and Florida where neither the Spanish, French nor English had penetrated in any numbers. At this period it is estimated that, with their kinsmen and allies the Seminole, the Creeks numbered some 24,000 people. Yet, though numerous, they were failing to stem the American advance westward. By treaty, cession or outright encroachment they were losing territory steadily. Many Creek tribes still sought security for themselves by peaceful methods; but some like Red Eagle who had been inspired to fight for his rights by Tecumseh raised their braves and went on the warpath. On 29 August 1813 Red Eagle with one thousand of his warriors attacked without warning, Fort Mims,[9] thirty miles north of Mobile in Alabama. The stronghold consisted of a stockade built around the fortified house of Samuel Mims, a Creek half-breed, and was garrisoned by seventy Louisiana militiamen. Rumours that the Indians were on the rampage had packed Fort Mims with refugees from the surrounding countryside, mainly planters and their families with their Negro servants. However, as the danger was not thought to be imminent, few precautions had been taken, and the gate was open when the Creeks attacked. Although the Indians had no firearms, they were so numerous and the surprise was

[9] About 150 miles N.E. of New Orleans.

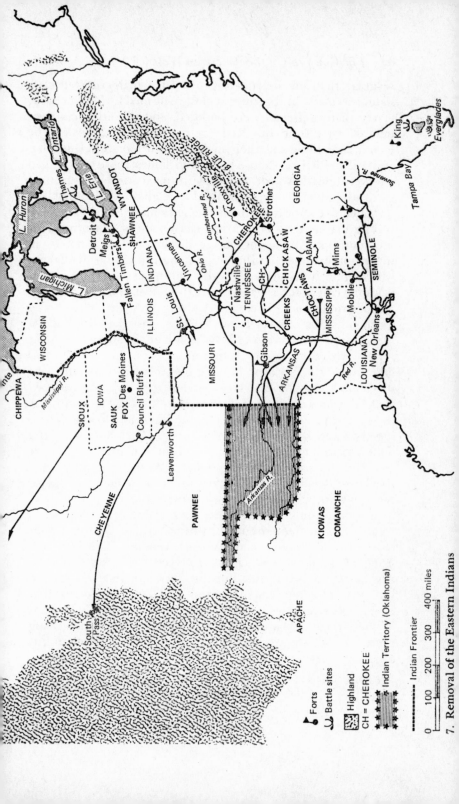

7. Removal of the Eastern Indians

so great that the defenders could offer little resistance. A
stand was made in the inner enclosure formed by Mims's house
where many refugees were huddled, and the attackers were
held off for a time, but Red Eagle ordered fire arrows to be
loosed, and these did their evil work all too well. The roof
and walls of Mims's house burst into flames; those who dashed
out were tomahawked; and those trapped inside were burnt
to death, men, women and children alike. Only thirty-six
managed to escape from the whole settlement.

The massacre at Fort Mims caused bitter resentment in
the South, and following outraged demands for retribution,
three columns were set in motion to punish the hostile Creeks
who had been involved. Georgian volunteers were dispatched
from the east; a force was sent out from Mobile; and a column
3,000 strong under General Andrew Jackson[10] was moved
south from Tennessee. It was on these last that the bulk of
the subsequent fighting fell. Jackson had already won a great
reputation. 'He's tough—tough as hickory,' his soldiers had
said, and 'Old Hickory' became his nickname. Starting out
in October, having first cut a wagon road over the wooded
Racoon and Look-out Mountains for his baggage train, he
thrust down towards Mobile with the intention, first of defeating the Creeks responsible for the Fort Mims holocaust, and
then invading Florida and dealing with the Seminole who were
reported to be on the rampage there. When Jackson reached
the Coosa River[11], he built a fort which he named Strother to
act as a base for his operations. Then on 3 November 1813
he attacked and destroyed a nearby hostile Creek settlement.
In this engagement the famous frontiersman Davy Crockett
took part. He went some way to revenging Fort Mims by
using the same ruthless tactics that Red Eagle had done, setting fire to a house and burning to death forty-six Indian
warriors. Moving forward again, Jackson now learnt that
Red Eagle's men were besieging a band of friendly Indians
in the village of Talladega, thirty miles to the south. Using
pincer movement tactics, he closed in on the settlement, but
although heavy casualties were inflicted, mostly in hand-to-

[10] Andrew Jackson, 7th President of the United States, 1829–1837.
[11] Tributary of the Alabama River which flows south through Mobile.

hand combat, several hundred warriors escaped through a gap in the encirclement before Jackson's cavalry could close it.

For a period Jackson was preoccupied with large-scale desertions from his force, and then with taking steps to make good his losses with adequate replacements. But eventually he amassed a new army of some two thousand and was ready to take the field again. In March 1814, when he discovered that Red Eagle had stationed 800 braves at Horseshoe Bend on the Tallapoosa River, thirty-five miles south of Talladega, he decided to attack. The position was a strong one, for the Creeks had built log breastworks, and they had moored canoes close to the river bank to provide an escape route. Before the Americans closed in the Indians were allowed to ferry their women and children to safety. Then scouts swam across the river under enemy fire and cut loose the canoe moorings to close that way of escape. The battle proper began by the American six-pounders opening fire. The cannon balls embedded themselves in the log breastworks and had little effect, whereupon Jackson sent in an infantry charge, and a bloody hand-to-hand battle ensued. The Creeks, though out-numbered, fought very gallantly but many fell, and after the remnant, who had manned a small roofed fort, were burnt to death by the use of fire arrows again, the battle was over and the Creek power broken. It only remained to hunt down Red Eagle who had escaped; but Jackson was spared this trouble, for not long after the battle the chief came to the American camp and surrendered. Red Eagle was released and eventually became a prosperous planter, but most of his people were less fortunate. Both the hostile and friendly Creek tribes lost their territory to the Americans, and what compensation they received for their land was very small indeed.

Having dealt with the Indians of Alabama, Jackson next turned his attention on those who were disturbing the peace on the frontier of Florida. In 1816 Florida was still nominally a Spanish province, but Spanish authority was little exercised beyond a few forts like Pensacola in the north-west, and most of the country was in the hands of the Seminole, a southern tribe of the Creek nation. The name Seminole signified runaways or those separated from the main body of the Creeks. The true runaways of the region were the fugitive Negro slaves from South Carolina and Georgia. Some of these had interbred with the Seminole, but most were now serving the Indians as slaves. It is interesting to note that the Seminole remained slave owners even when later they were moved to new lands beyond the Mississippi.

Frontier hostilities[12] broke out owing to Indian resentment at the United States Army's hunting runaway slaves on the Spanish side of the border. A major incident occurred at the Negro Fort on the Apalachiocola River. This fort contained three hundred men, women and children, who were ex-slaves, either recent fugitives or descendants of those who had escaped earlier from their American masters. In the autumn of 1816 an American expedition containing friendly Creek allies was sent to collect the escapees. A band of hostile Seminole garrisoned the stronghold, which was well supplied with cannon, and powder and shot in two large magazines. When the American column arrived, the garrison was immediately called upon to surrender. It replied by opening a furious but ineffective fire on the surrounding American troops and on two gunboats which had come upriver. The boats sailed in close and returned the fire, and a furnace-heated roundshot from one of them struck a powder magazine, blew it up with a tremendous blast, destroyed most of the fort, and killed all but fifty of its occupants. The survivors then capitulated, and all those who were claimed as slaves by American owners were restored to them.

A war party of Seminole marching to the fort's relief had quickly withdrawn on the news of its fall. But the tribes did not long remain quiet, for in 1817 a Seminole ambush trapped a lieutenant and forty men escorting some women and children, and killed them all except six of the soldiers who ran away and one women who was spared. The Seminole next raided Georgia, killing and scalping, after which they retreated to their Florida fastnesses again. In 1818, such countermeasures as were possible locally having failed, General

[12] Seminole wars were fought between 1816–18, and again during 1835–42.

Andrew Jackson marched south from Tennessee to subdue the Seminole with a force of two infantry regiments, a battery of artillery, 1,000 militiamen and a band of friendly Creeks. Jackson marched his column into the interior of north Florida, and, on reaching the Suwanee River, took prisoner two Britishers who were arming and rousing Seminole bands. He brought them before a court-martial, which had them executed. Next he took and hanged two hostile chiefs who came into his hands. After this he moved over to the west, and following a three-day siege took by storm Pensacola, the only strong Spanish fort in Florida. At first it appeared that Jackson had achieved all he had set out to do. Then, it seemed that everything was lost; for confronted by Spain's irate protests at the general's highhandedness, the United States disavowed him and directed that Fort Pensacola be returned. However, negotiations followed, and the end result of Jackson's military operations was the cession in 1819 of Florida by Spain in return for a sum of five million dollars.

During the Presidency of James Monroe, 1817–25, demands began to be made to concentrate Indian tribes west of the Mississippi so that they should no longer impede further settlement of the newly occupied areas east of that river. Indians and half-breeds with well developed farms were given the choice of removal or staying and becoming American citizens. Those who preferred to leave exchanged their property for new lands in the West and were promised payment for travel expenses and the value of improvements on their relinquished property. During the presidency of John Quincy Adams, 1825–29, this removal policy was slowed down, as Adams was not convinced that it was entirely ethical; but after the inauguration of Andrew Jackson (1829–37) it was put into vigorous operation again. In 1830 Congress passed an Indian Removal Act, appropriating half a million dollars for transferring the Indians. Under the Act the President was authorised to grant lands in part of the Louisiana Purchase in exchange for those relinquished in the east. The Indians were to be protected in their new reservations and have their removal expenses and one year's subsistence paid for by the Federal authorities. They were also entitled to compensation for improvement on their old land.

The liquidation of northern Indian territories was largely accomplished between 1829 and 1843, when bands of Shawnee, Wyandot and Delaware from the area of Lake Erie were persuaded to accept reservations in the country of the Osage, west of the Missouri in what are now the States of Nebraska and Kansas. It was not a very happy transportation, for their numbers were drastically reduced by disease on the journey owing to epidemics of cholera and measles, and many groups were unable to make the journey in one season and suffered in improvised winter quarters en route. The removal of Black Hawk's Sauk and Fox was resisted, as the chief was determined to retain his ancient tribal capital at the mouth of the Rock River in Illinois.[13] But white settlers encroached on the Indian settlement and took over the Indian cornfields, and after the Governor of Illinois had threatened to remove the tribe forcibly, Black Hawk agreed that after crossing the Mississippi to the west for his annual winter hunt, he would not return. While over the river, however, the Sauk and Fox were attacked by hostile Sioux and could not stop long enough in one place to plant their crops. In desperation, in the spring of 1832 they returned to the east of the river in search of a vacant prairie on which to plant their corn. The Governor of Illinois then called out the militia—among whom was the young Abraham Lincoln—and drove the Indians up Rock River into the wilds of Wisconsin. The Indians resisted gallantly until Black Hawk was captured, after which they gave in and lost their ancient lands.

The great Indian nations of the south,[14] Chickasaw, Choctaw, and Creek were moved along with the rest, as also were the Cherokee, although the Cherokee's independence in the area between the Cumberland and Tennessee rivers had been guaranteed by the United States in a treaty of 1791. When in 1838 there was resistance among the Cherokee, regular troops under General Winfield Scott rounded them up and

[13] 150 miles west of Chicago.
[14] The Choctaw, Chickasaw, Cherokee, Creek and Seminole were known as the Five Civilised Tribes (1876).

started them off on their long trail to the area of Fort Gibson on the Arkansas River to the south of which the Chickasaw, Choctaw and Creeks had already moved (see map 17). The journey of the Cherokees cost then a quarter of their number, but the remainder reorganised their national government and prospered. They have retained their language and alphabet to the present day.

In the removal arrangements of the Eastern Indians to Louisiana, the military played an important part. At first mounted Rangers were embodied to settle the Indians on their new reserves in the West, but these irregulars were later replaced by new dragoon regiments to which some of the Rangers were transferred. In the new 1st Dragoons were several noteworthy figures drawn from the Rangers. These included Philip St George Cooke, later to become a distinguished cavalryman, and Jefferson Davis, the future President of the Confederation.

The 1st Dragoons were mustered near St Louis in 1834. Under Colonel Dodge also from the Rangers, they marched 400 miles south-west to Fort Gibson on the Arkansas River, and then west into Comanche country. Their object was to visit and impress the tribes who were to be the neighbours of the Indians moved there from the East. The expedition had been planned for May when there would be good pastures, but owing to recruiting and equipping difficulties the column did not set off until June. The cavalry formed the advanced part of a force under General Leavenworth, and the late start was nearly the cause of destroying them. It turned dreadfully hot, and the humid air of the Mississippi basin caused the troopers to suffer severely from heat exhaustion. To this was added fever caused by drinking the impure water found in the prairie water-holes, so that after a journey of only eighty miles half the men collapsed from heat or dysentery.

When the rear party came up, a camp was established for the sick men and unsound horses. With the good May grass gone, however, the latter were slow to recover. In spite of all these difficulties, after a short halt, the undaunted Colonel Dodge led forward two hundred troopers on those horses capable of continuing. They were followed by General

Leavenworth and some of the infantry. The General was soon in trouble. First he fell sick with fever, and then, when he had recovered he was thrown from his horse while hunting buffalo and killed. Dodge, however, unaware of his superior's death, pushed on, passing through brush country where in places the undergrowth was so dense that it had to be hacked down to make a path. When they reached the open prairie beyond the brush they entered territories inhabited by the Osage and Kiowa. These two tribes were carrying on a desultory war with each other, but the presence of the long blue column of disciplined troopers marching through their country had a good effect. Not only did the Indians agree to stop their warlike activities, but they also said they would visit Fort Gibson in the autumn to parley.

Dodge now decided to return. Reaching the rearguard, whom he found enlarging the sick camp for more invalids, he took over command and led the effectives back to Fort Gibson, leaving the ailing men and horses to come along behind at a slower rate. Although the casualties had been severe, being ninety out of a total cavalry force of six hundred, the results were not unsatisfactory. Soon after Dodge's return on 24 August 1834 the Osage and Kiowa started coming in to treat for peace, and were followed by other tribes. What was more, the Indians transferred from the East were left unmolested by their neighbours sufficiently long enough to allow them to settle down in their new and rather disappointing country.

There followed several other expeditions westward over the plains to try and stabilise the area. One, led by Colonel Dodge again, was from Fort Leavenworth to the Arkansas valley to visit the Comanche. They found the country relatively peaceful, and this although the Comanche complained that the Cheyenne were stealing their ponies. Meanwhile, Colonel Stephen Watts Kearny, who had taken part in the first expedition, established Fort Des Moines farther north on the Des Moines river in Sioux country. At this time the possession of Oregon on the west coast was in dispute with Britain, and from Des Moines Kearny made a noteworthy exploratory march with 300 dragoons, westward up the

Oregon Trail as far as South Pass and the Rockies Divide in the present state of Wyoming. Including the return journey, Kearny and his dragoons covered over a thousand miles. On the way back they met many potential settlers moving westward up the Oregon Trail. Later when the great gold rushes began, the cavalry were required to guard passengers on the trail from attacks by Sioux aroused to resentment by the sight of the numerous intruders.

The Seminole of Florida proved the most difficult to move; it took the Army, Navy and Marines combined six years to drive them from their strongholds in the Everglades and to evacuate them to Oklahoma, and even then remnants were left, descendants of whom live in Florida to this day. Hostilities began when Osceola, the chief of the Seminole, took prisoner and executed the Indian Agent who was trying to make him sign a treaty agreeing to evacuate his lands. Then, about the same time, an American column 112 strong under Major Dade, marching from Tampa Bay to reinforce the garrison of Fort King 130 miles to the north-east, was ambushed and almost wiped out. These incidents aroused the American nation, and forces were sent to Florida to subjugate Osceola and those supporting him, which included some free Negroes. An expeditionary force from the north was led by General D. L. Clinch, and another from New Orleans by General Gains. Both forces were over a thousand strong, but neither had much success. Although they defeated the Seminole when they met them in the field, and drove them into the swamps, the Indians regrouped, and were soon back attacking again, apparently as strong as ever. Nor did the American generals manage to combine and co-operate.

The next attempt was made by General Winfield Scott, the future captor of Mexico City, but he had even less success than his predecessors, mainly because he was handicapped by losing a number of short term volunteers, and had his manpower further reduced by camp epidemics of mumps and measles. Scott's showing was so feeble that he was recalled to face a court of inquiry. But in the end he was exonerated.

The subsequent commander in Florida was General Thomas S. Jesup, and as he was well supported by his subordinate commanders, one of whom was Zachary Taylor, and also well supplied, he achieved more success. In the summer of 1837 he defeated the Seminole in three engagements and as a result of his victories 3,000 Seminole men, women and children gave themselves up. However, before the prisoners were brought to Tampa Bay to board the transports to take them to the West, Osceola and his braves arrived and by persuasion and intimidation swept the entire encampment away back into the swamps before the Americans could get organised sufficiently to restrain them.

General Jesup had believed he had won the war, and had let down his guard. He now felt so frustrated that he stooped to treachery to retrieve his mistake. He called a council and persuaded Osceola and seventy-five of his warriors to attend under a flag of truce. Then he made them his prisoners.

Jesup's coup, however, had little effect on the war, which continued to drag on as bitterly as ever. Because of his indiscretion Jesup was soon replaced by Colonel Zachary Taylor, whose rugged appearance, brusque ungrammatical speech, and down-to-earth methods earned him the nickname 'Rough and Ready'. From the outset Taylor had his hands full. Even before he took over from the departing Jesup, Seminole chiefs and tribesmen were burning to avenge Osceola. There was no question of them surrendering again and agreeing to leave for the West. It was a matter of routing them out of the maze-like morasses of middle Florida.

Towards the end of November 1837 Taylor disembarked his troops, his baggage train of eight wagons, and his pack mules at Tampa Bay. Then he marched inland at the head of 1,000 men: 727 regulars of the 1st, 4th and 6th Infantry, the 4th Artillery, and the Missouri mounted volunteers. Two forts were built along the route. In the second of them the artillery and baggage was left, and then the army moved into the swampy ground surrounding Lake Okeechobee, north of the Everglades. On rising ground, not far from the north-east lake shore, the Seminole waited under Chief Alligator, the leader of the earlier ambush on Major Dade's column. The position chosen was a strong one amid cypress and palmetto groves and surrounded by swamps and creeks studded with sharp pointed grass. Taylor attacked on Christmas Day 1837. He sent in dismounted cavalry in the first wave, and when these brave men were shattered by enemy fire from Seminole perched up in the branches or behind the trunks of trees, he ordered forward first his regular infantry and then his reserves. These combined proved formidable enough to cause the Seminole to give way and run, but the Battle of Okeechobee had proved the bloodiest of the whole Seminole War, with an American loss of 26 killed and 112 wounded. It was impossible to estimate the enemy loss. Most of their casualties were carried away. But 12 Indians and 1 Negro were found dead on the battlefield, along with 9 severely wounded warriors.

This victory no more ended hostilities than others before it. The Seminole faded back into their swamps, and then issued forth again in sudden, deadly raids. Taylor, brevetted a general after his victory at Okeechobee planned to divide the country into squares and systematically blot out the Seminole refuges. When his proposal received no support from higher command, he asked to be relieved of his command.

His successor, General William J. Worth, however, was permitted to carry out a plan similar to Taylor's. Through the spring and summer of 1841 he methodically eliminated centres of resistance. Although he was able to kill or round-up few hostiles, he could and did destroy huts and crops. Facing winter starvation, and threatened with the hanging of several captured chiefs, the tribe at last surrendered and submitted to exile and resettlement in the West. By the signing of a final treaty in 1842 a total of 4,000 Seminole were deported. A few more were gathered in between 1850 and 1859. An unyielding group remained hidden in the Everglades and the Big Cypress where their descendants still live.

By 1850 the bulk of the Eastern Indians had been moved to the west of the Mississippi. Only a few minor tribes with assistance from missionaries or others managed to cling to their ancient lands. An example of one of these is provided by the Chippewa or Ogibwa Indians. Living along the Bad

River in Wisconsin they were taken under the protection of the Reverend L. H. Wheeler, the Protestant missionary at La Pointe. When in 1850, pioneers began lobbying Congress to remove these Indians to the west of the Mississippi so that they might acquire their lands, Wheeler visited the proposed site of resettlement and reported that it would be a deed of mercy to shoot every Chippewa rather than send them there. Congress reconsidered, and in 1854 guaranteed the Chippewa three reservations on the south shore of Lake Superior.

After the Eastern and South-eastern Indians had been moved beyond the established Indian frontier line which ran from the Great Lakes southward parallel and near the Mississippi in the north, but several hundred miles west of the river in the south, the whole region from the Appalachians to the frontier line was open to settlement, and in due course became sufficiently filled with homesteaders to create viable territories which later reached statehood with the Union. Arkansas became a State in 1836, Florida in 1845, Iowa in 1846 and Minnesota in 1858. Louisiana had reached Statehood in 1812 before the movement of the Indians, as had Mississippi in 1817, Alabama in 1819 and Missouri in 1821.

Chapter 4

The
Mountain Men

The area to the north-west of the Louisiana Purchase, beyond
the territory claimed by Mexico, was first reached overland
by trappers of the British North-West Company[1] and by sea
by American naval captains. It was on 11 May 1792 that
Captain Robert Gray from Boston entered the largest river
in the area and named it the Columbia[2] after his own 83-foot
armed merchant vessel. The next significant event in the
history of the area which came to be known as Oregon was
when John Jacob Astor's Pacific Fur Company's ship *Tonquin*
put in at the estuary, and its crew established in 1811 the
fort of Astoria six miles east of the site of Fort Clatsop where
Lewis and Clark had spent the winter after their journey
across America to the Pacific coast in 1805. In Astoria[3] an
active trade soon grew up with America's East in fish, furs

[1] Later amalgamated with the Hudson's Bay Company.

[2] The *Columbia* was also the first American ship to circumnavigate
the world.

[3] Erected in 1926 by members of the board of the Great Northern
Railway and descendants of J. J. Astor on a promontory that com-
mands a panoramic vista of the ocean and estuary is the famous
Astoria Column. This pillar, designed by the architect Electus Litch-
field after the Trajan Column in Rome, has on it a frieze by the
Italian artist A. Pusteria which depicts the local history. From bottom
to top are the the following scenes in succession: a primeval forest; the
discovery of the river by Robert Gray; Lewis and Clark boiling sea
water to obtain salt, and building Fort Clatsop; the *Tonquin* arriving;
the building of Fort Astoria; the arrival of Astor's Overland party;
Fort Astoria being handed over to the British in 1813, and being
restored to the United States in 1818; the coming of the first settlers.

and timber, and vessels of other nations began to visit the estuary. In 1811 two parties from Astoria visited the Nez Perce[4] Indians in their valleys on the slopes of the Bitterroot Mountains to try to persuade them to trade furs. Neither party met with much success, for the Indians lacked the necessary energy to go trapping and preferred to sell surplus horses to obtain the guns, ammunition, knives and blankets they required. Nor would they at first permit trapping by the Americans on their own behalf, and there were several nasty affrays before some sort of *modus vivendi* was arrived at with the Nez Perce and other local tribes.[5]

In 1813 during the war with Britain Astor sold Fort Astoria to the British North-West Company, and it became Fort George until it was restored in 1818. In 1816 Donald McKenzie who had already played a part in trying to promote trade with the Nez Perce accepted a position with the North-West Company and established a station on their behalf at Walla Walla near the junction of the Snake and Columbia rivers. This venture proved more successful than the earlier ones had been and Walla Walla became an important trading post for horses. In payment the Nez Perce secured the guns and ammunition they needed to meet on equal terms the savage Blackfeet[6] whose territory east of the Rockies they visited for their annual bison hunting. The Blackfeet had been the most hostile Indians encountered by Lewis and Clark. As already mentioned, during an affray two were killed, the only Indians slain during the expedition. Some historians attribute Blackfeet anti-Americanism to this incident; others to an occasion when a member of Lewis and Clark's band helped some Crows[7] defeat a group of Blackfeet. But the more general view seems to be that the Blackfeet were just naturally and impartially ferocious. They also practised torture and refused to observe even the mildest conventions of formal, temporary truce that most tribes felt bound by.

---

[4] So called because some wore nose pendants.
[5] The Cayuse in the west and Shoshoni to the east.
[6] So called because of the colour of their moccasins.
[7] The Crows were traditionally friendly to Europeans.

The Cayuse caused the most trouble at Fort Walla Walla. Their warriors were at odds with the Shoshoni because the latter, having bought guns at the fort, used the weapons against them. When the traders tried to patch up the quarrel they found it of long standing, caused, according to the Cayuse version, by the Shoshoni's stopping them hunting in the Blue Mountains south of the fort. The Cayuse had arrived in the area from the west comparatively recently so that it is possible they may have encroached on traditional Shoshoni hunting grounds. The Cayuse retaliated by preventing the Shoshoni from using the Dalles[8] trading station downstream, and from fishing for salmon in the lower Columbia. The enmity between the tribes continued unabated until the virtual destruction of the Cayuse by war and disease some forty to fifty years later. However, in spite of these troubles the traders at Walla Walla made their post a valuable centre for the area, and one which was held in high esteem for several years by most of the neighbouring tribes, some of whose members even began to adopt white customs and practices. The traders also started to teach a few Indians in close contact with them the rudiments of Christianity, so that the area was prepared to some extent to receive the missionaries about to arrive from the East.

The Nez Perce were the first to become aware of the possible advantages of white man's 'medicine', with the result that they dispatched in October 1831 three of their tribe along with one Flathead to St Louis to ask for missionaries to be sent to them.[9] The pleas of the heathens, only one of whom managed to return safely to his own people, met with a good response. On 17 July 1833 a party of Methodists under the Reverend Jason Lee took the Oregon trail through the mountains to the Hudson's Bay Company's Fort Vancouver, where they were received by its commander Dr John McLoughlin. McLoughlin, physically a giant and a natural leader, had forsaken medicine for an adventurous life in the West. He was with the British North-West Company at

[8] Dalles = flagstone, and refers to rocks in the local rapids (now dammed).

[9] This was not the prime reason for the Indians visiting St Louis.

Astoria until Astor's company and his own had between them
despoiled the coastal area and reduced its Indian population
by fifty per cent through the introduction of European
diseases [10] and alcohol. When the North-West Company was
incorporated in the Hudson's Bay Company, McLoughlin
became the local representative of the latter. Moving east
to Fort Vancouver[11], he ruled his new domain like an un-
crowned king. He practised the traditional sound trading
methods of the Hudson's Bay Company under which only a
calculated percentage of furs were taken in any given area,
after which it was allowed to lie fallow until the animal
population had been restored. The Company's employees
were subjected to strong discipline, and a rigid control of the
local Indians was also enforced. The missionaries were welcomed by McLoughlin as another means of helping to maintain law and order, but he did not want them to settle in
Indian country in case they interfered with trading, so he
directed them westward to the fertile Williamette valley,
persuading them that if they went to live among the Nez
Perce they would lay themselves open to attack from the
tribe's traditional enemies, the Blackfeet.

The response by the Methodists to the call from Oregon
sent the Presbyterians scurrying into action. Their parties
arrived in 1836, and this time, McLoughlin could not prevent
them settling among the Indians. One mission station under
the Reverend Marcus Whitman was set up at Waiilatpu near
Fort Walla Walla among the Cayuse and another at Lapwai
on the Clearwater[12] in Nez Perce country. Neither the Methodists nor the Presbyterians can be said to have been very
successful, but they did persuade a handful of natives to alter
their way of life in the hope of salvation, the most distinguished being Old Chief Joseph[13] of the Nez Perce. He was
an active Christian for twenty-seven years, though in his old
age he renounced white ways because he considered his treaty

[10] Smallpox and venereal disease.

[11] Across the Columbia from present-day Portland.

[12] A tributary of the Snake.

[13] Young Chief Joseph, his son, who will be met with later was also
a Christian.

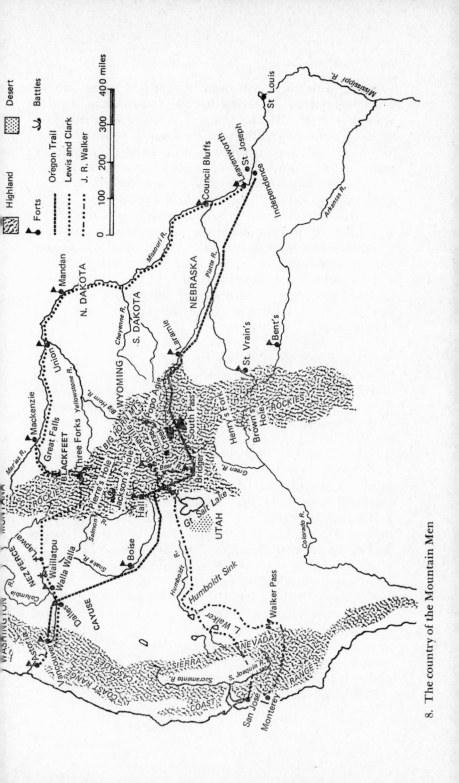

8. The country of the Mountain Men

with the white men had been broken when they annexed his tribe's territory. It seems that the Roman Catholic priests who came west with the trappers of the British companies made a greater impact than the Protestants. At any rate when Whitman's mission was withdrawn the number of Protestant converts left behind was small indeed, and the majority of Christian Indians in the North-West had received their faith through the Catholic Fathers. Although the missionaries failed to win many converts, they gave a great impetus to migration. By sending home glowing reports of the Snake, Columbia and Williamette valleys they not only brought more missionaries to the area but also drew permanent settlers. For example, it is recorded that in 1839 fifty settlers arrived and laid out farms, opened a store and built a saw-mill by the falls of the Williamette; and this was only one arrival among many.

It was not only the missionaries who drew the attention of prospective migrants to the North-West. The trappers who had blazed the trails and with whom the missionaries travelled through the mountains also sent back encouraging reports. As has been seen, some of these trappers approached their hunting grounds from the west; but the majority came from the east. From the latter direction there were several established routes into the Rockies where the fur-bearing animals lived. These included the famous Oregon Trail, a more northerly route from Fort Union on the Missouri up the Yellowstone, and one up the Big Horn to cross the Continental Divide like the Oregon Trail at South Pass (see map 8). To describe the nature of the activities of the trappers at this period it is proposed to follow some of the parties travelling in the mountains in 1832.

An early organiser of trapping parties in the Rockies was William Henry Ashley. Ashley was a Missourian whose business had failed in the 1819 financial crisis;[14] and he sought to recoup his losses by sending trading parties first up the Missouri and then into the Rockies. In 1823 one of his bands under Jedediah S. Smith was among the first to cross the

[14] The so-called Panic of 1819.

v Fort Laramie by A. J. Miller (*Walters Art Gallery*)

Colonel George A. Custer (National Archives)

VI Kit Carson (Library of State Historical Society of

Rockies in a westerly direction through South Pass, a broad sagebrush belt fifty miles or more wide, that was to become the pathway of countless overland pioneers. Smith's party discovered that the Green River basin west of South Pass was rich in beaver. In 1825 Ashley came West himself and organised the systematic trapping of the area, employing for the first time the famous rendezvous system whereby trappers were sent out in small bands to trap the beaver streams, and then gathered at an agreed-upon spot each summer to trade their year's catch for goods sent westward by pack-horse caravan. From then on the rendezvous system became a regular feature. In 1826 Ashley sold his interest to three of his employees headed by Jedediah Smith, and in 1830 Smith and his partners in their turn sold out to a number of traders whose leading members were Thomas Fitzpatrick, James Bridger and Bill Sublette. This group became known as the Rocky Mountain Fur Company and were soon in competition with Astor's eastern corporation which in 1828, under the title of the American Fur Company, began to trade in the Rocky Mountains area. Under the rendezvous system, instead of bringing back the bands of trappers to base they had to hole-up for the winter in the mountains, either in improvised forts like Fort Bridger and Fort Bonneville, or in sheltered valley bottoms like Jackson's Hole and Brown's Hole, after which they proceeded to the chosen rendezvous to dispose of their furs. The main annual rendezvous sites were Pierre's Hole between the sources of the Snake and Yellowstone, Popo Agie at the source of the Big Horn on the east of the Wind River Mountains, Henry's Fork and Horse Creek on the Green River, and Bear Lake, Utah (see map 8). In 1832 the chosen rendezvous was Pierre's Hole.

One of the parties engaged in the fur trade in 1832 was led by Captain B. L. E. de Bonneville, on leave of absence from the United States army. His principal lieutenants were the experienced 'Mountain Men', M. S. Cerré and J. R. Walker, and his rank and file were a typical bunch of Creole, French Canadian and American frontiersmen. Bonneville used wagons to cross the Continental Divide. His vehicles were smaller and more adaptable than the prairie schooners of the

Santa Fé Trail, but nevertheless they caused him much trouble. When he started to ascend into the mountains the high dry air shrank the spokes of the wheels and the tyres began to fall off. There were also tiresome delays getting the wagons across gullies and canyons, but in the end nearly all the vehicles were brought over South Pass. By using them Bonneville was able to take a far greater quantity of goods than pack animals would have allowed, and his men were also spared the irksome task of unloading and loading up at each night's halt. Bonneville's party travelled along the Oregon Trail[15] up the Platte to the mouth of its tributary the Laramie. After passing the many-coloured, contorted rock formations known as Red Buttes, the trail left the Platte and crossed to the valley of the Sweetwater, a smaller stream. Almost at once Independence Rock hove into sight. This they found inscribed with the names of many passing travellers, including that of the celebrated Mountain Man Jim Bridger. Five miles beyond the rock came Devil's Gate, a narrow vertical canyon through a 400-foot ledge. After Bonneville's party had traversed South Pass, and thereby crossed the Continental Divide, they entered the basin of the Green. This river flows south to join the Colorado and emerges eventually in the Gulf of California and the Pacific. The waters of the Sweetwater and Platte, which they had left behind, flow towards the Missouri and Mississippi to reach the Gulf of Mexico and the Atlantic. In the basin of the Green River Bonneville's party met an American Fur Company caravan led by Lucien Fontenelle. This party had come from Fort Union and up the Yellowstone and Big Horn to cross the Continental Divide at South Pass and then turn north for the rendezvous at Pierre's Hole with goods to exchange for furs when the trappers assembled there. Fontenelle had with him a small band of Delawares. Many years before in the East the ancestors of these Indians had been defeated by the Iroquois and classed by them as 'Petticoat Indians', useless as warriors. The Delaware tribe had moved to the Mississippi area, and

[15] After South Pass the Oregon Trail led across the basin of the Green River, north past Bear Lake to the Snake, and then down the Snake and Columbia to Fort Vancouver.

there, with the advance of the whites, had been largely dismembered. Some joined the Miami or Shawnees; others crossed the Mississippi and set up for themselves. It was from these last that Fontenelle's Indian Mountain Men were descended. They had mastered the Plains Indians culture and survival skills, and become expert horsemen, horse thieves, buffalo hunters and beaver trappers. Before Fontenelle left for Pierre's Hole, he bribed some of Bonneville's men to join him by offering them higher wages. As Fontenelle hurried off, Bonneville disconsolately ascended the valley of the Green River until he came to Horse Creek. In an angle between the two streams he built a log-stockade fort. His party had not managed to trap sufficient beaver to make it really worth while going on to Pierre's Hole, but after he had completed his fort he nevertheless made his way north to find out what was happening at the rendezvous.

At Pierre's Hole the trappers were beginning to assemble. Already in the valley were two parties from the Rocky Mountain Fur Company; the first, a caravan of trade goods under Bill Sublette, had arrived ahead of the caravan of the American Fur Company led by Lucien Fontenelle and would steal most of the rendezvous trade; the second was a trapping party under Tom Fitzpatrick and Jim Bridger. About to arrive were a body under the Boston merchant Nathanial J. Wyeth and another American Fur Company Group under William H. Vanderburgh and Andrew Drips, as well as a large Taos party, an Arkansas group, and scores of Indians. Competition had been severe that year.

As soon as everyone had reached the rendezvous the business of the meeting began. First, the season's furs were sold, then came the purchase by the trappers of the horses and goods required for the following season. Worn-down horses were traded for gunpowder and knives, and fresh horses were bought from the Indians at an average price of ten St Louis dollars. The Nez Perce had learnt how to breed horses selectively. They had produced the famous spotted Appaloosa, and traded these animals with neighbours who drove great herds to the rendezvous to barter. The Indians also had tasselled buckskin coats, breeches and leggings to dispose

of. Although uncomfortable, Indian clothing was more serviceable in brush country than the woollen garments the
caravans brought, and most of the Mountain Men wore
buckskins.

After the completion of the selling and buying the traditional rendezvous festivities began. The keen competition of
that year did not impair mountain fellowship. The employees
of the rival companies got noisily drunk together, the partners
doing so a little more formally at dinners, at which principals
like Lucien Fontenelle, Jim Bridger and others toasted one
another and exchanged reminiscences. As the kettles of alcohol
passed round day after day, night after night, the rendezvous
was transformed into a scene of roaring debauchery. During
this period of renewed fellowship, good food and abundant
liquor, the Mountain Men took part in, or more often stood
around applauding the horse-racing, shooting, and other competitions organised by the attendant Indians for their pleasure.
They also usually drank themselves silly, and although possessed of their own Indian wives bought other Indian women
for a yard of cloth or a string of beads. Some of them would
spend all the profits they had earned in a few days of barbarous
dissipation. Eventually, however, the alcohol—and the men—
were exhausted, and the trappers stumbled away into the
wilderness to start another season.

The 1832 rendezvous at Pierre's Hole nearly ended in
tragedy. When Sublette's brigade followed by Wyeth's party
were leaving, and had gone a few miles toward the west,
they saw a substantial body of Indians in the distance. These
were Gros Ventres (Atsina), a detached fragment of the Arapahos who had moved into Blackfeet country and attached
themselves to that warlike tribe. They had adopted Blackfeet
ceremonies and characteristics, and resembled their hosts in
every way, even accepting their feuds. They had been south
visiting the Arapahos in Colorado, and when returning north
had already brushed with bands of trappers. While at a
distance the two sides secured their positions and watched
one another. Both needed time, the whites to let their rendezvous companions come up, the Indians to complete the full
religious preparations necessary for an attack in force. A war

chief, wearing a scarlet blanket and carrying as a peace-pledge a tribal medicine pipe, rode out towards the trappers indicating that the Indians would like to parley. Sublette, however, rating them as Blackfeet and therefore treacherous, did not trust them to observe the truce they offered and sent forward to meet the chief a half-breed whose father the Blackfeet had murdered and a Flathead whose tribe was a traditional enemy. These two, instead of negotiating, grabbed and held fast the chief's offered hand of friendship, shot him dead, took his scalp, and galloped back triumphantly waving the scarlet blanket.

This breach of faith horrified the honourable Wyeth, but Sublette must have thought it was the right way to treat Blackfeet, or he would not have chosen such a pair of envoys. In any case it was a declaration of war. The Indians withdrew into a grove of willows and cottonwoods, piled up a breastwork of fallen trees, and when their squaws had dug fox-holes behind the barricade, took up their fighting positions with their weapons in gaps between the lowest logs. Meanwhile, the trappers, having sent back for support from those still at the rendezvous, started firing at the Indians behind their barricade whenever they showed themselves. After the arrival of more trappers and allied Indians, Sublette selected some sixty volunteers and staged an attack on the enemy position, the whites taking one flank and the friendly Indians the other. The Indians, well protected by their ramparts, opened a deadly fire which stopped most of the assailants in their tracks. One white, the worse for drink, managed to climb over the logs, but was shot while doing so, and fell dead inside the fort. With five others dead and many wounded Sublette decided to try another method, and ordered his men to take cover and shoot it out. This proved a slow business, and a noisy one! Besides the gunfire there were yells and howls from the Indians on both sides. Custom required them to taunt and deride one another, shouting that their enemy was a child, a squaw, a homosexual, or had hares or other timid animals in his ancestry. According to Indian practice, if you needled an opponent into rushing out where you could shoot at him, so much the better; if not, you might at least win a round of abuse.

By late afternoon some of Sublette's men had worked themselves under cover up to the logs again. It was planned to
pile up brushwood and burn the defenders out, but before
the fire could be kindled a voice from behind the rampart
delivered a message which sent most of the attackers scurrying
away. The Indian announced that he and his comrades were
more than willing to sacrifice their lives, for they knew they
were being avenged by a large force of their comrades who
were murdering those left at the rendezvous, stealing their
horses and plundering the camp. Most of the trappers feared
this might not be the ruse their stauncher companions asserted,
and galloped off to the camp to make sure. Only a handful
were left to watch the Indians left behind the barricade.
Then, by the time these few were rejoined by their friends,
coming back shamefaced after having found everything serene
at the rendezvous, it was nearly dark and too late to stage
another attack. That night the Indians stole away. Next
morning when the trappers were at last able to enter the
Indian compound they found it deserted. But nine dead
Indians and thirty dead horses lay behind the logs, and many
more corpses were scattered in the woods.

Although the Mountain Men had the better of this confused affray which is sometimes called the Battle of Pierre's
Hole, nevertheless the Blackfeet took their revenge. When
the Rocky Mountain Company party, led by Thomas Fitzpatrick and Jim Bridger, drifted northwards from Pierre's
Hole, followed at a distance by the American Fur Company
party under Vanderbrugh and Drips, both were eventually
attacked by Blackfeet seeking retribution for their losses[16] at
Pierre's Hole. Vanderburgh and a companion were killed in
one encounter; in the other Fitzpatrick and Bridger managed
to escape; but the latter carried a barbed iron arrowhead
in his back for the next three years as a memento of the
affair.

After poor seasons in 1832 and 1833 it became clear that there
were no longer sufficient animals in the mountain area to

[16] Besides casualties, a herd of Blackfeet horses had been captured
from a spot where the squaws had hidden it.

support the number of companies and individuals engaged in the trade, and so amalgamation became the order of the day. By 1834 the Rocky Mountain Fur Company and Astor's American Fur Company were convinced that the overtrapped Rockies could never produce enough furs to support both of them, and were ready to come to terms. The far-flung activities of Astor's company made withdrawal difficult, for if it abandoned its mountain trade its prestige among Indians in the still profitable areas would suffer. Hence, before the year was out it had reached an agreement to buy the goodwill and assets of the Rocky Mountain Fur Company. After this only Bonneville's outfit remained as a serious competitor. In 1833 Bonneville, having had a series of bad seasons, sent off some of his men under J. R. Walker to reconnoitre westward beyond the Great Salt Lake for an area better stocked with beaver. Walker and forty followers skirted the north shore of the lake, and then struggled across a barren, rocky and sandy region as far as the source of the Ogden, later Humboldt, River. After this they followed the river down into its Sink, and passed the lake which now bears Walker's name. Having crossed the Sierra Nevada, and the valley of the San Joaquin, they reached the mission station at San José near San Francisco, where they were welcomed hospitably by the Catholic Fathers. From San José they travelled along the coast to Monterey where they were again well received by the Mexican inhabitants, including the commander of the presidio (fort). As it was late in the season they decided to stop for the winter. It was not until mid-February 1834 that Walker and his men took the trail home. Then they crossed the Coast Range, which is a formidable obstacle at this point, and after passing over the San Joaquin valley, found a way through the Sierra Nevada by the defile later known as Walker Pass. The way back now took them over desert country, and the party suffered severely from lack of water until they reached their outward trail by the Humboldt River. Even with the better going they could only make slow progress owing to the fatigue engendered by their long and difficult journeyings, and it was several months before they arrived back to report to Bonneville. But their report was not a favourable one, for they had found the streams in the country to the west as over-trapped as those of the Green basin. Bonneville persevered for a time after this setback, but following the 1835 rendez-vous at Fort Bonneville he started back East never to return.

The next five years were fairly profitable for the combined concerns still left in the trade, but after 1840 its centre no longer remained in the heart of the Rockies, for by then the rendezvous system had been abandoned, and the trade was being carried on from forts on the fringes, like Fort Hall on the Snake, Fort Laramie on the Platte, and Bent's Fort on the Arkansas (see map 8). These forts were strong enough to withstand Indian attacks and were supplied with trade goods to barter for furs by the Hudson's Bay Company in the west and the American Fur Company in the east. Eventually, however, even this restricted form of trade ended, and so the fur trade in the United States died and a romantic era of exploration and endeavour came to an end.

The hard times in the East which followed the financial crisis of 1837 together with the glowing reports of Oregon from missionaries and fur traders alike started an 'Oregon Fever' and a flood of emigrants to the North-West. This was wel-comed by the politicians, for ownership of the area was in dispute between Britain and the United States, and the feeling was that possession being nine points of the law, the more Americans who went to Oregon the more certain it was of being joined to the Union. Some 3,000 emigrants, mostly in small parties, reached Oregon in 1845, and 1,350 in 1846, by which time a new president was taking a hand in the matter.

When James Knox Polk of Tennessee came to the White House in March 1845 he quickly made it clear that in his view the American claim to Oregon was unquestionable, for, as he said, 'already are our people preparing to perfect that title by occupying it with their wives and children'. Since 1806 the United States and Britain had been in active rivalry for possession, and since the War of 1812 the territory had been the subject of considerable diplomatic correspondence. In 1845 the British stated they were willing to negotiate a treaty to settle the matter of a common boundary, and their plenipotentiary suggested this frontier should be the 49th Parallel as far as the Columbia River and then follow the river to the sea. When the United States refused to accept this, there followed much debate and diplomatic manoeuvring until Britain offered as a compromise the 49th Parallel all the way to the coast but with the whole of Vancouver Island remaining British. Polk would not at first agree to a preliminary treaty on these lines which his Secretary of State had produced, but after some wrangling and two day's debate the Senate took the matter out of his hands, so that the United States gained not only Oregon but also the slice of land of the Columbia which was to become Washington. Oregon was recognised as a Territory by the United States Government in 1849, and was admitted as a State of the Union on 4 February 1859. Washington, meanwhile, was organised as a Territory in 1853, and was admitted as a State in 1889. The upper basin of the Green River, which had been the centre of the fur trade was first of all Mormon Territory, and then was admitted as the State of Utah in 1896. The lands of the Flatheads, Shoshoni and Nez Perce in the valleys of the Clearwater, Salmon and Snake, received an access of settler population when gold was discovered in the 1850s and 1860s. Once the powerful Nez Perce had been subdued and the routes from the East freed from Blackfeet and Sioux attack, population began to build up. The area was first split into administrative territories which later became the States of Montana (1889) and Idaho (1890). The lands of the Rockies could not be occupied until the North Plains Indians had been subjugated. When this had been achieved, and the coming of the railway had made access easier, sufficient settlers arrived to engage in agriculture and livestock production to allow the creation of the viable states of Nebraska in 1867, North and South Dakota in 1889 and Wyoming in 1890.

Chapter 5

Over the Rockies
with the Mormons

An impetus to westward expansion and settlement was given by religious bodies such as the Latter-Day Saints or Mormons, founded by Joseph Smith[1] in 1830. Ten years before, at the age of fourteen, when living in Manchester, Ontario County, New York where a religious revival was in progress, he had been puzzled as to which of the many thriving local churches he should join. While praying for guidance in the wood by his home two angels appeared and told him not to join any religious body, but instead prepare himself for the special work for which he was destined. Several years passed and then a further visitation occurred while he was praying in his bedroom. On this occasion a spirit in human form, who said he was Moroni the son of Mormon, told Joseph that a book explaining the task ahead was to be found buried on the slope of Cumorah Hill[2] at Palmyra nearby. He was told that the book had leaves of gold inscribed with an account of the former inhabitants of America and it also explained God's purpose for Joseph and his followers. Attached to a ceremonial breast-plate alongside the book were two seer-stones in the form of spectacles to assist in its translation and interpretation. Young Smith was greatly perturbed by the

[1] Joseph Smith was the son of a farmer from Vermont who had moved with his wife and children to the village of Manchester near Palmyra twenty miles east of Rochester and fifteen miles south of Lake Ontario.
[2] A forty-foot monument capped by a statue of the Angel Moroni has been erected on this glacial drumlin, which has become the Mt Sinai of the Mormons.

visitations and consulted his father about them. The latter was reassuring, saying that Joseph should have no fear, for surely he had been chosen to do God's work in America. Joseph paid two visits to Cumorah: the first, as he had been instructed, merely to locate the book; the second in 1827 to bring it home for translation. He described his first visit to the hill as follows:

'Convenient to the village of Manchester in Ontario County in New York stands a hill, and on the west side not far from the top under a stone of considerable size lay the plates deposited in a stone box. This stone was thick and rounding in the middle on the upper side, and thinner towards the edges, so that the middle part of it was visible above the ground, but the edge all round was covered with earth. Having removed the earth I obtained a lever which I got fixed under the edge of the stone and with a little exertion raised it up. I looked in and there indeed I did behold the plates, the seer-stone spectacles and the breast-plate as stated by the messenger from the Lord. The box in which they lay was formed by laying stones together in some form of cement. In the bottom of the box were laid two stones, crossways and on these stones lay the plates and the other things with them.'

Before Joseph's second visit to the hill news had got around that he had found a treasure-trove, and on the way back he had difficulty in avoiding some men who tried to intercept and rob him. Nor was he safe when he got his precious burden home, for he learnt that his enemies intended to search the house. After trying several hiding-places he found a secure one under a pile of flax in the loft of the cooper's shop across the road, so that when the intended robbers swarmed in and searched every inch of the Smith's home they found nothing.

With the assistance of the spectacles, Joseph translated the hieroglyphics on the golden plates of the book, and then returned it to the hill as he had been instructed. The resulting Book of Mormon was printed and published in 1830. To witness to the book's authenticity eight people including Joseph's father and two of his brothers testified in the preface that Joseph had shown them the golden plates and they had seen the engravings on them. Mormons believe that this work is comparable to the Bible. They acknowledge that Jesus is the Son of God and that He established the Christian Church through the apostles, but they also consider that after the death of the original apostles divine guidance ceased, and that Joseph Smith was chosen to establish a new true Church of Jesus Christ, first in the New World of America and then in the Old.

In essence the Book of Mormon is the history of the peoples of America in ancient times. The first people it describes were the Jaredites, who were Israelites whom God had led across the oceans. Internal dissensions resulted in their extermination near Cumorah in 590 B.C., but about the same time the followers of the Jewish Prophet Lehi were landing on the west coast. This new group split into two factions: the civilised Nephites and the savage Lamanites from whom the American Indians are descended. In a great struggle about 400 A.D., which also took place near Cumorah, the Lamanites almost destroyed all the Nephites. Shortly before this climactic battle Mormon, the chief prophet of the Nephites, had been told by God to write the history of his people on imperishable material and hide the work in the earth until God should see fit to have it brought forth and united with the Bible for the accomplishment of His purposes. This history was inscribed on golden plates by Mormon, and concealed on the hillside of Cumorah by His son Moroni who was one of the few Nephite survivors of the great battle. Moreover, it was he who appeared as an angel to tell Joseph Smith where the history was deposited.

When the Book of Mormon was brought to the notice of the people of Orange County there were some who believed what Joseph Smith had testified and, with the members of his own family, were ready to accept him as chosen by God to create a new Church in America. On the other hand, the majority in the neighbourhood considered him a self-seeking humbug and much ridicule and even active opposition came his way. Some of the hostility took a drastic form, for Joseph Smith's house was assaulted by mobs, and he and his followers were shot at in the streets. It was not only the uneducated who attacked the Mormons. Church leaders of other denominations also denounced them. One group even put forward the theory that Joseph had got his ideas from a romance written by a quondam clergyman, Solomon Spaulding. However, although not particularly well educated, Joseph Smith held his own in controversial discussion with his religious rivals. What was more, he drew sufficient support to establish officially the Church of Jesus Christ of Latter-Day Saints in the State of New York on 6 April 1830.

In January 1831, after prayers for guidance as to how to deal with the hostility displayed towards the new Church, further revelations led Smith and his followers to move west to Kirtland in Ohio, and from there a smaller group went on and settled far in the west across the Mississippi at Independence in Jackson County, Missouri. For a time both these new centres thrived. At Kirtland Twelve Apostles for the Church were appointed and the Council of the Seventies named. Also, a mill, a store, a bank and a printing press were set up, and the building of a temple began. In 1837 a mission under Brigham Young left Kirtland for England, where it converted and baptised into the Mormon faith some 2,000 people. The colony at Independence in the west was equally successful to begin with. But this success caused jealousy among the rest of the populace. Disorders similar to those that had occurred in New York State followed, and by 1833 most of the Mormons had been driven out of Independence into Clay Cross County across the river, some later going back to join the main body in Kirtland.

The period of relatively peaceful progress lasted longer in Kirtland, but by 1838 it had come to an end there as well. Envy and hatred led to persecution in the now traditional manner, so that the Saints felt compelled to move once again, this time to north-west Missouri, where they set up a main settlement in Calwell County, which they called Zion, and subsidiary settlements in the neighbouring counties. However, the stay of the Mormons in Missouri was even less happy than it had been in Ohio. In the very first year of their arrival attempts to stop them voting in elections led to dis-

orders in which the rioters got out of hand and laid waste
property regardless of to whom it belonged. The Missouri
State Militia was embodied to try to quell the uprising, and
when it failed to do so, the Governor sent in troops. When
order was restored, the Mormons were unjustly held responsible for all the trouble, and as a punishment their leaders
were imprisoned, and their rank and file ordered to leave the
State forthwith. Joseph Smith and the other prisoners were
at first condemned to death; but they were later released on
the undertaking that they too would leave with the rest. In
the winter of 1838, therefore, almost all the Mormons moved
eastwards back across the Mississippi into Illinois where with
the permission of the authorities they set up yet another new
settlement at Nauvoo on the east bank of the Mississippi.

There followed several years of comparative peace and
prosperity during which the numbers of Mormons in Illinois
grew by 1844 to 20,000 and Nauvoo became the State's largest
and most prosperous city with 15,000 contented Saints within
its gates.

In 1844 Joseph Smith[3] received a revelation which he said
allowed certain Mormons to practise polygamy, and several
men who were well enough off to enlarge their household
made use of this divine sanction to take more than one wife.
For example, John Scott, who was bodyguard to Joseph Smith,
and later played an important role in the Mormon westward
migration, had five wives and sired thirty-six children; while
Brigham Young, is said to have married as many as twenty-
seven women and to have been the father of fifty-two children.
By this time the prosperity of Mormons in Nauvoo and their
dismissal as erroneous of all faiths save their own had already
made them unpopular, and the introduction of polygamy
was sufficient to produce a new wave of anti-Mormonism, with
the usual accompanying riots and disorders. In an attempt to
appease the anti-Mormon faction the authorities issued war-

[3] Some Mormons did not approve. They said that it was Brigham
Young who had received the revelation not Joseph Smith. They
broke away from the main body of the Church and remained in the
East after the migration to Salt Lake City.

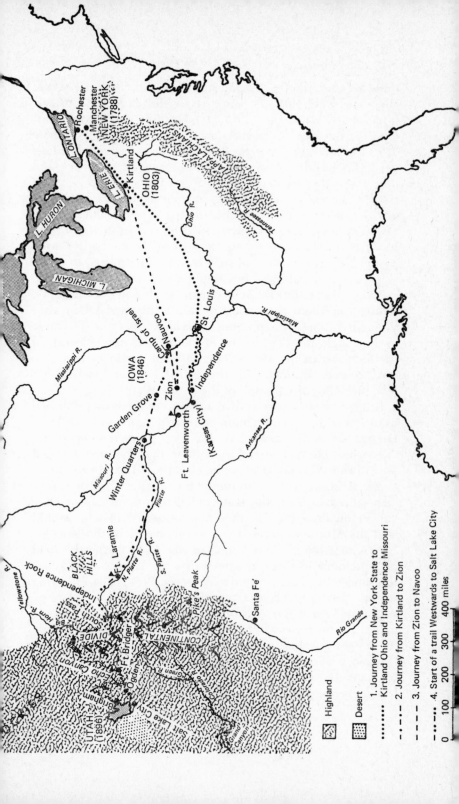

L. ONTARIO

Rochester
Manchester
NEW YORK (1788)

L. ERIE

Kirtland

OHIO (1803)

L. HURON

L. MICHIGAN

Ohio R.

APPALACHIANS

Tennessee R.

Misisippi R.

St Louis

Mississippi R.

Camp of Israel

Nauvoo

IOWA (1846)

Garden Grove

Zion

Independence (Kansas City)

Ft. Leavenworth

Missouri R.

Arkansas R.

Winter Quarters

Platte R.

Platte R.

N. Platte R.

S. Platte R.

Ft. Laramie

BLACK HILLS

Pike's Peak

Independence Rock

Yellowstone R.

Big Horn R.

SOUTH PASS

CONTINENTAL DIVIDE

Ft Bridger

Green R.

Santa Fé

Rio Grande

Echo Canyon

Ogden

Brigham

Bear R.

Salt Lake City

UTAH (1896)

ROCKIES

Colorado R.

Grand Canyon

Highland

Desert

1. Journey from New York State to Kirtland Ohio and Independence Missouri
2. Journey from Kirtland to Zion
3. Journey from Zion to Navoo
4. Start of a trail Westwards to Salt Lake City

0 100 200 300 400 miles

rants for the arrest of Joseph Smith and his brother Hyrum, and they were duly imprisoned in the gaol at Carthage, fifteen miles south-east of Nauvoo. But this was not sufficient to satisfy the angry mob, and on 27 June 1844 a group of some 200 rioters broke into the gaol and shot the two brothers dead. There followed first a mass outbreak of prisoners, and then the gathering together of several mobs of anti-Mormon rioters who roamed the countryside, crying out for the blood of more of the Saints, and threatening to storm their city.

The Mormons were stronger in Illinois than they had been in Ohio or Missouri, for the State Legislature had granted them a liberal charter, and they had been permitted to establish their own militia. They might very well have been able to defend themselves in their compact settlement, but Brigham Young, on whom the mantle of leadership had fallen after the martyrdom of Joseph Smith, decided otherwise. He came to the conclusion that, as the Mormons had suffered both in the East and in the Mississippi valley, it would be better to sever communications with the settled areas of America and seek their 'Promised Land' in the empty West.

Brigham Young had studied accounts of the West published in the Report of J. C. Frémont on his expedition in 1843–1844. He had also read Lansford W. Hastings' guide to Oregon and California. He had learnt from these that the most isolated area in the West lay around the Great Salt Lake in the heart of the Rockies, where the mountains of the Wasatch Range shut off access from the east, and deserts form a protective barrier on the west. He therefore suggested that he should lead the Mormons across Iowa to this haven in the Rockies.

At a meeting of the Council of the Twelve Apostles held in September 1845 it was agreed that the Saints should adopt the suggested plan and move off to the West. The following spring, having received a promise of immunity from persecution in return for agreeing to vacate Nauvoo, and having made the necessary preparations during a peaceful winter, the migration began. In February 1846 a thousand left Nauvoo, crossed the Mississippi over the ice and set up on the far bank the great settlement called Camp of Israel which was to become the first staging post on their journey. The arrangements for the series of trails westward were then placed in the hands of Brigham Young. Young, aged 43 and tending towards corpulence, looked, it is said, more like a prosperous farmer than a religious leader. He had already shown that he was capable on the Mormon mission to England from Kirtland. Now he displayed an indomitable will, consummate organising ability, and superlative leadership qualities. He dispatched his people not as a large group but in a series of parties. The early ones set up a small staging camp at Garden Grove 155 miles west of Camp of Israel, and a larger one which they called Winter Quarters on the western bank of the Missouri in the neighbourhood of present-day Omaha in Nebraska. Here they established a meeting-house, workshops, a gristmill, and, over the course of the summer built a 1,000 log-cabins. The first party left Camp of Israel on 1 March 1846, and the others followed at regular intervals. Each train with its desert-schooner tented wagons[4] was divided into hundreds or fifties under a captain. These in turn were subdivided into tens controlled by a lieutenant who kept order and supervised the day's march and the night's emcampment. There were hardships from shortage of food, from marching through snow, sleet or rain, and from spending nights stretched on the frozen ground. But the pilgrims plodded on without complaint like a disciplined army, convinced that it was under God's guidance that they were being led forward.

The first group to move west from Winter Quarters on the Missouri was commanded by Brigham Young, and consisted of 146 people with their belongings carried in 73 wagons. To avoid travellers on the traditional pioneer trail south of the River Platte they blazed a new path along the northern bank. They followed a rigid routine evolved by Young which was to become standard Mormon practice. Each morning a bugle sounded at five o'clock, followed by prayers and breakfast while the draught animals grazed. Another bugle blast signalled the start of the day's march. The caravan moved forward under the supervision of captains and lieutenants in single file, except in dangerous Indian country when a double column was used. At 8.30 each evening the train halted, after

[4] There are examples in the Fort Leavenworth Museum.

wheeling the wagons into a protective circle. Supper and
prayers took such a short time that by nine the whole company
was usually asleep.

The organisation was efficient, and rapid progress was made.
They moved along the North Platte, past Fort Laramie and
Independence Rock, and then up the Sweetwater River to
South Pass. When at one stage they had to cross the river,
they made boats to do so and afterwards lent them to a party
of settlers bound for Oregon in return for food and supplies.
Finally, they left a party to operate the crossing service for
late-comers.

In the foothills of the Rockies they encountered the
renowned trapper and fur-trader, Jim Bridger, who had
already spent twenty years roaming the mountains and was to
spend more than twenty more assisting the United States
authorities and the pioneers moving west. Bridger was not
encouraging. He said that the Great Salt Lake region was too
dry to support anything but sagebush and cactus. However,
Brigham Young was not to be deterred. Moving over South
Pass and the Continental Divide they reached the basin of
the Green River, a tributary of the Colorado, where they had
another unexpected encounter, this time with Samuel Brannan who had earlier taken 238 Mormons to California by
sea and had come to try and persuade Young to join them.
However, Young was still determined to go to the Great Salt
Lake area. He believed it was God's will for him to take his
followers there; and not one of his band challenged their
leader's decision.

They moved south-west by Fort Bridger—named after their
trapper friend on South Pass—and having crossed the upper
valley of the north-flowing Bear River, turned down one of
the many parallel valleys on the eastern edge of the Wasatch
Range in order to try and find a way through to the west.
They had proceeded some way north before they succeeded
and came upon a narrow defile they called Emigration
Canyon[5] which took them through the mountains towards
their goal. As the canyon broadened near its southern end

[5] The parties which followed took much the same route as Young's
but came down a parallel defile named Echo Canyon.

the Saints had the first glimpse of their future home, and they found it, as Bridger had warned, a barren plain studded with sage bush. But there was plenty of room. It stretched down south as far as the eye could see to what came to be called Lake Utah, and across to the Great Salt Lake and Salt Lake Desert in the west. It was encircled on the north, east and south by high snow-capped mountains. Most of them felt disappointed, and fearful at the prospects of having to try and cultivate such a barren area. Not so Young, however. 'This is the place,' he announced confidently.[6]

One by one the parties arrived, and by the autumn of 1847 1,800 Saints had reached the shores of the Great Salt Lake. There was time for a few log-cabins and dug-outs to be constructed, but most of the settlers had to live in tents or canvas-covered wagons during that winter, which proved a very cold and trying one. With the spring of 1848 all turned to planting the huge 5,000 acre field that had been laid out the year before. In June calamity struck. A swarm of crickets descended and began to eat up the crops. In this their darkest hour the Saints turned to prayer. And their prayers were answered. As if by a miracle clouds of seagulls suddenly appeared and fell on the insects. However, only about half the crop survived, and even less than that was harvested owing to a droughty summer, so the settlers—who by this time numbered some 4,000— faced a difficult prospect of survival. It was now that Brigham Young came to the rescue. During that autumn he worked out a complicated programme of systematic settlement and cultivation, making use of irrigation, which eventually put the Mormon colony on a sound basis.

No longer, Young told the settlers, should they live and farm individually. In order to survive it was necessary for them to work together under the direction of their Church. By a joint effort let them build a city of magnificent proportions. In the centre would be a square of ten acres with a giant temple surpassing all edifices the world had yet seen. About this would stretch wide streets at right angles marked off in blocks of the same size as Temple Square, divided into eight portions for houses and gardens. Major farming would

[6] According to Mormon legend.

be carried out in fields around the city. Nearby would be a number of five-acre plots for young artisans and mechanics who had little time to cultivate. Beyond, would be ten-acre lots for larger families, and still farther out, farms of twenty to eighty acres for agricultural specialists. All this was eventually carried out just as Young had planned. Water was essential in such an arid country, and a main irrigation ditch was built by co-operative effort to convey water from the mountains. From this, side ditches were then dug, and irrigation ditches along each of the streets of the city for garden use. Finally the whole water-supply system was placed under the direction of the bishops, who supervised water disposal and controlled over-greedy individuals.

Next, Brigham Young set about drawing up a constitution for his settlement, which was called Deseret.⁷ This, he patterned on those of the other American states, with four-year terms for a governor and members of a two-house legislature. Executive matters were in the hands of the governor and a council, and there was a separate judiciary. There was manhood suffrage and religious toleration, but no mention of slavery. After the constitution had been ratified in March 1849, Young was named as Governor in the subsequent elections, and through his influence, although also by election, Church members were placed in all offices. The country was also divided into wards over each of which presided a bishop who helped the people establish their homes, advised them on the cultivation of their fields, and gave them every form of help both material and spiritual. In this way Church and State were intimately connected in all walks of life.

In July 1849 a petition was dispatched to Washington begging Congress to accept Deseret as a State within the Union. This Congress refused, but they agreed that it could be affiliated, with the status of a Territory. On this, boundaries were drawn up which followed roughly those of Utah and Nevada of today. Congress also required some alterations in Young's constitution, but these were not significant. Young was named Governor, but it was decreed that the executive council must have four Gentile members to work alongside

⁷ Deseret, from a term signifying 'honeybee' in the Book of Mormon.

four Mormon ones. In the event, the presence of the non-Mormons did not alter the character of the government very much, and over the years no attempt was made to meddle with Young's autocratic, stern rule. His word remained law and his Church ruled supreme in both religious and secular matters.

Having attained recognition as a viable Territory, the next vital step was to build up sufficient manpower to function as such. In 1849, therefore, an emigration fund was established to provide loans for emigrants to Utah. Ships were chartered to carry them by sea and river, and agents appointed at points to organise their transportation. On the basis of the successful visit to England in 1837, wholesale missionary activities were launched, and within a few months Mormons were at work enlisting followers not only in the Eastern States, but in many European countries as well. Such was the zeal of the missionaries that there was a good response; in England alone some 33,000 were said to be ready to depart by the end of 1851.

The transportation to Utah was then carried out with customary Mormon efficiency. Central embarkation points were designated, at which converts were allotted space on ships apart from other passengers; each group was given a leader who assigned sleeping space, supervised meals, directed social activities and conducted religious services. When immigrants from abroad reached America, there were agents to arrange further passages upriver to St Louis, and from there up the Missouri to Fort Leavenworth or Winter Quarters, where they were provided with teams and wagons and given instructions in plains travel. On the trail itself posts were set up at regular intervals and ferry parties were formed to help in the passage of rivers. When immigrants finally arrived in Utah work was provided until they were trained for their new life, and were ready to take their place in society on their own.

A minor setback in the emigration procedure occurred in 1855 when shortage of funds made a cheaper mode of travel necessary over the plains. With his usual ingenuity Young substituted handcarts for wagons and horses and that autumn

Mormon carpenters at Winter Quarters began building the carts which were ready waiting when new parties arrived in the spring of 1856. This experiment was not altogether successful. The first group employing 100 carts arrived safely, and in faster time than most of the wagon columns, but two subsequent handcart parties were delayed for one reason or another, and then got snowed up in the Rockies where 225 of their number died before a relief column from Salt Lake City reached them. However, parties following were not deterred, and some 8,000 converts reached Salt Lake City by this means.

With the increase in population, Brigham Young was not only able to establish viable settlements in the vicinity of Salt Lake City, but also to set up well planned colonies away from the capital. After a new outpost had been conceived, a party was sent out to survey town lots, locate irrigation ditches and mark out farms, as had been done originally in Salt Lake City. Then the settlers were carefully chosen to ensure a proper proportion of farmers, artisans, shopkeepers, millers, blacksmiths, and professional men, and were placed under the direction of a bishop. The principal settlements that emerged were at Carson City 400 miles west of Salt Lake City and on the borders of the Sierra Nevada Mountains of California; at San Bernardino 550 miles to the south-west in the mountains east of Los Angeles; and at Las Vegas and Cedar City between San Bernardino and Salt Lake City. Earlier settlements nearer at hand included those at Ogden and Brigham, 40 and 70 miles respectively north of the capital. and at Provo 50 miles south.

Agricultural progress was steady: orchards flourished, cattle herds grew in numbers, and wheat production multiplied from year to year. Less progress was made in industry owing to lack of capital and manpower. As one might expect with religion affecting directly all and sundry the prevailing standard of morals and behaviour was far in advance of other frontier territories. Yet the people did not lack social activities. The presiding bishops saw to that. Beer-halls and brothels it is true were conspicuous by their absence, but horticultural societies, literary groups and musical associations flourished.

In fact, the tone of society was encouragingly wholesome, with strife, vice and crime largely absent.

The Saints were not for long left to develop their way of life in peace. Discord first began when passing emigrants to the California mining areas complained that the Mormons overcharged for goods purchased from them. Then, in 1855, three Federal judges were appointed for Utah territory. The Mormons offended them by not using their courts, so that they returned to Washington raging at their treatment. Mormon attitude towards the Indians also brought disapproval. In accordance with the tenets of their religion they held the Indians in respect as one of the original races of the continent. They attempted to convert the red men to their faith, and were willing to treat them on terms of equality, whereas the average frontiersman considered them savages who should be driven out or exterminated. To frontiersmen and mining emigrant alike the only good Indian was a dead Indian. There were several incidents where it appeared that Mormons were taking the side of Indians against fellow Europeans,[8] and even rumours that they were arming Indians to aid in the massacre of non-Mormon immigrants, with the result that the Mormons were considered to be in open rebellion against the Federal Government. The result was that President Buchanan (1857–61) decided the time had come to assert authority and on 26 May 1857 ordered Colonel A. S. Johnston to assemble a force of 2,500 men to march into Utah to restore law and order. Young and his people were appalled when they heard the news of the federal invasion. Remembering what had occurred at Kirtland and Nauvoo, it was decided to get on the move again. It was planned to destroy their towns and crops and move south

[8] A party of emigrants to the mines known as the Missouri Wild Cats abused Indian converts, turned their cattle into Mormon fields and called Mormon women whores. Their treatment of the Indians led the red men to attack them behind their barricade of wagons at Mountain Meadows. Later the Indians with the support of 50 Mormons killed all the emigrants, numbering 120 men, women and children. This Mountain Meadows Massacre brought a new wave of hatred against the Mormons.

while Mormon guerillas held off the invading army in the Wasatch Mountains on the east.

The Mormon guerillas successfully held the Federal troops during the autumn of 1857 in the neighbourhood of Fort Bridger by laying waste to the country around the fort so that Johnston's transport animals were too short of fodder to proceed, and the Federal forces compelled to take up winter quarters in the fort. Then, during the winter, Thomas L. Kane, a Philadelphia lawyer and friend of the Mormons since the time of the Nauvoo persecution, offered to mediate on their behalf. Having received permission to do so from President Buchanan, he reached Salt Lake City in February 1858 and persuaded Brigham Young to step down, and the Mormons to accept a governor appointed by the Federal authorities. There was a setback in April when the new governor[9] insisted on Federal troops being permitted to occupy Mormon territory. A number of families in the north were so perturbed when they heard that Johnston's force was being allowed to move in that they began to evacuate their homes. When the public in the East heard of what was happening however, their sympathies suddenly switched towards the side of the persecuted Mormons, and in an atmosphere of growing sympathy, their leaders accepted the generous terms President Buchanan now offered. These gave a free pardon to all Mormons who agreed to submit to the authority of the United States, and stated that the army of occupation would not set up its camp nearer than 40 miles from Salt Lake City; but insisted that Federal officials be included in the administration. Thus the so-called Mormon War came to an end, and the territory was allowed to develop in peace.

The only real discord after 1858 was in relation to polygamy. An anti-polygamy law was passed by Congress in 1862, but it remained practically a dead letter, only one conviction being secured in twenty years. For some time after the passing of the act, polygamy was openly practised. For example, one Mormon delegate to Congress with several wives was permitted to hold his seat for many years. In March

[9] Alfred Cummings.

1882, however, an act supplementing the law of 1862 was passed, and this was more rigorously enforced. Finally, in 1890, a local convention of monogamous Mormons, who were vastly in the majority, added a clause to the written constitution of Utah Territory prohibiting and punishing polygamy. At the same time an application—the fifth—was made for admission to the Union as a State. This application, like the others before it, was at first refused. However, after a proclamation by the Mormon Church in 1890 accepting the law of the United States prohibiting polygamy, and after enabling acts had been passed during 1893 and 1894, and following a convention held in Salt Lake City in 1895, Utah became a State within the Union in 1896.

NOTE

When I was in Salt Lake City in April 1973 I visited Temple Square early one morning and asked if I could attend a service in the Tabernacle. There were vast crowds in the Temple grounds, and the usher informed me that a convention was in progress, there were 10,000 people[10] already assembled in the Tabernacle, and the queue by the gate was forming for the service at 2 p.m. I was strolling disconsolately studying the architecture of the vast building when suddenly a side door opened, and another usher appeared who asked, 'How many in your party?' 'One,' I replied, on which I was whisked inside and given the only remaining seat in the vast concourse. The service, which was being televised and broadcast to the world, was most impressive: the vast Temple choir of both sexes sang superbly; the organist played the famous huge organ skilfully; and the addresses of the five principal leaders of the Church were most inspiring. The main theme was the importance of the family in shaping the lives of children. One preacher told the story of the Mormon soldier who always carried two watches. Asked the reason for this, the soldier replied that one watch told him the proper time and the other the time in his home State of Utah. 'At 5.30 each evening my family say their prayers together,'

[10] Probably an exaggeration: the Tabernacle holds 8,000.

he continued. 'When my second watch records that time I drop on my knees knowing I am praying with them.'

Later, in New Mexico, I was given a lift while walking to the Pueblo Indian settlement $2\frac{1}{2}$ miles north of Taos. The good Samaritan said he was a Mormon who was doing social work among the Indians. This seems to have a bearing on the traditionally friendly attitude of the Mormons towards the Indians which was mentioned earlier.

The present number of practising Mormons is reckoned to be three million, and according to Gentile[11] opinion sounded in the United States the Church is considered to be one of the wealthiest and most flourishing in the country. It also seems to be held in high esteem, mainly because it is reckoned to be doing valuable work for those in need everywhere throughout the world.

[11] i.e. non-Mormon.

Chapter 6

The Occupation of Texas: The Alamo

The Spaniards were not the only people interested in Texas. In the eighteenth century French fur-traders started moving in and seemed likely to claim the area for France. Spain's reaction was to set up military posts to protect the territory. One of these was established at Nacogdoches near the northern frontier and others farther south at Goliad and San Antonio. In 1718 war broke out between France and Spain and after skirmishes on the frontier the Spaniards were forced to retreat, though later they fought back and reoccupied Nacogdoches. In the nineteenth century Americans began to enter the province. The first intruders occupied an area near the presidio at Nacogdoches, where they were allowed to remain, and later more Americans arrived who had been turned out of settlements by the Red River to make way for Indians moved from the East. There was an impetus given to settlement after Mexico became independent of Spain in 1822, for the new republic's authorities adopted a policy of encouraging immigration to provide sufficient population to resist Indian attacks.

One of the first to contemplate settlement was Moses Austin.[1] Austin had drifted into Missouri when it was still under Mexican rule and had become a Mexican citizen. Aware of his advantage, he set out for San Antonio to lay before the governor a plan to bring into Texas a group of settlers pledged to become loyal Mexicans like himself.

[1] There is a monument to Moses Austin by Waldine Tauch in the City Hall grounds near the old plaza San Antonio.

Austin's proposition was provisionally approved, but unhappily, while returning to Missouri, he fell ill and died of pneumonia. However, the task of colonising in Texas was taken over by his son Stephen F. Austin, who like his father was a man of probity and good judgement. Stephen Austin began by carrying out an extensive reconnaissance of the central regions, after which he chose for his American colony an area between the Brazos and Colorado rivers where the soil was deep and fertile. The task of recruiting settlers proved easier than anticipated, for following the hard times in the United States after the Panic of 1819 many Americans felt attracted by offers of free land in Texas. Requests outnumbered those required and Austin was able to pick and choose. The Austin colony suffered the customary teething troubles of drought and Indian attack, but by far the worst setback was the news that permission to establish the settlement had not been confirmed by the central authorities. This necessitated a visit to Mexico City by Austin to plead his cause, and it was not until a year later that his grant of land was finally approved. Under the terms eventually arrived at, heads of families were allotted without payment 1 labor (177 acres) of land for farming and 74 labors for stockraising. Austin for his services was allowed to collect $12\frac{1}{2}$ cents per acre from the settlers and was given a bonus of 65,000 acres for every two hundred families he brought in. There were a number of not very severe stipulations in the contract. For example, settlers had to be of good repute and willing to adopt the Roman Catholic faith. Although slaves might be brought in, they were not allowed to be bought or sold in Texas and their children had to be freed at the age of fourteen.

Once its early difficulties had been overcome the colony began to flourish. By the end of the summer of 1823 the original three hundred[2] families permitted by the authorities had arrived and Austin was authorised to recruit an additional five hundred. However, the Mexican government considered that the northern province required a still larger population to keep the Indians at bay, and in 1824 passed a law under which contracts were awarded to land-agents

[2] 'The Old Three Hundred'.

(*empresarios*) in rivalry with Austin to settle 2,400 families. Not all the *empresarios* succeeded in creating viable colonies —some never even started to do so—but a considerable migration was put under way by this edict. Among heads of families who formed colonies at this time in the manner of Austin were Vehlein, Milam, De Witt, De Leon, Woodburgh and two men of Scottish origin, McMullin and McGloine. Vehlein established his settlement north of Austin's; Milam, De Witt and the others mostly to the south-west.[3] In 1830 the Mexicans attempted to encourage European immigrants, but were not very successful. In the inrush that followed the majority were illegal American entrants and only two ship-loads of Irish and a few German families arrived.

From the start there was friction with the Mexican authorities. Few settlers were willing to become Roman Catholics and it was resented that no services for other sects were permitted. Another grievance concerned slavery. Mexico practised a bonded service known as peonage, but there were no peons available for the settlers, who had to rely on the slaves they brought in. Also in 1829 a decree abolished bondage and the settlers feared that the slaves on whom they depended would be freed. Thanks to the representations of Austin, the authorities agreed to allow labour-contracts made outside the state to continue, but the Americans remained apprehensive for the future. There were also direct clashes, the worst being the Fredonian Revolt of 1826. This began when Hayden Edwards attempted to remove squatters from the territory he had been granted near Nacogdoches. The squatters protested strongly, and the Mexican authorities upheld their claim, annulled Edwards's contract and expelled him from the province. Edwards's supporters retaliated by forcibly taking possession and announcing the territory to be the Republic of Fredonia. As the father of Texan colonisation, Austin then took a hand in the matter. He raised a counter-force and quickly dispersed the revolutionaries. But a good deal of bitter feeling still remained. Probably most dissatisfaction was felt because the settlers were allowed so little say in running their own affairs, for although conventions were held

[3] A contemporary map in the Alamo museum gives the locations.

from time to time to try to find ways of enlarging their responsibilities little was conceded. Then, in 1834 President Santa Anna repudiated a reform programme which was to have introduced democratic methods of government and set about creating a unified military state with himself as leader and generalissimo. In accordance with the new policy the garrisons at Nacogdoches, San Antonio al Bexar and Goliad were strengthened, and Anahuac was established at the mouth of the Trinity River to stop the entry of further American immigrants. Word had already spread that Santa Anna intended to abolish local governments, disenfranchise Americans and eventually drive them back to the United States. The reinforcement of the garrisons, therefore, appeared to be the first stage in the new programme.

Matters came to a head when the commander at Anahuac, rigidly interpreting instructions previously disregarded, refused further American immigration, and also imprisoned two settlers who refused to loan their slaves for government work. Supporters of the two settlers seeking revenge assembled at San Felipe de Austin. While one armed group under W. B. Travis went off to get a cannon to assist the warlike operations, another marched directly on the post at Anahuac. Those who attacked the post did not achieve much; but Travis's party not only dispersed a Mexican covering force when returning to join their companions but afterwards stormed the fort. Austin, anxious as always to act as peacemaker, managed to obtain a breathing space by persuading the Mexicans to leave Anahuac unoccupied for a time so that tempers might cool, but this respite did not achieve very much. The settlers remained seething with resentment, and soon the majority, including Austin, were convinced they would have to fight for their rights.

In the event they did not have to wait long to do this, for Santa Anna, having restored law and order in the metropolitan parts of his kingdom where some areas had rebelled following his dictatorial actions, now moved north to quell the revolt in Texas. While still some way off he became so concerned by the news that reached him that he sent forward his cavalry to nip the rebellion in the bud. The cavalry, having occupied San Antonio al Bexar, sent a detachment to Gonzales in De Witt's colony to impound a brass six-pounder which the Mexican authorities earlier provided for defence against Indians. The inhabitants, however, decided not to give up the cannon and delayed matters by evasive replies while they sent off for reinforcements. While waiting, they withdrew the ferry boats and buried the cannon in a peach orchard against a surprise attack by the Mexicans on the other side of the River Guadalupe. When support arrived they crossed over bringing their cannon, and under cover of fog advanced on the Mexican position. When the fog lifted the two forces were confronting each other a few hundred yards apart. Both sides agreed to parley, but when the Mexicans renewed their demand for the cannon to be handed over so that it might not be used against the authorities who had provided it, the men of Gonzales once more refused to do so. There followed a battle to decide the issue, in which, with the advantage the cannon gave, the Gonzaleans were able to drive back the Mexican cavalrymen on San Antonio, and inflict losses without suffering any themselves.

News of the Battle of Gonzales soon reached the other settlements and Stephen Austin, William Travis and James Bowie, among others, hastened to help their friends. Also in New Orleans, which had been the port of departure for immigrants to Texas, a meeting was held to raise war funds and two companies of New Orleans Grays were mustered. On arrival, Austin was unanimously elected commander-in-chief. He decided to march on San Antonio, which the Mexican commander General Cos was said to be fortifying, and sent forward a detachment to reconnoitre an assembly place near the town from which to launch his attack. After examining and rejecting a spot near the old mission of San José, five miles south of San Antonio, the final site chosen was by the nearer empty Conception mission. Soon after Austin's men reached Conception they were attacked by Mexicans sent out from San Antonio, but were able to beat them off and capture one of their guns.

On 1 November 1835 Austin advanced and laid siege to San Antonio. General Cos had placed one part of his force

in the Alamo[4] and the other around the main plaza. He
fortified the houses surrounding the square, built barricades
at the four open street corners and placed sharpshooters and
guns on flat roofs to command the area. Because of shortage
of numbers Austin decided on a protracted siege. This did
not suit his undisciplined followers who began to drift away.
After a week or two of siege operations even after the arrival
of the New Orleans Grays the besiegers numbered consider-
ably less than they had at the start. At this juncture Austin,
who had proved less able as military commander than he had
been as colonial administrator, was called away to become a
commissioner to the United States and was replaced by Burleson. But Burleson was no more successful than Austin had
been, and the troops still continued to desert. After a series of
councils of war from which nothing practical emerged it had
just been decided to abandon the siege when an unexpected
piece of news caused a change of plan. Following desertions
on both sides, a Mexican lieutenant appeared in the besiegers'
lines with the encouraging information that the force in the
plaza was too weak to resist an assault. Several leaders at once
pressed the reluctant Burleson to attack. One of the most
vociferous was Milam who had just returned from a visit to
Mexico.

'Who will go with old Ben Milam into San Antonio?' he
cried. A ringing affirmative shout was the reply, and volunteers promptly fell into line ready to follow Milam in an
attack on the town.

This began at dawn on 5 December 1835, five weeks after
the siege began. There were three columns involved. The
first made a feint attack against the Alamo; the second
advanced along Acequia Street towards the barricades around
the main plaza; and the third approached up Soledad Street
(see map 10). As the Mexican deserter had suggested,
opposition was slight, and the columns were quickly able to

[4] The mission station of San Antonio de Valero occupied several
sites before moving to the Alamo. The Alamo was so called perhaps
because it was surrounded by cottonwoods or alamos, or possibly
because the first company of soldiers to occupy the long barracks
alongside came from Alamo de Parris in Mexico.

Panning for Gold (*Denver Public Library, Western History Depart-ment*)

Sitting Bull (*National Archives*)

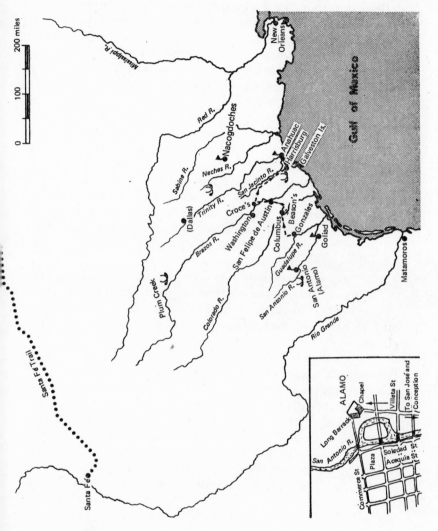

200 miles
100
0

Mississippi R.

New Orleans

Gulf of Mexico

Red R.

Nacogdoches

Sabine R.

Neches R.

Anahuac
Harrisburg
Galveston Is.

San Jacinto R.

(Dallas)

Trinity R.

Croce's

Beason's

Brazos R.

Washington

San Felipe de Austin

Columbus

Gonzales

Goliad

Plum Creek

Guadalupe R.

San Antonio
(Alamo)

Colorado R.

San Antonio R.

Rio Grande

Matamoros

Santa Fé Trail

Santa Fé

ALAMO

Chapel

Long Berrack

San Antonio R.

Villeta St

To San José and
Conception

Commerce St

Plaza

Soledad St

Acequia St

10. Texas

establish themselves without significant loss in houses around
the plaza, though a lucky shot from a Mexican piece on the
roof of a church in the centre of the square dismounted
one of the besieger's guns. There followed a period of stale-
mate. Further advance was difficult because of fire from
enemy cannon in position at street corners. The pieces were
masqued and roofed in and because of the small openings
for their muzzles were difficult to silence. There was also
heavy cross-fire from the Alamo, where the ominous black
and red flag signifying no quarter was flying.

At daylight on the second day of the attack the Mexicans
opened a brisk fire from a trench made during the night on
the east side of the river. There was also fire from a gun in
position in the cross-street leading from the plaza across the
double stream to the Alamo. The Texans managed by
counter-fire to silence both these, and followed up by breaking
holes with crowbars in the walls of one of the houses adjoin-
ing the square and taking possession of it. During this operation, however, a serious loss occurred. While crossing over
towards the newly acquired stronghold Milam was struck
by a rifle-ball in the head and killed. It was thought he was
hit by a sharpshooter hidden in a cypress tree on the river
bank.

During the third day of the assault more walls were broken
through in houses surrounding the square, and a whole row
on the south-side was occupied. Next, a concerted attack by
the New Orleans Grays and the Brazonians seized a priest's
house on the north side of the square. Its capture proved
most valuable, for the upper storey dominated the area, and
the result was that during the night General Cos withdrew
all his men into the Alamo. He had intended to make this
post secure and then launch an attack on the Texan camp
at Conception, but by this time desertion had become so
serious that he changed his mind and offered to capitulate.
Burleson, realising the Mexican force still outnumbered his
own, agreed to parley, and immediately chose commissioners
to go to a house[5] in Villita Street to arrange terms. By the
following day an agreement had been reached. For the time

[5] Now named Cos House and bearing a suitable tablet.

being General Cos and his men could stay in the Alamo, but except for the sick and wounded they would have to leave San Antonio within six days of the signing of the capitulation; though they would be allowed sufficient provisions at current prices to last them until they reached the Rio Grande. On 14 December 1835 General Cos and his thousand men marched out of the Alamo and proceeded to the mission of San José. On the following day they continued their march towards the Rio Grande.

At the end of the first phase of the Texan Revolutionary War a meeting was held at San Felipe de Austin at which were present representatives of all the American colonies in Texas. After three days of bitter debate Henry Smith was elected temporary governor of the new state, twelve men were chosen to form a council and, Stephen Austin having lost favour, Sam Houston was named commander-in-chief of the army. No decision was then reached about independence. However, the dire consequences of an unsuccessful revolution were realised from Santa Anna's threat[6] to shoot all rebels, and after a second meeting which included Mexican liberals in March 1836, a declaration of independence was made and a constitution was drawn up based on that of the United States. Thus came into existence the Republic of Texas.

Sam Houston was born in Virginia in 1793, but was brought up in Cherokee territory in Tennessee after having been adopted by an Indian chief. In 1813 he enlisted in the United States Army and by persistent gallantry under fire in the war with England rose to the rank of lieutenant. He left the army in 1818 to study law and subsequently became a member of Congress and the Governor of Tennessee. In 1829 he returned for three years to live among the Cherokees in the region beyond the Mississippi where they had been removed along with other Eastern Indians. In 1832 Houston returned to civilisation again, and having learned of the Indians' grievances during his stay with them petitioned on their behalf. He managed to bring about the removal of several Indian Agents on charges of fraud, but got into difficulties

[6] By this time Santa Anna was investing the Alamo.

with their supporters in Congress, with the result that he was anxious to leave the United States, and Texas appeared to offer a new field for his ambition. From the first Houston faced difficulties. He found it difficult to get his officers to carry out his instructions and although he had the support of Governor Henry Smith, the Council were prone to issue orders directly to his subordinates which were quite contrary to his wishes. Houston decided to abandon the forward posts at Goliad and the Alamo, concentrate farther north, and protect the Texan colonies by sending out strong columns against the advancing Mexicans; but he had great difficulty in implementing this plan.

In charge at Goliad was James Bowie. Born in Tennessee in 1759, Bowie had led an adventurous life fighting Indians and engaging in speculative adventures which were said to include smuggling. One of his claims to fame was the invention of the 'Bowie Knife'[7] an article much approved of by frontiersmen. After drifting into Texas he had distinguished himself under Austin at the Battle of Conception. Houston ordered Bowie to abandon Goliad and join Colonel Neill who was in charge temporarily at the Alamo. He also ordered Neill to send all war material back to Gonzales preparatory to abandoning the Alamo as well. Meanwhile Neill was in the process of handing over to the youthful William Travis, who had recently joined him along with twenty-five regulars. But there were soon to be two more principals in the Alamo besides Travis. During February Bowie came in with thirty men from Goliad and Davy Crockett arrived with sixteen mounted volunteers from Tennessee. Crockett was born in Tennessee in 1786. After serving as a scout under Andrew Jackson in the Creek War 1813–14 he became Justice of the Peace in Tennessee. He later boasted that none of his decisions, which were based always on natural born sense instead of law learning, was ever reversed. His main claim to fame was as a bear hunter, having killed over a hundred in one year alone. A humorous suggestion that he run for Congress led him to do so, and he was subsequently elected

[7] It was an all-purpose one-edge blade with guarded hilt, so nicely balanced that it could be thrown with deadly effect.

for three terms, becoming known as the 'Coonskin Congressman'. His opposition to the policies of Andrew Jackson cost him his seat, and the call to Texas found him at a loose end.

Despite Houston's orders, the leaders at San Antonio would not abandon the Alamo. They thought the post too valuable to leave to the enemy, and demanded reinforcements to enable them to hold out. There was, however, a good deal of discontent among the garrison, mainly due to the behaviour of Bowie. The volunteers objected to being commanded by a young regular like Travis, and, after having been allowed in traditional American fashion to elect a leader of their own, chose Bowie. Bowie's response was to join in drinking bouts with his men and allow them to behave as they fancied. Also, on his own authority, he ordered prisoners to be released, and stopped the civilian authorities evacuating private families. It was fortunate in some ways that he was taken ill with typhoid-pneumonia and Travis was allowed unfettered command. The Alamo was in much the same condition as when General Cos left after his capitulation. A part of the chapel had been unroofed but a platform in front still remained and this was large enough to mount cannon; the long barrack, which contained living quarters, a dining-hall and kitchen, protected part of the west side; and around the compound was a perimeter fence. Not much had been done to improve the defences of the fort before the Mexican attack, but a protective entrenchment had been placed in front of the chapel and the perimeter barricade had been strengthened with cedar-post stockades, breastworks and ditches.

The first Mexican troops reached the post on 23 February 1836, and their commander, Colonel Almonte, immediately demanded its unconditional surrender. Travis's reply was a cannon shot at an enemy group gathered where Commerce Street enters the main plaza. This Almonte correctly interpreted as a refusal. The siege operations that followed were conducted by Santa Anna himself, and his first move was to subject the post to a sustained bombardment lasting twenty-four hours. Surprisingly, casualties inside the Alamo were few, and Travis made use of the first lull to draft and send out his famous appeal for help. This read:

Commandancy of the Alamo
Bexar, Feby 24th 1836—
    Fellow citizens and compatriots,

I am besieged by a thousand or more of the Mexicans under Santa Anna—I have sustained a continual bombardment and cannonade for 24 hours and have not lost a man. The enemy has demanded a surrender at discretion, otherwise the garrison are to be put to the sword, if the fort is taken. I have answered the demand with a cannon shot, and our flag still waves proudly from the walls. *I shall never surrender or retreat.*

Then, I call on you in the name of liberty, of patriotism and everything dear to the American character to come to our aid, with all dispatch. The enemy is receiving reinforcements daily and will no doubt increase to three or four thousand in four or five days.

If this call is neglected, I am determined to sustain myself as long as possible and die like a soldier who never forgets what is due to his own honor or that of his country.

Victory or Death.

William Barret Travis
Lt. Col. Comd.

P.S. The Lord is on our side. When the enemy appeared in sight we had not three bushels of corn. We have since found in deserted houses 80 or 90 bushels and got into the wall 20 or 30 head of beeves.

Travis

On 25 February, having been reinforced, the Mexicans attempted to set up a battery south of the Alamo. They were hampered in this by sharp fire from the ramparts and a Texan sally during the night, but next day they managed to set up another battery to the north-east, nearer the fort. The following day they attempted unsuccessfully to cut off the fort's water supply; but in a second attempt managed to damage the main aqueduct.

On 1 March a lucky shot from the twelve-pounder in position on the roof of the chapel struck the house in which Santa Anna was lodging in the town; and on the same day there arrived a reinforcement from Gonzales of thirty-two men. These managed to get through the enemy lines safely under cover of darkness.

The 3 March was an important day in the history of the siege. About two hours before sunset there was a lull in the bombardment, and Travis made use of this to call together and rally his men. According to an account said to have been given by Moses Rose, Travis paraded them in a single file, and, after standing in front for a few moments speechless from emotion, declared that he was determined to stay and fight it out, even if left on his own, but every one of them must do what he thought best. Then he drew a line with the point of his sword along the ground, and exclaimed, 'I now want every man who will stay and die with me to come across this line.' The first to cross was Tapley Howard. He leaped over the line in one bound, saying, 'I am ready to die for my country!' His example was immediately followed by every man except Moses Rose. Bowie, who could not leave his bed, asked his companions to carry him over, and four men lifted his cot and bore it across. Every sick man who could not walk made a similar request, and had his bunk moved in the same way.

Moses Rose recorded that he, too, was deeply affected, but differently from his companions. He wrote: 'I stood till every man had crossed the line. Then I sank to the ground, covered my face with my hands, and thought what best I might do. Suddenly an idea came. I spoke their language, and could I once get safely out of the fort might easily pass for a Mexican and effect my escape. I stole a glance at Colonel Bowie in his cot. Colonel Davy Crockett was leaning over talking to him. After a few seconds, Bowie looked at me and said, "You don't seem willing to die with us, Rose." "No", I said. "I am not prepared to die, and shall not do so if I can avoid it." Then Crockett looked at me, and said, "You might just as well, for escape is impossible." I made no reply but looked up at the top of the fortress wall. "I have often done worse things than climb that wall," I thought. Then I sprang up, seized my travelling bag and unwashed clothes and ascended it. Standing on top, I glanced down to take a last look at my friends. They were all now in motion, but what they were doing I heeded not. Overpowered by my feelings, I turned away. Then I threw down my bag and leaped after it. I took the road which led down to the river, crossed by the ford, and went through the town past the church. I saw no one. All the doors were closed. San Antonio appeared as a deserted city. After passing through the town I followed the river southward. When I had gone about a quarter of a mile my ears were saluted by the thunder of the bombardment which had begun again.'

Meanwhile, the Mexican leaders were meeting to decide when they would launch their attack. After a long discussion Cos and some others suggested they should wait for the arrival of two twelve-pounders which were due on the 7th; Santa Anna and Almonte, on the other hand, wanted to attack next day. During the night a Mexican woman deserted from the fort and told them how small the garrison of the Alamo was. Emboldened by this, they decided to attack at once, though not without some misgivings, apparently. According to Santa Anna's Negro servant Ben, he was serving coffee just before the assault began, and heard Almonte remark that it would be a very costly undertaking, to which Santa Anna replied that it would have to be done whatever the cost.

On the morning of the 6th, the Mexicans, under cover of darkness, approached the barricade round the fort. While the infantry surrounded the compound, the cavalry formed a circle further out to catch any who passed the infantry line. Just as daylight was approaching, the infantry planted scaling ladders, climbed up to the top of the wall, and jumped down within, many to their instant death. But according to one account, 'as fast as the front ranks were slain, they were filled up again by fresh troops'.

The Texans resisted staunchly, but there were so many Mexicans—seemingly several thousands—that the 182 defenders could not keep the attackers out, however hard they tried. The outer walls had soon to be abandoned, after which it was a case of holding the buildings, room by room. When ammunition was expended the Texans used the butts of their muskets to defend themselves, but, within an hour, they were overwhelmed.

What little is known of the last moments of the principals came from the few non-combatants who were spared, particularly Mrs Dickinson, Joe, the Negro servant of Travis, and Ham, the Negro servant of Bowie. Travis seems to have done deadly work with his cannon on top of the chapel, and his body was found beside the gun. Crockett appears to have been shot down outside a room in the long barrack, for Mrs Dickinson recalled that when being led away from the macabre scene, she recognised him lying dead between the chapel and the barrack, even remembering seeing his famous coonskin cap lying by his side. His body, however, was found just inside the Bapistry, the first room on the right on entering the present Alamo—and this is now his memorial chapel. It was said that Bowie was carried from the Confessional— the first room on the left on entering the Alamo—over to the Bapistry where he met his fate, the Chapel being the last place to be taken.

After the battle, Santa Anna directed that the bodies of the fallen Texans be placed on two great pyres. Alternate layers of wood and men were laid, and then oil was poured over the pyres and they were set alight. It seems to have taken two days for the bodies to be consumed. After the war the ashes of the heroes were collected, and, following a memorial service in the town, were buried in the grounds of the Alamo.

In January 1836, while Houston was on leave, the Council ordered his deputy, James W. Fannin, to lead a force of some 400 men against Matamoros near the mouth of the Rio Grande. But before Fannin had gone very far news came that the place had been heavily fortified and that Santa Anna was already advancing at the head of a large army, so in a change of plan Fannin fell back on Goliad which following Houston's orders to Bowie had now been evacuated. The presidio at Goliad was situated upon a rocky height above the San Antonio River and its compound was surrounded by a ten-foot stone wall, so, believing it might easily be defended, Fannin left some detachments at outposts to the west and consolidated the rest of his force at the post.

On 19 February a messenger[8] arrived from the Alamo to ask Fannin to come and help Travis; but Fannin refused to leave. Then came Travis's 'Victory or Death' announcement and Houston urged Fannin either to go to the relief of the Alamo or to fall back. On this Fannin set out for San Antonio with some 300 volunteers, but after going only a few miles returned with them to the fort. Precisely why he did not continue is not known. One view is that with such a small force mostly on foot and with a limited supply of provisions to march a hundred miles through uninhabited country for the purpose of relieving a fortress beleaguered by 5,000 men was madness. Next, Fannin heard that his outposts were being assaulted, and dispatched some of his Georgians to help them. This proved of no avail, for after the arrival of the reinforcements the posts were attacked by a large Mexican force and liquidated. On hearing the sad news Fannin decide to fall back on Gonzales, but by this time advance parties of the enemy were approaching, and before getting ready to leave he had to make two sallies to drive them off.

The march began at dawn on 19 March, and with a heavy fog giving an opportunity of leaving unobserved, they made six miles with no reports of any pursuit. Then, instead of making use of the fog which still hung about to put even more distance between themselves and the Mexicans, it was decided to stop and graze the animals on the grassland leading to the woods bordering Colete Creek, their first objective. Following the halt the march proceeded slowly, and after a few miles Mexicans were noticed in the rear. Immediately a hollow square was formed and a few artillery rounds unleashed, after which they moved on. At this stage the Texans believed they were being followed only by skirmishing parties in search of plunder, which they would have no difficulty in holding off. Then an accident occurred which seriously affected the issue. While approaching Colete Creek an

[8] James Buller Bonham: he managed to return to the Alamo.

ammunition wagon broke down. Instead of abandoning it and continuing towards the protective woods, Fannin allowed his men to halt and try and transfer the load to another cart. While they were doing this the Mexican cavalry completely surrounded the Texan column. According to some reports they had time to form themselves into a hollow square which was three lines deep, with wagons and oxen in the centre; but other accounts say this was done during the battle.

The Mexicans were led by José Urrea, one of their best generals. When he found he could not overwhelm the outnumbered Texans by cavalry charges, he ordered his sharpshooters to pick off the draught animals and make his enemy immobile until his artillery came up to bombard them into submission. Early next morning the Mexican artillery arrived, along with reinforcements in manpower which brought up their numbers to well over a thousand. By this time 9 of the 400 Texans were dead and 51 wounded, Fannin being slightly wounded in the thigh, while 50 Mexicans had been killed and 140 wounded.

The Texan artillery had not proved very effective, and after its commander was killed were even less so. With the arrival of the Mexican artillery, the Texans in their open position were at their mercy. Indeed, when Urrea opened fire with his guns, the Texans made no attempt to reply. Instead, a white flag was raised and Fannin and two companions went forward to seek the best terms they could get.

The exact nature of these terms have remained in doubt. The Texans claimed they were accepted as prisoners of war and promised repatriation to the United States from where the bulk of them derived; the Mexicans, on the other hand, stated that the surrender had been unconditional. Certainly under a decree of 1835 Fannin's men ranked as pirates—for they had entered the province armed and had taken part in a rebellion—and were legally subject to the death penalty. Urrea may have offered them a safe conduct; but Santa Anna would not allow this. He pointed out that the prisoners were subject to the 1835 decree, and he ordered them to be executed. Then, because he was not confident that Urrea would carry out such instructions he detailed another officer to see that it was done. The men were thus first taken back to Goliad, and then marched out and shot.

In March 1836, after the declaration of independence and while delegates were engaged in drawing up a constitution at Washington-on-the-Brazos, a courier arrived from San Antonio with an appeal from Travis for help. Immediately someone hastily made a resolution that members of the convention be excused to go and fight, but Houston pointed out that the business of the meeting was to establish a governmen, not to fight Santa Anna. The latter was the task of the army, he said, and with the convention's approval he would go immediately 'to take command of the Texian (*sic*) forces in the field'. Chastened, the delegates returned to finish their work on the constitution, and having selected a government headed by D. G. Burnet and the Mexican liberal Lorenzo de Zavle they adjourned.

When Houston reached Gonzales he found his army consisted of 374 volunteers, poorly armed and inadequately supplied. These he formed into a regiment under Burleson with Sherman as second-in-command. There had already been reports that the Alamo had fallen and that an army under General Sesma was advancing towards them, and this news was confirmed by Mrs Dickinson on her arrival in Gonzales. Immediately, and without consulting anyone—a trait which irritated everyone again and again before the campaign ended—Houston decided to fall back. Thus began the so-called 'Runaway Scrape' during which soldiers, settlers and their wives and families retreated eastward before the Mexicans in a ragged stream. When the army reached the Colorado in the vicinity of Columbus a plan to stand on the river line was considered, but later discarded. Instead, Houston first placed guards on the crossings at Columbus and then led his army downriver to Beason's Crossing. At this stage about a hundred volunteers joined, but twenty of the original party left to go and see how their families were faring. On 21 March Sesma's army arrived opposite Beason's and took cover in a belt of trees a few hundred yards from the river. Sherman pressed Houston to attack, but the army commander

refused to do so. He was even more definite in his refusal a
little later when news arrived of Fannin's surrender. When
Houston gave orders for the retreat to be continued there
were mutterings and some hundred more deserted to assist
their families. The rest reluctantly followed Houston eastward and reached San Felipe de Austin on the Brazos next
day after an exhausting forced march of thirty miles. This
withdrawal left many settlers between the Colorado and
Brazos without protection, so that panic similar to that at the
beginning of the 'Runaway Scrape' was reborn, and more
families loaded their possessions in carts and joined the
stream of refugees. On reaching the Brazos, Houston ordered
a further withdrawal, this time upriver to Croce's Landing
which was in the opposite direction from where the enemy
were now heading. This caused more mutterings. Two
companies were so anxious to stand and fight that they flatly
refused to follow Houston. But with his customary sound judg-
ment Houston avoided trouble by ordering them to stop and
guard the river crossings at San Felipe de Austin. For weeks the
rain had been unusually heavy, and as the army struggled
through the mud the downpour became almost incessant. Men,
wagons and teams floundered and slipped and slid over the
soggy ground beside the river. It took the better part of four
days to slog the twenty miles to Croce's Landing, and by
the time the army arrived there on 31 March it had dwindled
by desertion to 900 men. While at Croce's Houston attempted
to drill and train his undisciplined troops and make
them more like soldiers, but there was not time to do much.

Not only the troops disapproved of Houston turning away
from the enemy. The government, now at Harrisburg on the
estuary of the San Jacinto, was also perturbed by his tactics.
Governor Burnet considered the army should have marched
down to protect the cabinet, or at least placed themselves in
the path of the enemy. He sent his Secretary of War, J. J.
Rush, to Croce's to order Houston south, stating that if he
refused Rush must take over command himself. Rush, however, was a personal friend of Houston and when he arrived
was easily persuaded to fall in with his plans. Houston's oft-
quoted statement about his decision to wait on the advancing

enemy's northern flank was: 'Had I consulted the wishes of all I would have been like the ass between two stacks of hay. Many wished me to go below; others above. I consulted none. I held no council of war. If I erred, the blame is mine.'

Meanwhile, Santa Anna, on receiving reports from Sesma of Houston's movements, changed his mind on an earlier decision to return to Mexico and, having sent orders for his armies to converge on San Felipe de Austin, hurried forward to join Sesma. Santa Anna reached the Brazos on 7 April, and was held up for a time by the flooded waters and the men Houston had left on guard. Turning downriver, he eventually effected a crossing, but had to leave most of his heavy equipment to await the construction of rafts. He hurried forward to try to capture Burnet and his government at Harrisburg; but before he reached the town Burnet and his ministers had galloped off to the coast. The enraged Santa Anna sent Almonte and fifty dragoons in hot pursuit. Almonte very nearly succeeded in overtaking them. Burnet and his companions jumped precipitately into a boat and shoved off and rowed away to seek sanctuary on Galveston Island only moments ahead of the first dragoon.

Meanwhile, Houston was on the move. Although as was customary he did not divulge where they were being taken, his troops thought it might be either a further retreat eastward to Nacogdoches or a move south to fight Santa Anna. As they all wanted to fight they were delighted when at a road junction where one fork led to Nacogdoches and the other to Harrisburg their leader chose the latter. The two armies eventually met near Buffalo Bayou on the shore of San Jacinto estuary close to Harrisburg. The Texans, now numbering 800, occupied a position among some trees by the bayou, while the slightly more numerous Mexicans approached from the south and took up a position in a belt of woods along the shore of the estuary.

The battle began with the Mexicans opening fire from a single gun concealed in the wood, after which they began to advance across the open space between the armies, but were met with such a rain of fire that they hastily withdrew again to the cover of the trees from which they had emerged. Sherman pressed Houston to attack, but all Houston would allow was a small cavalry reconnaissance party to go forward. This clashed with Mexican cavalry, and in a sharp encounter had two men wounded and several horses killed before galloping back to safety, some men two to a mount. The ever-cautious Houston was afraid the skirmish might develop into a general battle and the Texans be caught at a disadvantage, but the rest of the day passed uneventfully.

After a quiet but anxious night the Texans were alarmed on the following morning to see General Cos approach with 500 reinforcements. This tilted the odds to 1,400 Mexicans and 800 Texans; but it also contributed to the Mexicans' undoing, for when the Texans failed to mount an expected dawn offensive, tension was relaxed in the Mexican camp, and rest and refreshment became the order of the day, with a minimum of guards.

In mid-afternoon after an indecisive council of war—said to be the first and only one he ever called—Houston assembled his commanders and ordered a general assault. The Texan army, in three divisions with the cavalry on the flank, then charged forward shouting excitedly, 'Remember the Alamo! Remember Goliad!' The wild Texans tore in among the slumbering Mexicans in their lines, striking with a blood lust that increased the more they killed, for when ammunition was expended, they took to clubbing their opponents or stabbing them mercilessly with Bowie knives. Neither Houston nor his officers could check the wanton carnage, and although the battle was won in twenty minutes it was not until nightfall that the senseless killing ended. Then a crude prisoner-of-war camp was set up and the several hundred terrorised Mexicans who had escaped the holocaust were huddled there under guard. The next morning the round-up of prisoners began anew, and continued until the following day. The most important capture of all was Santa Anna, who was taken travelling on foot dressed as a private. The acclaims of other prisoners of 'El Presidente! El Presidente!' gave him away. The Battle of San Jacinto gave Texas her independence, as although 2,000 Mexicans were in the country at the time of the battle, these made off home as soon as the news reached them, and the capture of Santa Anna made a strong bargaining point in deciding the terms of the peace that followed.

Six months after the battle, elections were held to form a new government. Austin and Houston both stood for President, but Austin's popularity had declined during the war years and Houston was chosen, with Mirabeau B. Lamar as Vice-President. The establishment of sound government was hard to achieve because of the inadequate state income, but Houston produced a workmanlike administration. His efforts to join the United States were not successful because the Northerners were reluctant to admit another slave state,[9] but he managed to obtain recognition in 1837. The years following the war were ones of substantial immigration. The Panic of 1837 caused hundreds of Americans to seek a new life in Texas, and many Germans also arrived. At first the new-comers came as individuals or single families, but in 1841 the *empresario* system was revived and group colonisation began again, one of the most successful being the Peters Colony established near present-day Dallas. This prolonged wave of immigration swelled the population of Texas from 30,000 to 142,000.

In 1838 Houston's term of office ended and Lamar succeeded him as President. He was more forceful than Houston had been and began a policy of subjugation of the local Indians whom Houston had left in peace. Under his direction an operation was staged against the Cherokee which ended in their defeat on the River Neches in 1839; and the hostile Comanche were attacked and overcome at Plum Creek in 1840. Lamar's foreign policy was equally dynamic. By diplomatic pressure he managed to get France to grant recognition in 1839 and soon afterwards England, the Netherlands, and Belgium followed suit, though not Mexico. Determined to make Texas a great and powerful state, Lamar sought to extend her frontiers westward. In 1841 he dispatched an expedition to Sante Fé to try to persuade the people of New Mexico to cast off the Mexican yoke and throw in their lot

[9] The USA were careful about having equal numbers of slave and non-slave States.

with Texas. When approaching Sante Fé, exhausted after a long journey, the Texans were attacked by a large Mexican force sent out by the Governor Manuel Armijo and forced to surrender. They were marched off 2,000 miles to Mexico City and those who survived were incarcerated in the capital. This ill-starred expedition sealed the fate of Lamar and his supporters, and at the elections in 1841 he was replaced by Houston for a second term. In spite of efforts at retrenchment and peaceful co-operation with neighbours, Houston became involved in a new and costly war with Mexico who, angered by the Sante Fé expedition, raided and plundered western Texas. The three forces Houston raised were not successful. The first, after crossing the Rio Grande, was surrounded and captured, and the men marched off to join their unhappy comrades in the dungeons of Mexico City; the second composed of Mountain Men were chased away from the Mexican town they attacked; and the third consisting of Missourians did no more than kill a lone Sante Fé trader. Yet another force sent out later to raid caravans on the Santa Fé Trail meekly retreated when the yearly caravan was seen to be escorted by United States dragoons.

In 1843, after hostilities had ended Houston attempted to get the United States concerned with annexation by playing off a tentative Mexican offer of independent statehood within the Mexican Republic. This brought an offer from the United States to negotiate, but when the matter was voted on in the Senate it was turned down. However, the tide was turning towards United States expansion. President Tyler at the end of his term promised annexation would come, and Polk who succeeded him won his election on an expansionist ticket. Then, when a move was made by other European governments to support independence, and its acceptance was wrung from Mexico, the United States were at last encouraged to let Texas join them. This came about in 1845 when on 29 December President Polk signed a message that admitted Texas to the Union.

Chapter 7

The Conquest of California

In 1827, when the northern Mexican provinces were beginning to be settled by Americans, New Mexico with 44,000 inhabitants was ten times as populous as Texas or California. This was because it possessed good pastureland and mineral resources. Sheep-raising was the principal industry, and there were some four million animals on the *ranchos* along the upper Rio Grande between El Paso in the south and Taos amid the Rockies in the north. Mining was scarcely less important. The Santa Rita mines on the site of present-day Silver City produced a thousand tons of copper yearly, and the Dolores gold mine south of Santa Fé was almost as productive.

The early history of New Mexico was stormy. The Indians were not as docile as the coastal tribes of California, and the Holy Fathers had difficulty in training them to become herdsmen and husbandmen. The first Spanish settlement at San Gabriel north of Santa Fé was not a success and had to be abandoned, but in 1610 a mission-station was established at Santa Fé itself and a new attempt was made to save the souls of the local Pueblo Indians and teach them civilised ways, including the weaving of textiles. Meanwhile, successive governors sought to produce financial benefit for themselves by herding, and sending the animals[1] south for sale. Marauding Indians were troublesome. Apache raided from the west, Navaho from the north-west, Comanche from the east; and in 1680 the local Pueblo Indians rebelled and drove out all the Spaniards they had not killed.

[1] Mainly horses and cattle.

The province was reconquered by Don Diego de Vargas in 1692, after which he was established as governor and rebuilt the Governor's Palace[2] at Santa Fé. From Spanish archives it is learned that in 1739 a group of Frenchmen reached Santa Fé to trade, and were well received. In 1744 three more Frenchmen arrived, this time at Taos; when the Governor heard they were tradesmen[3] he allowed them to settle in the area. With the Frenchmen came Comanche tribesmen saying they wanted to trade. They soon, however, began raiding outlying settlements, so military action was taken to drive them away. In 1776 there was a large-scale Comanche raid following which another military operation had to be staged. After this, peace talks were initiated with the Indians, and some Navaho chiefs, who had earlier been menacing the Spanish settlements, even came and stayed with the Governor in his palace at Santa Fé to talk peace.

In the early nineteenth century the first Americans came to New Mexico. One of these was Zebulon Montgomery Pike. Pike's first important expedition had been towards the source of the Mississippi. Setting out in a keel boat from St Louis with twenty soldiers in August 1805, he made for the head-waters of the Mississippi with the object of exploring the source, and also showing the Indians and British that the United States was sovereign in the area. The winter was spent in what is now Minnesota. Here Pike constructed a camp where most of his men remained, but after the snow fell he explored the neighbourhood with a selected few using dog sleds. In his search for the source of the Mississippi he penetrated deep into the lake-dotted forest region which surround its headwaters, and he explored the Leech Lake drainage system which he mistook for the true source. In the spring he floated downstream with his party and reached St. Louis on the last day of April 1808. In July 1808 he was sent out again, this time to explore the country towards the head of the Rio Grande, where the boundary between Mexico and Louisiana was very vaguely determined. His party,

[2] Now a museum.
[3] One had three trades, being a tailor, barber and bloodletter, the other two were carpenters.

numbering twenty-three, was accompanied by fifty Osage Indians—including women and children—who had been captured by the Pottawattamies, and whose release and return to their homes had been brought about by the efforts of the United States Government. Their presence had the advantage of procuring a friendly reception in Osage country. The party ascended the Osage River as far as it was navigable and then, having obtained some horses, travelled on to the large village called the Pawnee Republic after which the Republic River was named. A Spanish expedition several hundred strong, whose intentions were to impress the Indians with the might of Spain, had anticipated Pike's men by travelling through this debatable land. Pike, however, had little difficulty in getting the chiefs to hoist the American flag instead of the Spanish one that had been left with them.

From the Pawnee village the explorers crossed the Great Plains and travelled towards the upper waters of the River Arkansas. Like all early travellers they were impressed by the sea of grass and the multitude of buffalo they encountered. When the party reached the Arkansas, late in October, five men who had had enough journeyed downriver to go back home; but Pike and the rest pressed on westward into the mountains. Late in November they reached the neighbourhood of the high mountain[4] which was named later after Pike himself. In the second half of January, while installed in improvised shelters in Wet Mountain Valley, the party became very short of food and nine men were crippled with frostbite. At the point of crisis, Pike and Dr Robinson went out hunting and found and killed a lone buffalo, which saved the situation. After leaving Wet Mountain Valley, Pike and his men reached the Rio Grande, where the weather was milder and deer abounded. Here they built a fort over which they flew the United States flag, though Pike well knew that he was in Spanish territory. When the Spanish commander at Santa Fé learnt of their presence he sent out a detachment of troops to bring them in, tactfully pretending they had lost their way. Pike accepted this explanation of his party's presence in Spanish territory, and the result was a happy

[4] Pike's Peak, 14,147 ft.

one, for the Spanish army not only did not molest the Americans, but after entertaining them in Santa Fé escorted them
back to the frontier.

The news of Mexico's independence in 1821 was slow to
reach New Mexico but was received with jubiliation when
it did arrive. In 1827 the Republic appointed General
Mamuel Armijo as Governor of New Mexico, and he remained
in charge until 1846 except for a period of a few years from
1837 when a half-breed ranchero seized control of the province.
Under the republican regime outside trade was no longer
prohibited, and the era of the Santa Fé Trail began with
American caravans arriving with manufactured goods to
exchange for gold, silver and furs. For two decades caravans
of wagons laden with goods of very description regularly plied
the thousand-mile long trail between western Missouri[5] and
Santa Fé. The first trader to conduct a successful round trip
was William Becknell. In 1821 he returned with sufficient
Mexican silver dollars to make him want to go again; and
others soon followed his example. There were two main problems on the Santa Fé trail. One was to chose the best route,
and the other how best to guard the caravans against Indian
attack. In 1825 an official survey was carried out by three US
commissioners to select a trail for the traders. Starting from
Fort Osage the surveyors moved west, testing fords over
streams, levelling banks of canyons, and throwing up mounds
of earth to mark the way. In the first section the commissioners also made treaties with the Osage and Kansa Indians
whereby in exchange for goods or cash they promised not to
molest the caravans. On arrival at the Mexican border one
member of the commission went forward to Santa Fé to seek
permission to continue the survey across Mexican territory.
When this was granted the survey was continued and completed. The traders approved of the trail the commissioners
selected as far as the Mexican border, but the subsequent
section that followed a route to Bent's Fort and then south

[5] Starting first from Franklin, then Independence, or Fort Osage;
then from Westport where the Kansas river joins the Missouri in
Osage country, not far from the site of present-day Kansas City; or
from Fort Leavenworth—see map 11.

through the mountains by the Raton Pass was not popular; most of them preferred the more direct southern route across the Cimarron Desert, in spite of having to cross a barren region.

Indian attacks had made the journey hazardous from the first. Marauding Indians molested William Becknell's caravan in 1822, and another party was attacked in 1823. The negotiations carried out by the commissioners with the Osage and Kansa in the east stopped attacks in that section to some degree. But Pawnee raids in the border area and Comanche attacks in the New Mexican section continued, and the Indians could not always he held off even when larger wagon-trains were used. In 1829 the yearly caravan was escorted as far as the frontier by a company of foot soldiers under Captain Riley. On arrival at the Mexican border Riley and his men halted to await the traders' return, amid much protest from the latter who could not see why they should not be escorted the whole way instead of being left to traverse the most dangerous section of the route alone. After the train had gone six miles from the frontier they were attacked by a band of Comanche and had to fight it out. They sent off a messenger to Riley asking for assistance, and then, although thoroughly frightened, put up a good resistance, and for the loss of one of their number, drove the Comanche away. On receipt of the call for help Riley agreed to continue to escort them for two days, and after this the caravan got through on its own without mishap; but Riley when back on the border was now himself beset by Indians. Before the caravan returned he had two soldiers killed and several of his few horses stolen. As a result of this, and the caravan of 1831 also being shot up, it was decided to employ cavalry for escort duties, and a measure was passed by Congress which enabled the War Department to recruit mounted men to police the western plains. The first force embodied was a temporary regiment of Mounted Rangers, some of whom accompanied the 1833 caravan and a larger number the train of 1834. Then, in 1833, a regular regiment of cavalry was formed known at the 1st Dragoons to which was assigned the escort duties. With cavalry protection, trading along the Santa Fé Trail proceeded smoothly for several years, but conditions became difficult in 1837 when the people of New Mexico were in rebellion against their government. At this period caravans were sometimes turned back before they had a chance to sell their goods.

Besides the visitors with the caravans a few Americans were living permanently in New Mexico by this time, and among these was the later famous frontiersman Kit Carson. Carson was born in 1809 in Kentucky, but when one year old moved with his parents to Missouri. As a youth he was apprenticed to a saddler, but tiring of this trade he decamped and sought a life of adventure in the West, making his headquarters at Taos,[6] seventy miles north of Santa Fé. From Taos he joined trapping parties in the mountains, or acted as guard and guide to caravans, and by his staunch qualities soon made himself an acceptable partner in any frontier enterprise.

At the time of his arrival in Taos in 1829, licences were not granted to citizens of the United States to trap in Mexican territory, but many surreptitious expeditions were nevertheless carried out, and in August Carson joined such a one led by Ewing Young. To avoid officials discovering what they were about, the party travelled north for fifty miles before swinging south-west towards the rivers where the beaver lived. While moving down the valley of the Salt, a tributary of the Gila, they encountered a band of Navaho. These Indians had attacked and turned back a previous party of Young's, so as on this occasion he was well armed, he decided to adopt an aggressive attitude towards the tribesmen. He ordered his trappers to set up a breastwork of baggage, pack saddles and the like. Then they took up a defensive position among this impedimenta and waited until the Indians attacked before opening fire. By these tactics Young's men managed to kill fifteen of the Indians and drive the rest away, but a few still had the audacity to crawl into camp that night, steal some traps, and cut loose and drive off three horses. The party trapped down the Salt until they reached its junction

[6] There is now a monument to him at Taos, and his house is a museum to his memory.

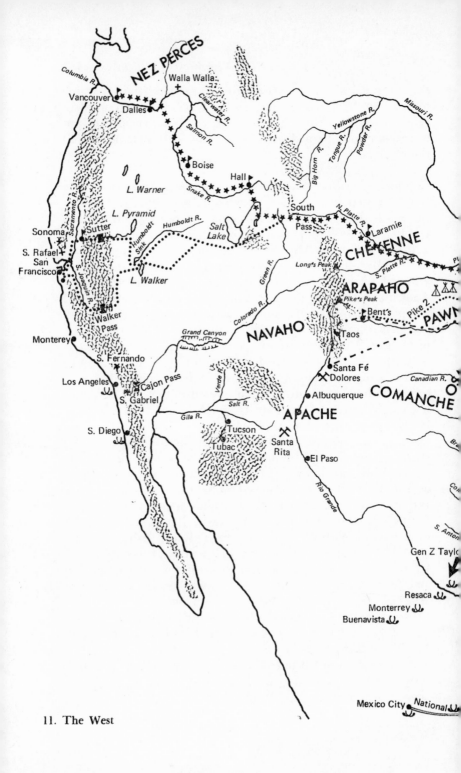

11. The West

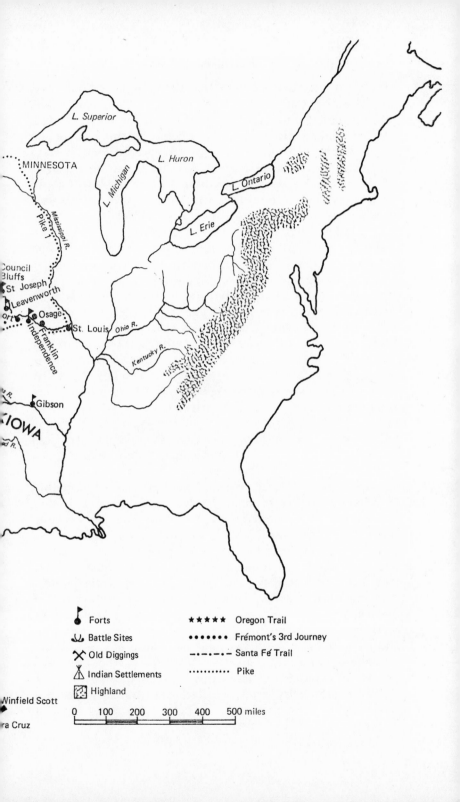

L. Superior

MINNESOTA

L. Michigan

L. Huron

L. Ontario

L. Erie

Mississippi R.

Pike 1

Council Bluffs
St Joseph
Leavenworth
Osage
ort
St. Louis   Ohio R.
Franklin
Independence

Kentucky R.

s R.

Gibson

IOWA

d R.

Winfield Scott

ra Cruz

♪ Forts

♫ Battle Sites

✕ Old Diggings

⛺ Indian Settlements

▨ Highland

★ ★ ★ ★ ★   Oregon Trail

• • • • • • •   Frémont's 3rd Journey

—·—·—·—   Santa Fé Trail

· · · · · · · · · · ·   Pike

0   100   200   300   400   500 miles

with the Verde and then divided. One group under Young, and including Carson, set off west towards California, while the rest returned to Taos to replace the stolen traps. Young's party crossed an area of near-desert before reaching the region of the Grand Canyon of the Colorado where local Indians provided them with welcome provisions. From the Colorado they struck out across the southern part of the Great Basin until they came to the sink of the Mohave River which they followed up to its source in the San Gabriel range east of Los Angeles. They crossed the mountains by the Cajon Pass and after travelling for a few more days reached the mission station at St Gabriel, which at that time housed fifteen soldiers and some thousand Indians. According to Carson it was a veritable paradise on earth, but they were not able to acquire much of its providence as they had nothing left to trade but a few butcher's knives, and these only got them the odd bullock. From San Gabriel they travelled north to the mission-station of San Fernando, and then over the mountains into San Joaquin valley where they were glad to find good pasture-land for the horses. Noting signs of the activities of another trapping outfit in the neighbourhood, they followed its trail and overtook a sixty-strong party under Peter Skene Ogden, belonging to the Hudson's Bay Company. Ogden had been with the British North-West Company, but following its takeover by the Hudson's Bay Company in 1821 was now employed by the latter. He had become, like McLoughlin in the north, a powerful figure in the life of the region.

Together the two parties trapped down the San Joaquin, taking to shooting the game, of which there was plenty, when they found no beaver in the stream. At the junction of the San Joaquin and the Sacramento they separated. Ogden's party took a northern trail for the Columbia River while Young's men remained to spend the summer hunting in the basin of the Sacramento. While there, one of Carson's less pleasing qualities was illustrated. While he was a brilliant horseman and shot, and the staunchest and most loyal of companions, he was also implacably harsh towards Indians, whom he rated the worst enemies of the whites on the frontier. At San Rafael, north of San Francisco Bay, some Indian workers at the mission-station ran away and took refuge in a local Indian village. A party was sent in pursuit, but the villagers refused to hand over the fugitives. As a last resort the Holy Fathers sought help from Young to regain possession of their workers. Carson and eleven of the trappers were given the job of bringing back the escapees, and Carson at any rate entered on the task with enthusiasm. His party rode to the village and charged in without meeting much resistance, and then having put many of the habitations to the torch, demanded the return of the runaways on pain of not leaving alive one of those who harboured them. On this the fugitive workers were handed over and returned to the mission station.

About this time an American schooner sailed into San Francisco harbour, and Young's men were able to trade their catch of furs with the captain, and obtain fresh horses with the money they had received. They were not, however, allowed long to enjoy the use of their new mounts. Perhaps in revenge for their earlier rough treatment, a band of local Indians raided the camp at night and ran off sixty of the animals. As only fourteen of the stolen horses were recovered next morning, Carson was dispatched with a party to try and get back the rest. As so often in the days to come, when he became expert in retrieving stolen horses, Carson was also highly successful on this occasion. He followed the trail of the Indians for a hundred miles into the Sierra Nevada Mountains to the east of the Sacramento basin, and came upon them in camp feasting off the flesh of six of the stolen animals they had killed. He ordered an immediate attack, whereupon the trappers put spurs to their horses and charged into the village, killing eight warriors, taking some children prisoner, and recovering all the stolen animals except those that had been in the process of being eaten.

On 1 September 1829 they set off for the south, and after travelling for a few days reached Los Angeles. Here the authorities demanded their passports, and when they said they had not got any, they had great difficulty in preventing the Mexicans from locking them up. However, in the end the officials could not resist the profit to be gained from selling them liquor, and a drunken rough-house followed, during which one of the trappers shot a fellow American dead. The Mexicans then reasoned that if their visitors were capable of shooting one another they must be dangerous indeed, and it would be better to let them go. The result was that first Carson, with some others of the party, was able to slip away; and then Young rounded up the more drunken ones who remained and followed.

From Los Angeles they returned to San Gabriel, and from there set off across the mountains at the southern end of the Great Basin towards the Colorado, following roughly their outgoing route. When they reached the Colorado, they first trapped south down the river, and then turned and trapped north as far as the mouth of the Gila. Here they encountered a band of Apache escorting a large herd of horses, which they later learned had been stolen from Mexican settlements in the south. Young's party immediately charged, shooting from the saddle, and managed to drive off the Indians and take possession of all the horses. In the night the Indians came back and retook 200 of the animals, but Young's men heard them being driven off, and sprang to arms and recovered them all again. Carson[7] records that they now had more animals than they needed; so they picked as many as they required, killed ten to produce dried meat to take with them, and turned the rest loose, no doubt to fall into the hands of the Indians again. After this successful encounter they continued up the Gila until they reached the Santa Rita copper mines where they cached the furs they had taken on the Colorado and Gila in one of the deep holes dug earlier by the miners. Then they went up to Santa Fé and procured a licence to trade with the Indians, which unlike trapping was permitted. Following the receipt of this, they sent back to the mines to collect their cache which by this subterfuge they were able to sell to advantage in Santa Fé.

For the next ten years Carson went trapping in the Rockies and Sierra Nevada, and explored nearly every important

[7] Carson started as a trapper; but when the fur trade died he became a guide for settlers moving west. Then he took part in Frémont's scientific expeditions; next he became a soldier, then an Indian Agent, and finally a soldier again, reaching the rank of Lientenant-Colonel.

stream and mountain pass from the headwaters of the Platte and Missouri to the West Coast, working in partnership on and off with most of the famous Mountain Men of the period. For example, in 1832/3 he went with a party led by Tom Fitzpatrick[8] along the Bear and Green Rivers, and wintered on the Little Bear, a tributary of the Green. In 1829 he joined Jim Bridger[9] and trapped with him in Blackfoot country, engaging in many conflicts with Indians and always coming out best. When he gave up trapping in 1841 he obtained a job as a hunter at Bent's Fort on the upper Arkansas, and during the following winter provided it with an adundance of flesh. The founder of this trading-post was Charles Bent from St Louis. Bent entered the fur trade in the early 1820s, and in 1826, with his younger brother William and Aaron St Vrain, established the firm of Bent and St Vrain, setting up Bent's Fort on the Arkansas near present-day La Junta and Fort St Vrain on the south fork of the Platte in the Park area north of Pike's Peak. Charles Bent made his home at Taos while his brother and St Vrain conducted the business at the forts. Charles had married Maria Jaramillo in 1835 and later Carson married her sister Josephine, so they became connected by marriage. Bent's Fort had strong adobe walls seventeen feet high and six feet thick at the base, and was comparable with Fort Hall and Fort Boise which were used by the Hudson's Bay Company on the west of the Rocky Mountain Range. All four forts and the American Fur Company's Fort Laramie were important fur-trading centres and rendezvous for both Indians and white men over a wide area.

In 1842 Carson left with Bent and St Vrain's Missouri caravan to St Louis for the purpose of placing his daughter

[8] Fitzpatrick left the mountains in 1841 to guide Bedwell-Bartleson party of immigrants from Missouri to Fort Hall. In 1846 he was appointed Indian Agent for the Cheyenne, Arapaho and part of the Sioux on the upper Platte and Upper Arkansas.

[9] Bridger quit trapping in 1842 to establish the important Oregon Trail supply post at Fort Bridger on the Green River. When driven out by Mormons, he became an official interpreter with Indians and an Army guide.

in a school and visiting relatives and old haunts. When returning by steamboat up the Missouri he met Lieutenant John Frémont with a party setting out to explore the Rockies, and he was interviewed by the explorer on board. Frémont had planned to employ the experienced Captain Dripps as chief scout and guide, but had failed to get him. He asked Carson if he could do the job, to which Carson replied, 'I have been some time in the mountains and believe I could guide you to any point you would wish to go.' On this, Frémont engaged him at the rate of a hundred dollars a month, and a famous and valuable partnership began.

Frémont was a son-in-law of Senator Thomas Hart Benton of Missouri, a leading member of the western expansionist group in Congress. When it was realised that the experienced scientific explorer J. N. Nicollet was too ill to conduct the projected government-sponsored expedition to the West, it was natural that Frémont who had trained under Nicollet was selected to take his place. The first expedition,[10] led by Frémont and guided by Carson, was away from 1 June to 1 October 1842. It was planned to acquaint the government with the nature of the rivers and country between the Missouri and the base of the Rocky Mountains; to examine the character and ascertain the latitude and longitude of South Pass, the great crossing-place of the mountains on the immigrant route to Oregon; and to select the best positions for military posts. But the expansionist senators believed it could do more. They intended in the next session of Congress to bring in a bill for the occupation of Oregon, and they hoped that Frémont's expedition might encourage settlement by advertising the convenience of the Platte-South Pass route for immigrants wishing to go to the North-West.

    Frémont's party started from Westport—on the site of present-day Kansas City—and proceeded first up the Kansas River and then across and up the Platte. When they reached the forks of the Platte the main body which included Carson continued along the North Platte to Fort Laramie, while

[10] Frémont made five expeditions in all: the most famous being the third expedition which led to the conquest of California.

Frémont with four companions followed the South Platte towards Fort St Vrain. On 9 July 1842 Frémont's party caught their first glimpse of the snowy summit of Long's Peak[11]; and next day they halted at St Vrain's Fort[12] where the courtly Aaron St Vrain welcomed them. Already they had disproved an earlier report on the nature of the great plains they had crossed to arrive at the mountains. In 1820 the government had sent Major Stephen H. Long to explore the West. He penetrated as far as the peak named after him, visited the gorge of the Colorado, and returned down the Canadian River through New Mexico and Oklahoma. Writing of the country he traversed, he said, 'I do not hesitate in giving the opinion that it is almost wholly unfit for cultivation, and of course uninhabitable by a people depending on agriculture for their subsistence.' Frémont's view was quite contrary. He described the region as potentially a fertile country. And he was to be proved correct. The area now includes the great farming states of Nebraska, Kansas and Oklahoma.

Later, when Frémont joined the main body at Fort Laramie, he was met with alarming news. Jim Bridger, who had just come down the North Platte trail with a company of traders, brought word that the Sioux, Blackfeet and Cheyenne had combined and were on the warpath, and that the route to South Pass was very perilous. These tribes had recently let a caravan led by Fitzpatrick go through their country, he said, but had served notice that the path was no longer open, and that any new group found upon it would be destroyed. Both traders and friendly Indians advised them to wait until the war parties had completed their raids, and then return home; but Frémont felt he could not honourably do this. His orders for the expedition included South Pass, and a main purpose of the reconnaissance was to determine the best points at which to set up forts for protection against Indians. It would hardly do, therefore, to refuse to face Indians in the field. There was an Oregon caravan not far ahead and if it were in trouble his duty was to follow at once. Moreover, Frémont well knew with what sneers he would be greeted in

[11] 14,255 feet high.
[12] About 40 miles north of present-day Denver.

the East if he returned confessing that an Indian scare had forced him to abbreviate his plans. He was a newcomer in the army, and very decidedly on his mettle. If he flinched, his fellow officers would never cease reminding him that he had allowed a trail—a settlers' trail at that—to be closed in his face. He therefore ordered his men to continue their march. Only one refused to do so, and, as it turned out, the party sighted few Indians, and none who contested their passage.

On 8 August they reached South Pass where there was no gorge, as found in the Allegheny gaps, but a wide sandy belt studded with sagebrush rising to 7,000 feet by such a slow and regular grade that they had great difficulty in determining the precise point of the Continental Divide. The party, which had now travelled 950 miles, continued to the headwaters of the Green River and then turned and explored the Wind River range, a magnificent group of snow-capped mountains. On the clear morning of 15 August Frémont set out to climb what he believed to be the highest peak,[13] and the one which was later named after him. On reaching the top without much difficulty he was much impressed by the view. To the west was the vast shining network of the lakes and streams which feed the Green and Colorado Rivers; to the east lay the forested valley of the Wind River and the streams flowing north to join the Yellowstone and Missouri; while far to the north were the snowy peaks of the Three Tetons marking the source of the westward-flowing Snake.

On the return journey an attempt was made to use an improvised boat made of buffalo skins on the Platte. This nearly caused a disaster, for it sank and dispersed their possessions in the river. Fortunately only a few instruments and records were not recovered. The topographer Preuss had sufficient material to produce a splendid map of their travels, and Frémont found enough of his records intact to make a detailed report of the rocks, animals, vegetation and the general geographic conditions in the territory they had passed through. Indeed, the government were so pleased with the report of the expedition which Frémont produced with the

[13] In fact Gannett Peak, five miles north, is a little higher.

help of his wife that it was soon decided to send him exploring again.

This time Frémont was instructed to go westward into Oregon and link up his reconnaissance of 1842 with the earlier surveys which Lieutenant Charles Wilkes had made along the west coast in 1838, and if possible to penetrate into California. Never before had an American scientific expedition been better fitted out. There were a dozen carts each drawn by two mules, and a light covered-wagon for the scientific instruments. Packed with the tents were large supplies of gifts for the Indians; and a rubber boat and a twelve-pounder howitzer were also taken. The three principals were Thomas Fitzpatrick who was chief guide, Louis Zendel the Prussian veteran who had been with Nicollet and was in charge of explosives, and Charles Preuss who was the topographer; the thirty odd rank and file were mostly French Canadians and Creoles.

After leaving Westport the expedition[14] kept at first to the Oregon Trail, where were encountered several caravans of emigrants and travellers, including the party of the missionary Dr Marcus Whitman. Soon, however, Frémont struck off south and blazed a trail up the Arkansas with the intention of trying to find a new pass through the mountains. On 4 July 1843 they arrived at St Vrain's Fort, and joined the fur trader in suitable celebrations. On 9 July, when on their way again, they had a momentary glimpse of Pike's Peak through the clouds, and soon afterwards met by chance Kit Carson on his way back to St Vrain's Fort. Deeming it too good an opportunity to miss, Frémont immediately re-engaged the famous frontiersman, which meant he now had two principal guides. Carson's first task was to ride off to the south to obtain some fresh mules from Charles Bent at Bent's Fort. After the replacements had arrived, Frémont sent Fitzpatrick with the heavy baggage and the majority of the men to South Pass. He himself, with Carson, Preuss, and a smaller group set off westward to try and find a way through the barrier of the Rockies which faced them. They failed to do so on this occasion, so turned north and followed behind Fitzpatrick

[14] This Second Expedition lasted from May 1843 to July 1844.

through South Pass and across the Green basin. While in the valley of the Bear they overtook and were warmly greeted by a single emigrant family travelling courageously alone with four span of oxen. They moved on leaving the emigrants in the rear, but next morning, on breaking camp, came upon a larger party resting by the roadside, and farther down the road yet a third. The Oregon was becoming as busy a highway as the Cumberland Road had been a generation earlier. They were now approaching the Great Salt Lake, but were separated from it by the Wasatch Range. Frémont decided to go round, and to do this followed the valley he was in northward and then turned and followed another valley southward. While in the second valley they came upon a band of Shoshoni Indians from whom they bought fresh horses, vegetables and berries, but it is recorded that in spite of this welcome addition to their food supply they were still sufficiently hard pressed to enjoy a stewed skunk for supper. Frémont described in his journal the natural curiosities they came across as they moved on towards the lake. He was much impressed by the red and white hills, the hot springs, an extinct volcano, and above all the lake itself. Looking down on it from a high butte, he recorded that to travellers so long shut up among the mountain ranges, 'a sudden view over the expanse of silent waters had in it something sublime'. Before leaving, one of his conclusions was that the region was suitable for a settlement or military post.

Fremont did not catch up Fitzpatrick's party until the latter had begun the long descent towards the Columbia River and reached the Hudson's Bay Company's Fort Hall on the Snake. At this post the whole expedition had a thorough refit and they were able to buy some more horses and some even more needed bullocks. Already the weather warned them that winter was approaching. On 19 September 1843 it snowed all day, and Frémont called his men together and gave leave for those unwilling to face the rigours of winter exploration to go home, whereupon eleven decided to return. On 25 September the rest resumed their journey down the Snake, Frémont having made up his mind before leaving that there ought to be a strong American military post at or near Fort

Hall. It was deplorable, he wrote later, that emigrants, exhausted after a journey of 1,320 miles from Missouri, should have no assistance save the aid furnished by a none-too-friendly British fur post.

At the end of the first week in October the expedition reached Fort Boise, another Hudson's Bay Company post near where the Boise River flows through high basalt precipices to join the Snake; and a few weeks later reached Dr Whitman's mission station at Waiilatpu near Fort Walla Walla. Frémont now felt he was approaching civilisation again, and in his report wrote, 'I found Dr Whitman[15] absent on a visit to the Dalles of the Columbia; but had the pleasure of seeing a fine-looking family of emigrants . . . and a small town of Nez Perce Indians gave an inhabited and even populous appearance in the station.' From Whitman's mission to the Dalles took them until 5 November. At Dalles the bulk of the party was left to refit for the return journey and obtain more horses, and cattle for meat on the hoof, while Frémont with a few companions went downriver to Fort Vancouver to get a fresh supply of flour, peas and tallow. At Fort Vancouver Dr John McLoughlin provided not only the stores, but also a rough sketch-map of the Great Basin. (He was always helpful to Americans and eventually became an American citizen.)

Frémont realised that if he were to carry out the wishes of the western expansionists back home and visit California, the most significant part of his second expedition still lay before him. What he had done so far was simply to complete a scientific journey of a much travelled trail, but he would now have to travel through a region largely unknown and at the same time execute a peaceful invasion of a foreign country. He did not hesitate, however, and on 25 November the perilous journey began and the long cavalcade of horses, mules and cattle, with twenty-five men and some Indian guides hired to go part of the way, set off south into the unknown.

[15] Whitman, his wife and twelve white men were massacred by Cayuse Indians four years later on 29 November 1847. The other women and the children of the mission were taken captive but were ransomed by Peter Ogden, the Hudson's Bay Company factor.

They pushed steadily on across the eastern slopes of the Cascades, their commander meantime making his usual assiduous notes on topography, botany, zoology, geology and soil fertility. The scenery was magnificent but the nights were cold and the marches exhausting, and they were soon to enter a country where the Klamath Indians were reputedly dangerous. A few days before Christmas 1843 they camped on the shores of Warner Lake, but the only Indians they encountered were some who came into camp to trade in a friendly fashion. They celebrated Christmas by firing a few rounds from the howitzer, and then pressed on into northwest Nevada. By this time they had fifteen pack-animals dead, abandoned or stolen by Indians; water and grass was scarce; and they had killed the last of their cattle. Then on 10 January 1844 they arrived at a large lake which was full of salmon trout, and their worries concerning food were temporarily ended. Frémont named the water the Pyramid Lake after a tall narrow rock rising from its midst. He called the fresh stream flowing down into it from the Sierra Nevada the Salmon Trout River, though it is now known as the Truckee. Moving south the expedition next camped near the site of present-day Reno, and on 19 January 1844 Frémont called his men together and put to them the perilous proposition of scaling the Sierra Nevada in winter. When he had received their consent to follow him, the expedition started forward again, proceeding up the Salmon Trout or Truckee River towards the mighty range of precipitous snow-capped peaks which barred their way.

On 24 January they met an old Indian of the Washoe tribe who consented to act as guide, but he gave up after going a few miles and handed over to a young tribesman. Next, the substitute, having led them into the heart of what seemed a likely valley, advised them against continuing, and decamped. In spite of these setbacks Frémont was determined to continue, and to encourage his men got Carson—who had been there before—to dilate on the delights of the sunny fertile Sacramento Valley which lay beyond the mountains.

On 2 February 1844 the ascent began, with ten men on the strongest horses leading the column as pathfinders. On 3

February they went forward seven miles, but next day were brought to a halt by deep snow. Most of the animals had been pushed thus far by leaving their packs behind, and the trail was strewn with stores, but in spite of lacking much of their equipment the party had no choice but to spend the night on the mountains seeking what shelter they could, and building great fires to keep themselves warm. Next day, Frémont set the majority to work making sleds to bring up the scattered baggage from the rear, while he and a few others tried to find a way over the heights. On discovering a weaving circuitous path which offered possibilities, he sent forward a patrol wearing snow-shoes to trample down the snow so that after freezing at night the path might bear the weight of the pack-animals when led up on the following day. In this way, after much effort, the party reached the crest of the range. And from there a most welcome sight met their eyes. Below them, wooded slopes descended steeply; in the distance was the Sacramento valley, its greens and browns untouched by snow; and a hundred or so miles away was the long line of the Coast Range. It proved difficult to fetch the rest of the animals, and then carry the whole outfit over the summit, for the beaten trail had become filled with snow again; but after thirty or so of the horses and mules had been brought over, the little, ragged and tattered column abandoned the rest and began to wind its way down the long trail towards the Sacramento valley. On reaching the lowland they first encountered a small band of Indians, and were greeted in a friendly fashion. Next, they came upon a populous Indian village whose inhabitants wore clean cotton shirts and other civilised apparel. They were employed on the ranch of Captain Sutter, they told the travellers, and their master's station was only a few miles ahead.[16]

Johann August Sutter was of German descent, but had been brought up in Switzerland and called himself Swiss. He arrived in New York almost penniless in the summer of 1834; in 1835 he accompanied a trading party from Missouri to Santa Fé; he repeated the trip in 1836. In the spring of 1838 he set out with a missionary party bound for Oregon

[16] On the south bank of the American River, a tributary of the Sacramento; a few miles east of present-day Sacramento.

with the intention of going on to California. On arriving at Fort Vancouver in October, he was told that snow in the mountains and hostile Indians made it impossible to reach California by land, and was urged to work for the Hudson's Bay Company instead. Undaunted, he took ship to Honolulu and waited for a vessel to take him to San Francisco. During his stay in the islands he evolved a scheme to bring Kanaka labourers from Hawaii to work on the settlement he intended to establish in California. Once landed there, he saw the Governor and sought official permission to establish a post and bring in Kanakas to till his land and herd his stock. He said he would establish such a powerful state that it would protect northern California from Indian attack. Duly impressed, the Mexican authorities granted him substantial territories on the American River, and within a year or so he had 500 head of cattle, 75 horses, and had engaged in his employ a motley crew of workers, composed of sailors, Kanakas, Mexican cowboys and friendly Indians. Early on he constructed a ranch house along with storehouses and workshops, and he surrounded the whole with a strong stockade in the corners of which he emplaced cannon. In 1841 Sutter was joined by some overland American immigrants whom he was glad to employ as overseers. Later on other Americans straggled in, and those who did not take up land under his grant, or hire themselves to him, used his fort as a rendezvous. By the time Frémont arrived, the Sacramento and American valleys had thus become the seat of an extensive American settlement.

Having learned something about the situation in Northern California—where some American settlers, it seemed, were already plotting to detach the province from Mexican rule—Frémont set about refitting his outfit for the journey home. Breaking camp on 8 March 1844 he made off south in good style, having acquired the requisite replacements of horses, cattle and milch cows from the friendly Sutter in exchange for payment drafts on the US Topographic bureau. Frémont's party passed up the San Joaquin valley, crossed the southern mountains by the Tekachapi Pass, and then turned east and followed the Old Spanish Trail across the semi-desert of southern Nevada. On arrival in Utah, Frémont might easily have returned by the much travelled Oregon Trail. Instead, tireless explorer that he was, he penetrated the Wasatch and Uinta Mountains east of the Great Salt Lake, crossed the basin of the Green River well south of the Oregon Trail, and discovered the pass[17] through the Rockies which had evaded him on the outward journey. He next turned south through the Park Region in the vicinity of Pike's Peak and reached Pueblo on the upper Arkansas. On 1 July he arrived at Bent's Fort, where George Bent received him with his usual warm hospitality. The long journey eastward across the plains was relatively uneventful, and on 31 July he reached the banks of the Missouri from where he had begun his journey fourteen months before.

Frémont's second report was nearly three times the length of his first, and even more impressive. With as much scientific exactness and with the same clear data upon topography, climates, soils, vegetation and wild animals, it yet contained an even greater wealth of general information. Understandably it was received with great satisfaction. President Tyler awarded the explorer a brevet as captain 'for gallant and highly meritorious services', the newspapers seized on his exploits and made him the hero of the hour, and when Polk replaced Tyler, Benton took his son-in-law to the White House so that he might discuss the potentialities of Oregon and California directly with the new President. The result was that Frémont was chosen to lead a third expedition to the West, the one which was to become his most famous.

At the first session of Congress after Polk's election it had been resolved to annex Texas; and Polk's diary reveals that the Cabinet fondly hoped that the territory might be taken over peaceably and even the cession of New Mexico and California might be acquired by treaty and purchase. Nevertheless, as Frémont set about preparing his third expedition it became apparent that these territories were unlikely to be gained without war, and his instructions recognised the realities of the situation. His immediate superior, the Secretary of War, ordered him to carry out another scientific expedition, but the Secretary of the Navy, backed by Senator

[17] The Muddy Pass.

Benton as chairman of the Senate Military Committee, told him to include also military objects, and make another visit to California to spy out the land preparatory for the likely war.

Frémont's party on the third expedition in 1846 was larger than on the previous ones and was more mobile, since it dispensed with carts and relied solely on pack animals for transport. Its sixty-two members included Kit Carson again, Joseph Walker who had travelled to the West Coast in 1832 when with Captain Bonneville, and Edward M. Kern who was skilled in sketching from nature.

Frémont set off for Bent's Fort on the upper Arkansas River and then turned north and went through South Pass and across the basin of the Green River to the Great Salt Lake. Next he followed the Hastings Cut-off[18] for some 200 miles, after which he split his party in two. Kern, with Walker as guide, followed the Humboldt River to its sink and from there went on to the lake which had been visited by Walker on his previous journey and was now named after him. Meanwhile, Frémont and Carson with ten picked men and some Delaware Indians set out across the barren bed of the Great Basin with the object of joining the other party at Lake Walker after having made a wide sweep to the south. The two parties having joined up successfully at the lake separated again. The main body with the impedimenta led by Kern and Walker, followed a southern route. After travelling along the foothills of the Sierra Nevada, they crossed by the same pass Walker had previously used in the opposite direction and then moved north up the San Joaquin valley to the appointed rendezvous near Lake Tulare. Frémont's party took a northern trail to Pyramid Lake, crossed the mountains by a pass north of the defile they had found under the terrible conditions of the winter before, and then moved down towards Lake Tulare. This second separation and meeting up again did not go as smoothly as the earlier one had done. Kern and Walker's people went to the wrong place, and Frémont had to send Carson out searching for

[18] A route blazed by Lansford Hastings in 1842 from Fort Bridger southwest to the Salt Lake and thence down the Humboldt.

them. However, the two groups eventually reunited on the ranch of an American settler between San Francisco and Monterey.

Although California was in something of a turmoil when Frémont's party arrived, with the Military Commandant, General Castro, at odds with the Governor Pio Pico, which accentuated the traditional antagonisms between north and south, the appearance of the American scientific expedition did something to settle their differences. At least both leaders agreed that the intruders must go, and they sent messages to the Americans' camp, saying they must leave California instantly 'under penalty of arrest and forcible expulsion'. This placed Frémont in something of a quandary, for his orders had suggested he should hang about in California in case war broke out between the United States and Mexico, in which case he should assist the American settlers in their revolt. Being undecided quite what to do, he took his party to a strong defensive position on a flat-topped wooded hill overlooking the valley of the River Salinas to see how the Mexicans would react. Frémont and his men stayed in their position on the hill for three days, on the second of which they were approached by a body of Mexican cavalry who did not venture to attack. While on the hill they got in touch with Thomas O. Larkin, the American consul in Monterey. Larkin was insistent that hostilities ought to be avoided as the American settlers were nervous regarding the consequences. Frémont then came to see that he had been unwise in not immediately accepting his expulsion order. He realised when Larkin pointed it out that he might very well start a war that Washington did not want; and that if President Polk was still hoping to acquire California peaceably any belligerent action might make this more difficult. On 9 March, therefore, he broke camp and started off north. He reached Sutter's Fort on 24 March, but did not stay. Having travelled rapidly up the Sacramento valley, he crossed the border between California and Oregon, leaving behind him the Mexican officials breathing threats and boasts, the American settlers buzzing with excitement, and Consul Larkin writing feverish letters to Washington asking that a warship be sent

up from the naval squadron off Mazatlán on the west coast
of Mexico to protect American interests in the area.

The close of March saw Frémont on the upper Sacramento
200 miles north of Sutter's Fort at the farm of a Danish
settler, hesitating whether to continue towards Oregon or to
wait nearer at hand to help should war break out and the
settlers rise in revolt. On 8 May 1846 after he had travelled
a short way further north and reached the Klamath Lake
from where if required he could easily take the trail to the
Columbia River, the matter was decided for him when a
farmer rode into his camp with news that Lieutenant Gillespie
of the US Marines had arrived in California from Washington
bringing instructions for him.

Gillespie had been dispatched by President Polk to give
both written and memorised orders to the American Consul,
the officer commanding the Pacific Squadron, and the head
of the scientific expedition exploring California and Oregon.
In the role of a whisky salesman he had travelled unscathed
from Vera Cruz on the east coast to Mexico City, although
there was a revolution in progress at the time. Proceeding to
Mazatlán on the west coast, he took ship to Honolulu and
reached Monterey by ship again on 17 April 1846. The
written dispatches Gillespie brought contained nothing to
suggest that force should be employed. As to the memorised
orders, their content has never been divulged, but Frémont's
instructions at least appear to have reinforced those given
him by the Secretary of the Navy, namely that in the case of
war he should give every assistance to the settlers in their
struggle for independence. Although the first battles of the
Mexican War were already being fought, Gillespie, who had
left months before, could only tell them that in his view
hostilities on the Rio Grande might start at any moment. But
this was enough for Frémont. He immediately gave orders
for a return to California.

On re-entering the Mexican province in May 1846 Frémont
was welcomed by the American settlers, who were now in a
nervous state because the authorities were threatening to
loose Indians on them to drive them out. Thus, one of the
first operations Frémont carried out was a raid on Indian

villages north of Sutter's Fort to forestall such an attack. Soon after this there was a skirmish near Sutter's Fort when a dozen American settlers led by Ezekiel Merritt seized some horses being conducted south from the area of San Francisco Bay. Next there followed an attack on the Mexican post of Sonoma, fifteen miles north of San Francisco. At break of day some thirty odd settlers again under Merritt rode in and routed the garrison, taking possession of 9 cannon and 250 muskets and dispatching the 12 prisoners taken to Sutter's Fort which Frémont had forcibly taken over from its unwilling owner. With Sutter's Fort and Sonoma as firm bases in the north, the settlers felt strong enough to declare their independence. On 14 June the Republic of California was officially established. There was also produced the famous Bear Flag of white fabric on which was written 'California Republic' beside a large star and the figure of a grizzly.

The reaction of the Mexicans to the declaration of independence by the settlers was to dispatch a force under Colonel Tome from the south to recapture Sonoma. When the Mexicans approached the post the American garrison, having sent off a messenger to ask Frémont for help, marched boldly out to confront their attackers, and in the brisk encounter that followed quickly put the Mexicans to flight. Frémont arrived after the Mexicans had fled and went in pursuit, but by an adroit move Tome got clear away. He put into the hands of an Indian a false message announcing an immediate attack on Sonoma by General Castro; when the Indian was captured and the message read, Frémont and the settlers returned to protect the threatened post, while Tome got hold of some boats and rowed across San Francisco Bay to safety. Although it was too late to catch up with Tome when the subterfuge was realised, Frémont crossed the Bay and spiked the guns of the fort guarding the entrance. Then, amid all his pressing problems, he found time to bestow the now immortal name of the Golden Gate upon the entrance to San Francisco Bay.

By this time only the strongly held Monterey remained in Mexican hands in northern California, and Frémont immediately set about raising a strong force to try and seize the place.

The result was the Californian Volunteer Battalion which consisted of four companies totalling 234 men, composed of voyageurs, trappers, scouts, sailors, farmers and ranchers, many having affinities with earlier frontier fighters like Daniel Boone and Davy Crockett. Frémont was just making plans to get his men trained for the attack when the welcome news at last reached them that the United States had declared war on Mexico. They also learned that American warships were approaching California waters, and it was the sailors from these ships who were subsequently allotted the task of seizing Monterey. Frémont and the Californian Volunteers were now shipped down south from Monterey to complete the conquest of California. Within days of the fall of Monterey the American flag was flying over Yerba Buena, New Helvetia (Sutter's kingdom), and had replaced the short-lived Bear Flag at Sonoma.

Meanwhile, at the time when northern California was being taken over by its American settlers, an American army under General Zachary Taylor[19] was crossing the Rio Grande and invading Mexico proper, and a force under Colonel Kearny was assembling at Fort Leavenworth with the object of moving against New Mexico. Kearny's force consisted of the 1st Dragoons, a battery of artillery and two companies of infantry. It followed the Santa Fé Trail, and its initial objective was Bent's Fort on the Upper Arkansas. The first units arrived there on 22 July 1846 after taking some twenty-four days to cover 565 miles—twenty-four days of rain, mosquitoes and short rations. At the post they found the caravan of the year waiting to be escorted to Santa Fé, but in New Mexico, with insufficient soldiers and a lack of arms and money, there was indecision as to what to do. The people really had little reason to be loyal to their homeland; for years now their economic ties had been with the United States via the Santa Fé Trail, while Mexico seemed only to provide them with corrupt governors and oppressive taxes. Yet they were

[19] On reaching Monterrey and Buenavista in northern Mexico, Taylor's expedition came to a halt, but the war was won after an army under General Winfield Scott landed at Vera Cruz, and then marched on and took Mexico City by storm.

Mexicans and in time of crisis latent patriotic sentiments began to stir.

The governor was the notorious General Manuel Armijo who had captured the Texas caravan earlier and sent its members in chains to Mexico City. At heart he seems to have been as hesitant as his people; but he made a show initially of encouraging resistance. General Kearny, understanding the position, acted accordingly. From Bent's Fort he sent three captured Mexican spies south to Santa Fé with word that those in the city who did not resist would be protected; and he issued a proclamation promising civil and religious freedom for all who laid down their arms. The proclamation along with a letter to Armijo inviting him to give in was taken to Santa Fé by Captain St George Cooke accompanied by James W. Magoffin, a trader who bore secret instructions from President Polk to talk Armijo into surrender. Accompanied by twelve dragoons, the emissaries reached New Mexico's capital under a flag of truce on 12 August 1846, and immediately went into conference with the governor in his palace. Cooke later described their meeting as follows: 'I entered from the hall a large and lofty apartment with a carpeted earth floor and discovered the governor seated at a table with six or eight military and civil officials standing. There was no mistaking the governor; he was a large fine-looking man.' What the outcome of the conference was has never been discovered; but subsequent events suggest that Magoffin managed to persuade Armijo not to resist. At any rate, Armijo led his army out of Santa Fé and took up a position at Apache Canyon where it would have been possible to ambush Kearny's column. Then, before Kearny's men reached the place, he ordered his whole force to disperse, and they and their leader made off in flight to the south. The formal surrender of New Mexico took place on the Santa Fé plaza on 19 August 1846. Here Kearny addressed the people and promised them protection for their lives, property and religion. Three days afterwards he issued a proclamation declaring he would provide them with a democratic government without delay. Next, he had printed the famous Kearny Code consisting of the laws by which the people of New Mexico would be

174 The Conquest of the American West

governed, and finally, on 22 September 1846, Charles Bent of the trading firm Bent and St Vrain was named as governor of the new territory.

Although the takeover by the Americans had proceeded so smoothly, in the following autumn and winter racial tensions developed. By 1 December 1846 a number of disgruntled New Mexicans in alliance with the local Pueblo Indians started to plot a revolt. The uprising began on the night of 19 January 1847 at Taos during a visit by Governor Bent and his staff. Moving silently across the snow-covered plaza the rebels first killed the local sheriff and one of his assistants, and then entered Bent's house[20] and scalped him. The rebels paraded Bent's body through the streets, after which they fell on any American they could find, killing ruthlessly. The task of restoring order was given to Colonel Sterling Price. With five companies of troops he started for Taos, and after scattering large groups of rebels en route reached the town at the beginning of February 1847. When he entered Taos he found that some seven hundred of the rebels had taken refuge in the Indian village to the north. After cannonading failed to breach its stout adobe walls, the American soldiers advanced and smashed their way in with axes. By nightfall they had killed 150 of the enemy, mostly Indians, and the rebellion was over. New Mexico enjoyed a troubled peace while the conquest of its mother country was still going on; and in 1848 it became officially a part of the United States under the Treaty of Guadalupe. During the Civil War Texas volunteers invaded the country in an attempt to compel it to join the Confederation. They occupied Albuquerque and Santa Fé, but were soon driven out by elements of the Union army, and after the summer of 1862 fighting in New Mexico ended. The coming of the Santa Fé railroad paved the way for economic expansion and when modern machinery was brought in to work the Dolores mines something of a boom occurred. The territory became a State within the Union in 1912.

After the bloodless occupation of New Mexico, General

[20] Bent's House is now on show in Taos as is the Pueblo two miles north of the town with Indians in occupation; Kit Carson's house is now a museum.

Kearny set off at the head of 300 dragoons to assist Frémont and the settlers in their conquest of California. He started westward on 25 September 1846 and had scarcely taken the trail when he received news that a Mormon battalion had arrived in Santa Fé to assist him. Mindful of his self-imposed role of liberator of California he continued on his way and sent back Captain Cooke to lead the Mormons there by a different route. Neither of the liberating parties had an easy passage. Cooke's men attempted to blaze a trail over the deserts of southern Arizona and suffered pitifully from thirst and short rations before they straggled in exhausted to San Diego on 29 January 1847. Kearny's troopers also met with difficulties. While still in the valley of the Rio Grande they encountered Kit Carson and a few companions riding east with dispatches announcing the surrender of California to the American settlers. Kearny sent his wagons back to Santa Fé along with 200 of his troopers. With his supplies packed on mule-back and two twelve pounder guns, a highly reluctant Kit Carson as guide, and 100 troopers, mostly mounted on mules, he then headed due west from the Rio Grande across the southern end of the chain of the Rockies in a dash for the coast. Meanwhile, the dispatches were handed over to one of the others of Kit Carson's band.

Guided by Carson, the dragoons passed the Santa Rita copper mines, and coming to the headwaters of the Gila, followed the river westward to its confluence with the Colorado. The dragoons hit the river at a point high above sea-level where it flowed swift and clear through good grazing land for their mounts. Though it was deep in Apache country, a well-armed force had nothing to fear. Indeed, those Apache encountered proved friendly and willing to trade. On leaving the mountains it was learned that the Mexicans had retaken Los Angeles, so Kearny pushed on by forced marches. Short of San Diego they encountered a body of Mexican lancers, and Kearny immediately ordered his men to charge and disperse them. This proved disastrous, for the Mexicans having first given ground, turned and charged back, killing nineteen of the dragoons and wounding as many others. Kearny and the remainder finally extricated themselves with difficulty,

assisted by sailors sent up by Commodore Stockton in charge
of the US naval squadron off the coast, who had by this time
put his force at the disposal of the American rebels.

After the successful Bear Flag revolt and the seizure with
the help of the US navy of first Monterey and then Los
Angeles and San Diego, California was divided into three
sections with Frémont in charge of the north, Polk's messenger
Gillespie of the south and Stockton of the central districts.
Frémont was relatively strong, having the support of a large
body of settlers and two good bases at Sonoma and Sutter's
Fort. Stockton was strong too with his naval forces at his back.
But Gillespie had a pitifully small force to hold Los Angeles
and San Diego, and the southern region was the most turbulent. The result was inevitable. The Mexicans, realising the
numerical weakness of Gillespie's force, attacked and regained
Los Angeles. With the arrival of Kearny's troopers and the
Mormon battalion efforts were made to regain the city. The
first attempts were unsuccessful, but on 10 January 1847 a
composite force which included a sizeable detachment from
the naval squadron fought its way in and took the town.

The transition from military to civil rule was delayed
while Frémont and Kearny squabbled over who should govern
the province; but orders from Washington eventually settled
the dispute in the favour of Kearny. His subsequent able
administration and that of his successor Colonel Mason soon
convinced the Californians that the change of masters was to
their advantage. California became a State within the Union
in 1850, and Sacramento near Sutter's Fort was designated its
capital in 1854. Meanwhile, the region between California
and New Mexico was also in the process of being assimilated.
This area, which came to be called Arizona, had for many
years suffered from such severe raids by Apaches that American occupation had been prevented. Periodic uprisings
including the disorders at the time of the Mexican Revolution
of 1821 had forced the abandonment of many of the earlier
Spanish settlements and mission-stations until almost the
only ones to remain were Tucson and Tubac in the south.
However, during the second quarter of the nineteenth century

American hunters, trappers and miners drifted in. The Treaty of Guadalupe Hidalgo of 1848, which annexed New Mexico, ceded part of Arizona to the United States and the southern mining areas were purchased through the efforts of James Gadsden,[21] when minister to Mexico in 1853. Arizona was admitted to the Union as the 48th State in 1912.

[21] The Gadsden Purchase included additional territory in New Mexico. It gave America a 45,000 square mile strip of desert land below the Gila River for $10 million, which was needed for a southern continental railway.

Chapter 8

With the Miners to the West

Having already played a part in the early history of California, Johann August Sutter was also involved in the discovery of gold there. Encouraged by the arrival of more Americans in the province after the war, and by the availability of skilled workmen, some of them discharged members of the Mormon battalion, Sutter decided to add milling to his activities, and set about erecting a sawmill on the south fork of the American River, forty-five miles above his fort. In the search for the best spot for the mill Sutter enlisted James Wilson Marshall, a moody, eccentric carpenter with a knowledge of things mechanical, and Marshall chose Coloma where the river narrows and impounds the waters before opening into a beautiful valley. Sutter inspected the site, approved it, and on 27 August 1847 entered into a partnership with Marshall to build and operate the mill, whereupon, Marshall set out with a crew consisting of the Wemmer family—Mrs Wemmer to act as cook—some Indians and a number of Mormons, and started work.

Where the river swung wide around a bar, Marshall constructed a log and brush dam, and through its base dug a channel for a race. Before the machinery was installed, a test showed that the lower end of the race needed deepening to provide a more rapid run-off. Accordingly the channel was blasted and dug out by day, and by night the water was directed to scour it through. On 24 January when Marshall was inspecting the end of the race he chanced to see something glittering on the bedrock of the channel downstream, and on going to investigate noticed several shiny flakes about the size of a grain of wheat. Collecting them up and putting them in the crown of his hat, he rushed excitedly back to the mill, crying out that he had discovered a goldmine. Some of the others then went down and searched the tailrace, and their joint efforts increased the find to a pile of nearly three ounces. Unable to contain his excitement, Marshall rode to Sutter's Fort with the accumulation of gold dust and demanded an interview with Sutter behind locked doors. The two of them then put the flakes to every test their ingenuity and the American Encyclopedia could suggest and were soon convinced it was true gold. Sutter, foreseeing disaster from the discovery for his current enterprises, tried to swear Marshall and his men to secrecy. He did persuade them to stay for a few weeks to finish the mill, but secrecy was out of the question, and the news leaked out.

Mid-March 1848 saw the completion of the sawmill. The first log was sawn on 11 March; and on 22 March Sutter's Fort got a delivery of planks from Coloma. Their task completed, the Mormon workers at the sawmill began to leave. By the end of April not one remained, and Marshall was attempting to saw with a crew consisting of a teamster, a blacksmith and a few Indians. Once dismissed the Mormons set off to search the neighbouring mountain streams for gold. Many workers at Sutter's Fort also quit, even though it meant forfeiting back pay, and headed for the headwaters of the American River; so that with this exodus of the Mormon sawmill workers and the employees of Sutter at the fort, the gold rush may be said to have begun. For California it meant an influx of population and the start of an era of development and expansion; but for Sutter it brought about a poignant reversal of fortune. Just as the sawmill was ready to begin cutting, just as the mechanical difficulties in its construction had been overcome, just as the months of toil and investment seemed about to bear fruit, Sutter and Marshall had to shut down. There was a market for lumber certainly, but no wages could keep men lumbering where gold lay about. Sutter thus fell a victim to the overpowering force he had unloosed. Marshall too received no reward for his discovery. After some unsuccessful prospecting, he was unable to find a worthwhile job and died penniless.

The news of the discovery of gold on the American River did not at first arouse much interest. The press of California was cautious because earlier finds had proved transitory, and only a few people ventured to go and investigate for themselves. However, after the former Mormon leader Sam Brannan[1] paid a visit to his co-religionists in the mountains, the scene was quickly transformed.

Brannan had come out at the head of two hundred Latter-Day Saints by sea round the Cape Horn, and claimed ecclesiastical jurisdiction over the Mormons of the disbanded battalion, including those who had been working for Sutter. He was not only an important figure in the Church in the West, but also one of California's leading businessmen, with interests in an hotel, a newspaper, and stores in San Francisco and at Sutter's Fort. He probably set out from San Francisco only with the idea of establishing a store at Coloma; but he came back wildly enthusiastic about the gold-producing potentialities of the district, and by his actions on his return gave the place the utmost publicity. On 12 May 1848 he went out into the streets clutching a quinine bottle filled with gold dust from the diggings. Waving his hat, and holding high the glistening bottle, he cried out: 'Gold, gold, gold from the American River!'

Brannan's antics had an electrifying effect. The town of San Francisco that had shrugged off the earlier intelligence, suddenly went wild. All who could leave were soon on the move. By sloop, lighter and many a lesser craft the San Franciscans set sail across the Bay. On horseback and on foot they made their way towards the mines. By 11 June, the consul Larkin reported the town half emptied. The wave of excitement rolled out to Monterey, and even to Los Angeles. The spread was not instantaneous, and the force of the wave was somewhat diminished by distance, but by the end of the summer the whole province was contributing to the flow of manpower to the diggings. There were some who resisted

[1] See page 114.

the lure of the gold, the most significant being a contingent of Mormons which included early participants in the finds near Coloma. They had planned to depart for headquarters at Salt Lake as soon as the passes over the Sierra Nevada were open, and forty-six started off on 3 July 1848 on the hard climb over the mountains, followed by the difficult trek across the desert of the Great Inland Basin. Their departure illustrates a strength of religion and of the authority of Brigham Young that is almost incredible.[2]

Out from San Francisco on 31 May 1848 the schooner *Louisa* carried news of California's gold to Honolulu, and a stream of Hawaiian argonauts were set on their way. From Hawaii, Hudson's Bay Company men relayed the news to Oregon, and settlers in the Williamette valley, including Peter H. Barnett, California's first elected governor, set out— some by ship, more by covered wagon overland. Mexico got the news, and her north-western provinces sent a substantial flow of prospectors, Sonora contributing some skilled miners who gave the name of their territory to a town near the Stanislaus River. Late in the year gold seekers arrived from Chile, another land rich in mining experience, from Australia, then suspect because of its history as a penal colony, and from China, whose able-bodied and capable representatives settled in Chinese Camp south of Sonora. Men from the Atlantic world were to come later; in 1848 it was a Pacific monopoly; through its earlier months a Californian monopoly.

At Coloma further placer deposits were discovered downstream in what came to be known as the Mormon Diggings, and soon afterwards similar deposits were found in dry beds of streams to the north about the forks of the American River and centred on Auburn, and to the south at Dry Diggings, centred on Placerville, while farther north, on the Yuba, was a group outfitted by Charles M. Weber of French Camp, so that settlements were coming in being, stretching from the River Feather in the north to Bear Creek in the south, and the extent of the gold-producing area which came to be called the Mother Lode was rapidly being identified.

In these early days almost all the prospectors working

[2] Caughey, *Gold is the Cornerstone*, p. 22.

along the tributaries of the Feather, Yuba, American and Stanislaus rivers found valuable caches of gold. The most likely spots were nestled against the bedrock where water flowed or had flowed and where a boulder or an irregularity in the rock formation made a natural trap. Occasionally, the deposit had been washed clear. More often, there was a surface covering that had to be removed. Success stories piled one on another. One prospector found color in every pan along the Feather. A crew on the Yuba took $75,000 worth in three months. A Dry Diggings team near Auburn on the north fork of the American boasted a return of $16,000 on five cartloads of pay dirt. A lad got 77 ounces in one day and 90 in the next, in a ravine north of Coloma; and gold in quantity, coarser than any yet seen but easier to salvage, was found on the Stanislaus in the south.

In the bustling excitement of gold hunting, not many Forty-Eighters bothered to record the scene, so the best reports are the official ones by Thomas O. Larkin, the United States Consul, and by Colonel R. B. Mason, the successor to General Kearny as Governor of California. From San Francisco on 1 June 1884 Larkin sent a preliminary report to Washington. For two or three weeks, he said, men had been bringing in gold to exchange for supplies. All told he estimated such receipts at $20,000. According to his information, the placers along the Feather and American rivers, where two or three hundred men were at work, were yielding from ten to fifty dollars a day per worker. He went on to describe the excitement in San Francisco, the sudden rise in wages, the booming market in shovels, pans and anything required at the diggings, and the depopulation of town and port. On 28 June, following a visit to the mines on the American River, he amplified his first report. He said that downstream at the Mormon Diggings he found fifty tents pitched, and the one he visited housed eight miners who had two rockers in operation. These were machines having a short trough and a handle for rocking and jostling, a hopper at the upper end to sort out the larger rocks, and cleats across the floor. They were more efficient than the Indian baskets or tin pans more frequently used, and produced for this crew fifty dollars worth of dust a day apiece. Larkin estimated that there were more than a thousand men at work in the diggings, but there was no way of telling how extensive or rich the deposits were. The Mexicans however said they had never seen such placers in their own country, and predicted that the ground would yield gold for many years to come, perhaps for a century.

Mason's report was written on 17 August and was based on an excursion in July to the American and Yuba rivers. Mason stopped at Sutter's Fort to celebrate the Fourth, and found Sutter unable to get much of his work done for lack of labour, though at this time he was receiving an income in rents from stores on his land managed by Brannan, Smith and others. At Mormon Diggings, Mason found the same scene as Larkin, and set average earnings at five dollars a day. At Coloma, he found several parties at work, 'all of whom were doing very well'. Marshall explained to him how he discovered the first deposits, and some of the miners showed specimens weighing as much as five ounces. On the Yuba, Weber conducted him on a tour of ravines which had yielded from $12,000 to $17,000, and one miner displayed $2,000 worth of gold he had got in three weeks. Mason estimated 4,000 men as the working force on the two rivers, half of them Indians. He put the daily production at $30,000 to $50,000. He agreed with Larkin that there was still plenty of gold to be got.

As the complement of gold seekers increased and spread out over the Mother Lode country, a system of supply belatedly developed to cater for the miners. Storekeepers, such as Brannan and Smith at Sutter's Fort, Brannan at Coloma on the South Fork of the American River, Weber at French Camp on the Yuba, and Syrec at Mokelumne Hill on the Mokelumne, set up their tents or shacks and began to trade. Their stocks at first consisted of flour, ship's biscuit, jerked meat, salt pork, whisky, picks, shovels, and boots, shirts and the like. These goods were bought in San Francisco and dispatched by wagon to the stores set up at the diggings. Shortages and transportation charges meant that prices were fantastically high, but the gold miners were reckless spenders anyhow, so did not worry unduly. In fact, the 'Forty-Eighters' appear to have been as happy and good natured as they were generally prosperous. A pick or a shovel sufficed to mark a claim; belongings left in camp went unmolested; and although the goldfields lay beyond the effective arm of the law, there was little or no crime.

In 1849 the worldwide rush to California began. There were several routes by which the gold seekers came. The safest, though most expensive and slowest, was by ship round Cape Horn. A quicker way was by sea to Panama followed by a land crossing to the west coast and then a second voyage to San Francisco. This was not very popular at first, as the Panama land trail was muddy and unhealthy. Later when a railroad was built across the isthmus it became more attractive, but long waits on the west coast of Panama for the infrequent service to San Francisco detracted from its merits. Rather naturally, considering the defects of the sea routes, the American people's usual choice was overland. This appealed because it was near at hand. River steamboats offered easy transport to where the trails began, and in any case, many midwestern gold seekers were only a short distance from the customary starting places like Council Bluffs, Fort Leavenworth, St Joseph and Westport. Furthermore, whereas the ocean routes usually required a substantial cash outlay, the standard equipment on every farm could easily be converted into a trail outfit. A farm team, a wagon, an axe, a gun, and the homegrown staples such as flour, meal and bacon were just what was required. A farmer's work clothes were ideal garb for the trail. The wagon not only provided a home on wheels for the journey, but also along with the team and tools could be put to good use on arrival in California.

The main overland route followed the Oregon Trail to South Pass, took the Sublette Cut-Off across the barren Green basin, went north along the fertile valley of the Bear River where redress might be had after the desert section, and then swung west to follow the Humboldt to its sink.[3] Finally the Sierra Nevadas were crossed by the Truckee or Carson Pass. Some travellers, however, crossed the Green basin by

[3] Later called the Carson Sink.

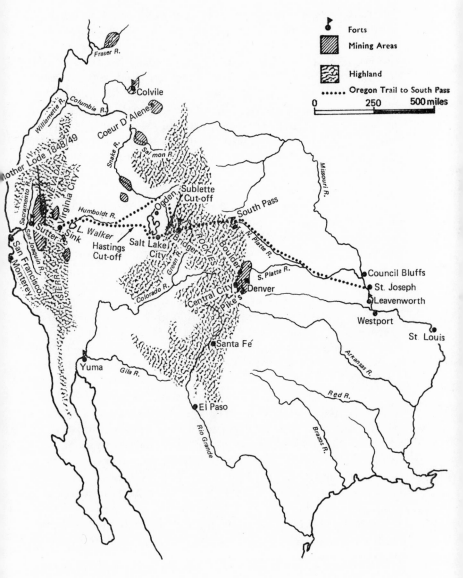

Forts

Mining Areas

Highland

⋯⋯ Oregon Trail to South Pass

0   250   500 miles

Fraser R.

Colvile

Columbia R.

Coeur D'Alene

Willamette R.

Snake R.

Salmon R.

Missouri R.

Mother Lode 1848/49

NEVADA

Virginia City

Sublette Cut-off

Ogden

South Pass

Humboldt R.

L. Walker

Sink

Sutter's

Hastings Cut-off

Salt Lake City

Bridger

ROCKIES

Boulder

Green R.

N. Platte R.

San Francisco

San Joaquin R.

Sacramento R.

SIERRA NEVADA

Monterey

Colorado R.

Central City

Pike's

S. Platte R.

Denver

Council Bluffs

St. Joseph

Leavenworth

Westport

St Louis

Yuma

Gila R.

Santa Fé

Arkansas R.

El Paso

Rio Grande

Red R.

Brazos R.

12. Mining areas

the main Oregon Trail to Fort Bridger, followed the Mormon routes through the Uinta and Wasatch Mountains to Salt Lake, and took the Hastings Cut-Off to join the trail along the Humboldt. The Mormons appear to have been hospitably inclined towards the travellers, but few gold seekers seem to have dallied to study the achievements of the Latter-Day Saints in and around Salt Lake City. A small proportion of prospectors took the Santa Fé Trail, followed the Gila River, and reached Mother Lode through southern California. Others took the land routes across Texas and the northern provinces of Mexico, and then the western trails paralleling the Gila which had been blazed by Kearny and his troopers or by the Mormon Battalion during the invasion of California at the beginning of the Mexican War (see map 12).

When sizeable settlements had been established on the diggings in the West, there came a demand for better transportation to and from the East, for better communications would mean lower commodity prices for the mining camps and more frequent news of the happenings back home. Both Easterners and Westerners agreed that improvements required government support, and their joint pressure forced Congress to grant a series of subsidies to shipping concerns, overland transport companies, and finally telegraph corporations and railroads.

A start was made when contracts were awarded for a semi-monthly mail service between New York and San Francisco via the Panama where letters were carted across the isthmus. This service took thirty days and the charges were high so there were soon demands for a quicker, cheaper overland service. The matter became a political issue between North and South. The Northerners favoured a direct route starting along the Oregon Trail. The Southerners preferred a route from St Louis crossing Texas, passing through El Paso in the south of New Mexico, crossing Arizona to Fort Yuma, and so into southern California to Los Angeles and north to San Francisco (see map). As the postmaster-general, Aaron V. Brown of Memphis, was an ardent Southerner it was not unexpected when he awarded a contract to two seasoned Eastern stagecoach operators, John Butterfield and William

G. Fargo who offered to provide a service of Concord express coaches on the southern route outlined above. The service over this 2,795 miles of route was started in 1858 and proved a success. President Buchanan (1857–61) was so pleased with John Butterfield's efforts that he sent him a telegram which read: 'I congratulate you on the result. It is a glorious triumph for civilisation and the Union.' For the next three years Butterfield Overland Express coaches raced over the southern trail, two a week in each direction, through rain and snow and desert heat, with scarcely a break in the service. Sometimes coaches and stage-posts were raided by Apache and Comanche, but almost always the coaches got through; and with generous subsidies, a steady increase in mail carried, and substantial local traffic on the way, the venture flourished.

The support given the southern route by the Democratic Party's officials who dominated national officers under President Buchanan led to the central and more direct route being operated by private enterprise. In 1855 the firm of Russell, Majors and Waddell was founded, of which Russell was the leading light. This company started a direct wagon service overland to the West, from the railhead at St Joseph in Missouri to San Francisco. It started with 300 vehicles and grew so rapidly that by 1858 it operated 3,500 covered wagons, employed 4,000 men and owned 40,000 draft oxen. Every wagon train sent out from Missouri contained twenty-five covered wagons, each carrying three tons of goods pulled by twelve oxen. For the next few years the company dominated freighting in the Central Plains, carrying food and industrial produce to army camps and mining fields, and bringing out hides and precious metals. So profitable was this freighting that the company was encouraged to start two other services. The first was a ridden-horse mail service known as the Pony Express from St Joseph to Sacramento. This was a dramatic affair. Stations were built at ten-mile intervals on the most direct route between St Joseph, Missouri, the western terminus of the railroads, and Sacramento. Five hundred horses carefully selected for speed and endurance were distributed along the route. Special lightweight saddles and flat mail pouches were purchased. The riders were chosen with equal care, lightweights possessing courage and stamina being sought—one of the men selected was young William Cody who became later a famous buffalo hunter, army scout, and showman in the East and in Europe. The service began on 3 April 1860 when crowds at St Joseph at the eastern end of the route and at Sacramento at the western end cheered away the first two riders. Each rode his horse at full gallop for ten miles, then came crashing into a station where another mount was held saddled and ready to be away. In a moment the mail pouches were fixed to the new saddle, and the rider leapt up and was off. Each rider rode seventy-five miles at breakneck pace, and then turned his pouches over to another, and rested for the return trip. Ten and a half days were taken on the first attempt, ten less that by a stagecoach. Unfortunately, the costs were not recouped by the charges made, and although the Pony Express was kept in business by support from the freighting concern until 1861, in that year competition from the new telegraph companies forced it to close down.

Russell, Majors and Waddell were no more successful with the third concern they started. It consisted of a stagecoach service from Fort Leavenworth to Denver on the Colorado goldfields, known as the Leavenworth and Pike's Peak Express. It never managed to make a profit, mainly because it had no government subsidies like Butterfield's southern company; but also possibly because it was not as well organised as their freighting business. In 1859 an additional small company running occasional stages from St Joseph to Salt Lake City was purchased to give the Pike's Peak Express a boost. Although through this a share of Butterfield's subsidy was gained for carrying mails to Salt Lake City, the subsequent 'shot in the arm' was not sufficient to keep the company from bankruptcy in 1862, when it was sold to Ben Holladay, already an up-an-coming man in the transportation business. Holladay although a coarse illiterate was endowed by nature with uncanny executive skill. Within a few months he managed to resurrect the bankrupt concern. With coaches running strictly to schedule and attracting more passengers, he was soon receiving handsome dividends. However, when

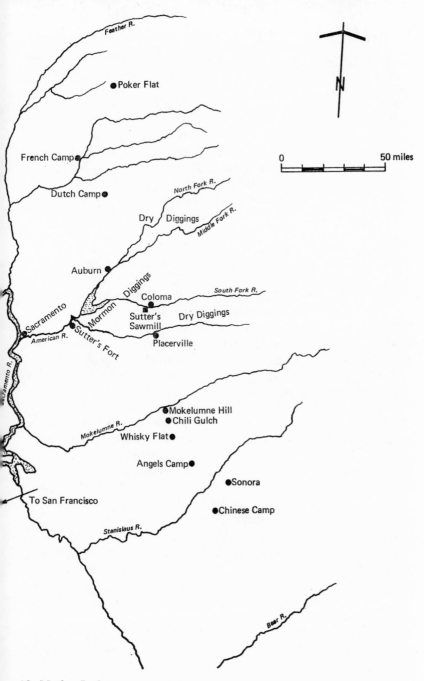

N

0   50 miles

Feather R.

● Poker Flat

French Camp ●

Dutch Camp ●

North Fork R.

Dry   Diggings

Middle Fork R.

Auburn ●

Mormon Diggings

Coloma

South Fork R.

Sutter's
Sawmill

Dry Diggings

Sacramento

American R.

Sutter's Fort

Placerville

Sacramento R.

●Mokelumne Hill

●Chili Gulch

Mokelumne R.

Whisky Flat●

Angels Camp●

●Sonora

To San Francisco

●Chinese Camp

Stanislaus R.

Bear R.

13. Mother Lode

there was a threat of competition from the new projected transcontinental railroad, Holladay was wise enough to see the writing on the wall, and in 1866 he sold out to Wells Fargo, a New York company that had previously purchased Butterfield's interests west of the Rockies.

During the decade when stage coaching was in its heyday in the West, railways were advancing slowly into trans-Mississippi territory, and by 1861 had reached as far as the 100th meridian, 200 miles west of Council Bluffs. The initiative for the construction of a transcontinental line belonged to Theodore D. Judah, backed by Collis P. Huntington and other prominent Westerners. Judah first persuaded his fellow Californians to build a line from San Francisco to the State border, and then sought federal support to contiue it to the Great Salt Lake to meet a railroad starting from the Mississippi valley. Late in 1861 Judah descended on Washington, and his persistent lobbying was rewarded in July 1862 when Congress passed a law launching the first Pacific railroad. Two companies, the measure decreed, would build the road. The Central Pacific Railroad was assigned the difficult task of bridging the Sierra Nevada from California, and continuing the line to Ogden, north of the Great Salt Lake. The Union Pacific was authorised to build westward from the 100th meridian, climb the Rockies at South Pass and meet the Central Pacific near Ogden. The building of the first transcontinental railroad proved a prodigious task. It took seven years, but in mid-May 1869, a little band of workers and officials at Promotory Point near Ogden watched the placing of the last ties, the fixing of the last steel rails, and the presentation of the golden spike which was to bind the two railroads together. A moment later, after a few well aimed blows, the tracks were joined and a new form of transportation[4] to the goldfields and the West had begun.

To begin with, gold mining was a task for individuals, and because of the numbers involved well populated settlements

[4] Later, other transcontinental railroads were constructed: including a northern one from Duluth paralleling Lewis and Clark's trail to Seattle; and a southern one across Texas via El Paso and Yuma to Los Angeles—see map.

grew up along Mother Lode, some being given fanciful names like, for example, Poker Flat between the Feather and Yuba rivers in the north, and Whisky Flat and Angels Camp between the Mokelumne and Stanislaus rivers in the south, while others were called more realistically, French Camp, Dutch Camp, Mormon Diggings, Chili Gulch and Chinese Camp. Buildings sprang up without thought to form or plan. Rough planks or canvas walls were the rule, and if fire burned the dwellings down, they were instantly rebuilt again. A valley empty in springtime might take on the appearance of a mushrooming metropolis by summer, and yet turn into a ghost town by fall when the last ounce of gold was mined. Or a once bustling town might be washed into the gulch by the hoses of the hydraulic machines attempting to wash out the gold. Every time the miner moved a retinue followed. Storekeepers were soon on the scene to provide necessities that were only a little less dear than luxuries. Governor Mason says he saw a miner pay Weber an once and a half of gold for a fifty-cent box of seidlitz powders. Consul Larkin reported pans worth twenty cents retailing at ten dollars. Some merchants amassed fortunes. Collis P. Huntington,[5] when stranded at Panama, seized the opportunity of going into business, and by enterprising in liquors, lotteries, games of chance and merchandise increased his capital of $1,000 to $4,000. He is also credited when in California with buying up shovels at $2.50 a dozen to sell at $10 each. Saloon keepers arrived early at new sites. They often opened with nothing more elaborate than a plank spanning two barrels, and hastily rigged canvas walls—or no walls at all. One bartender reported a profit of $700 on every barrel of whisky sold. The 'ladies' of the goldfields came next, filling the dance halls, gambling dens and inevitable bawdy houses with the soft smell of perfume and of cigar smoke—these were not the genteel gingham variety left behind.

The authentic flavour of life on the diggings has come from the pens of Bret Harte and Mark Twain, both of whom

[5] Uncle of Henry F. Huntington who donated his house and treasures at San Marino to the public as an art gallery and research library.

stayed for a time on the Mother Lode. Bret Harte arrived in 1855 at the age of 19 to be with his mother who had remarried after Bret's father died. For a time he mined in a desultory manner at Angels Camp by the Stanislaus River in the south. He was unsuccessful and in due course wound up his affairs; his partners paid his stage fare back to San Francisco. Mark Twain stayed in 1864 with some friends near Angels Camp where the barman at the Lode Hotel, an old riverboat pilot name Sam Coon, told him the story of how a frog jumping contest was lost by the champion after buckshot had been fed surreptiously to the famous leaper. This tale became the basis for *The Celebrated Jumping Frog of Calveras County*. When Mark Twain's version was printed in an Eastern magazine he became a sensation immediately. A year later he was to leave California never to return; but he carried a wealth of atmosphere with him that was to inspire his writings for the rest of his life. And his tale was to leave its effect on the Mother Lode. Every May contestants pour into Angels Camp bringing frogs, large and small, domesticated and imported, to compete in the Annual Frog Jumping Contest. For about a week the usually quiet town (pop. 1,575 —not quite a ghost town) teems with activity centred around a frog jumping competition that pays as much as $1,000 to the winner. In the public gardens a statue of Mark Twain, and one of a huge frog, commemorate the founders of the event, and while the contest is in progress Angels Camp recaptures a part of its colourful past.

The end of the old individual style of gold seeking came about when the placer deposits were used up. In 1848 and 1849 gold was got from bars, benches, beds and banks of rivers, and from ravines and gulches where streams flowed intermittently, but which were nevertheless part of the drainage system of the western foothills of the Sierra Nevada. Since these deposits were relatively shallow—two or three feet down was as far as miners usually bothered to go—and were of free loose gold, they were suitable for individual working; and that is how the early miners went about it, either entirely on their own or joining forces with a partner or two. There was also, however, gold embedded in the hard quartz of the hills, which required for its extraction the use of sophisticated machinery such as crushers, pulverisers and hydraulic washing machines. When the placer deposits had mostly been taken, therefore, the individual miners began to drift away and leave the work to companies possessing sufficient capital to bring in machinery. As these concerns required few men to work for them, the mining towns then became ghosts of their old selves—as most of them are now. But company production remained prosperous for those still involved. In 1852, with 108 mills representing a capital of $6,000,000 there was an annual output, including placer deposits, valued at $80,000,000. After this, although the number of stamp mills increased until it reached 300 in 1861, placer mining decreased so rapidly that annual output, mostly from hydraulic claims, totalled only between $15,000,000 and $20,000,000 a year. From 1884, interruptions from one cause or another, and fluctuations in the price of gold on the world markets, reduced the value of their average annual yield to some $12,000,000. In modern times there have been even greater fluctuations due to depressions, wars and debasement of currency.

The miners leaving the Mother Lode soon heard of other areas where they might seek their fortunes. An early exodus was to Fort Colvile on the Columbia River in Washington Territory. The gold deposits there were soon exhausted, and a move was then made towards reported richer finds on the River Fraser in Canada. Here for a time there was gold to be found; but also administrative chaos and social disorder. In 1859 the Canadian authorities resorted to licence fees, trade regulations and even a moral code. These brought law and order, but so stifled opportunity that most of the American miners returned to California.

There followed a new rush across the Sierra Nevada to seek gold in Washoe Indian territory, easily accessible by the Truckee and Carson passes. The vein, nearly half a mile wide, was sunk into the eastern side of the mountains, and extended five miles from north to south (the Mother Lode was 200 miles). The vein's surface outcroppings were few, and mainly hidden beneath rocky debris. At only two points were they partially exposed: at Gold Canyon, a shallow ravine cut by centuries of erosion down the south-eastern side of Mount Davidson; and a mile away at Six Mile Canyon which ran down the north-eastern side. Members of the disbanded Mormon battalion panned the first dust when bound for Utah in the summer of 1848; but it was not until a year later that news of their finds spread and the first prospectors began trickling in from California. These early comers met with little success, and it was not until January 1859 that the main lode was discovered by James Finny, a simple, generous man of bibulous reputation usually known as 'Old Virginny'. Finny noticed promising gravel on the side of a flat-topped hill in upper Gold Canyon and then located dust at a spot which he named Gold Hill. Returning with companions, having staked the customary forty-foot claims, he started digging. In early April, when they were ten feet down, they unearthed a vein of reddish decomposed quartz that was rich in gold. They had stumbled on Old Red Ledge, a vein of the main lode. At first their find aroused no excitement. A few nearby miners and ranchers took out claims on Gold Hill, but no successful exploitation followed, and not a word of the discovery reached the outside world. It was not until June 1859, when Peter O'Riley and Patrick McLaughlin uncovered the Ophir vein on the main lode at Six Mile Canyon that the Washoe field finally caught the imagination of the West. O'Riley and McLaughlin made their claims, and were already digging and washing furiously, when Henry T. P. Comstock—the man whose name was later given to the main lode—rode up. Comstock declared that he and Finny had bought the claim in Six Mile Canyon the winter before. O'Riley and McLaughlin did not really believe him; but claims usually played out so quickly that they were not worth arguing over, so they took Comstock and Finny into partnership. Later Comstock bought out Finny's share for a blind horse and a bottle of whisky. Within a few days the diggings were yielding well, and the partners then staked out some quartz claims to supplement the placers. A few weeks later

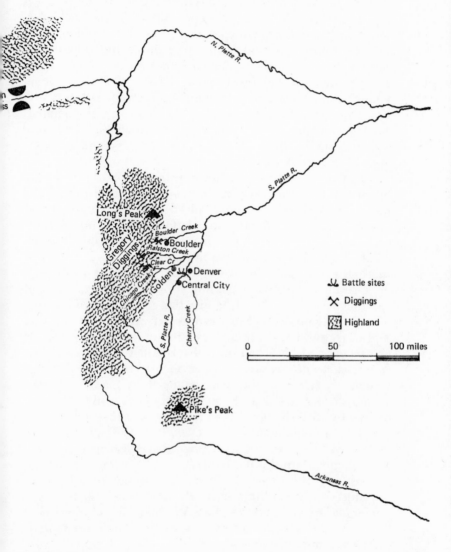

Long's Peak

Boulder Creek
Gregory
Diggings
Ralston Creek
Clear Cr.
Golden
Chicago Creek
S. Platte R.
Cherry Creek

Boulder

Denver
Central City

N. Platte R.

S. Platte R.

Highland

⚔ Battle sites

✕ Diggings

▨ Highland

0   50   100 miles

Pike's Peak

Arkansas R.

14. **Colorado**

they dug up blue stuff three fourths pure silver and one fourth
gold worth $3,876 a ton. The Ophir Mine, as the partners
called it, was a find indeed. The wild rush that inevitably
followed brought a few experienced men with capital ready
to form companies, and hordes of gullible individual prospectors. It was only the former that did well out of what came
to be called the Comstock Lode. Early on, some of them
bought out the partners. Comstock received $10,000; Mc-
Laughlin $3,500; and O'Riley, who held out the longest,
$40,000. The partners enjoyed their wealth only briefly before
squandering it on liquor, women and worthless mining stocks;
all died in poverty.

The Comstock Lode was awkwardly situated on a barren
hillside unsuitable even for a temporary settlement. The
matter of housing was only solved when the miners laid
out a shanty town on the flatter land below the hillside covering the Lode. By tradition it was named by Old Virginny
(Finny). Stumbling home in a drunken state he fell and broke
the bottle of whisky he was carrying. Staggering to his feet
he sprinkled the few remaining drops on the ground and
announced pompously: 'I baptise this ground Virginia City.'
The first saloon opened in a canvas tent with a box as a bar,
a pitcher and a few tin cups as equipment and two barrels
of flavoured alcohol optimistically labelled brandy. At first,
accommodation was so scarce that men were paying a dollar
a night to sleep on the floor wrapped in blankets rented
from a shrewd trader at an additional dollar a night. Nevertheless, by 1860 the town had grown so large that it boasted a
theatre, thirty-eight stores, eight hotels, nine restaurants and
twenty-five saloons, all charging outlandish prices. The
mining operations did not flourish at first. It was too difficult
to blast out the quartz by hand. When stamp mills were
introduced matters improved. By 1863 deep shafts were
producing richly, and by then Virginia City's population
had risen to 15,000. As regards Washoe, its palmiest days were
still ahead; but when Nevada in whose territory it lay became
a State in 1864 it was already passing beyond the frontier
stage.

Meanwhile, another rush had started, this time to the

country about Pike's Peak in Colorado. In 1858 William Green Russell made an important strike on the South Platte, and later joined forces with a party under J. H. Tierney and laid out a town (Denver) east of the junction of Cherry Creek and the South Platte. They then sent out false tales of imaginary strikes. This caused prospectors to converge on the area from both east and west. Though real discoveries of gold came only slowly, pay dirt was found in Chicago Creek in January 1859, and soon afterwards in Boulder Creek. A few months later John H. Gregory made a strike near Ralston Creek, which was later known as Gregory Gulch, and sold his claim afterwards for $21,000. Gregory's Diggings enjoyed only a short life; but during 1859 and through 1860 successful strikes were made at Jefferson Diggings, and also on the Boulder River and on Clear Creek. Denver reflected their successes by doubling in population in 1860; and other towns sprang up like Boulder on Boulder Creek, Central City near where Russell made the very first strike, and Golden. By the autumn of 1860 Denver boasted a theatre, two newspapers, and a circulating library, and its wild and woolly days were over. On the heels of the gold rush came the discovery of silver, whereby the wealth of the above towns became fabulous. An earnest of this was when solid silver bricks were laid in a pavement in Central City (pop. now 228) to welcome President Grant on a visit in April 1873. These were valued at $12,000, and were really meant as a protest against inflation. Later Colorado became known as the Silver State. Now it ranks second in the United States in diversity of metallic minerals and compounds. Leading the nation in production of molybenum, it also ranks high in coal, tin, uranium and zinc mining. Colorado became a Territory in 1861 and a State in 1876, one hundred years after the signing of the Declaration of Independence. From this circumstance it gets its popular name, the Centennial State.

Idaho is another State that owes its development to minerals. It was first visited by Lewis and Clark when they led their expedition into the area in 1805–6. Until 1860 the territory was inhabited my missionaries, fur trappers and Indians, and was looked upon as a liability rather than an asset to the Union. Discovery of gold on the Snake and Salmon rivers in 1862 and 1866 brought about the first substantial influx of population; and about the same time agricultural settlements by the Mormons were made in the south-east. Idaho was organised as a Territory in 1863, but the population did not increase greatly until the discovery of gold and silver in the far north at Coeur d'Alenes in 1883. In 1890 Idaho became a State within the Union. Lead, zinc, silver, phosphate rock and gold are now the chief mineral products in the order of their value. Over the years Idaho has ranked first in the production of silver and zinc, and second in lead. Also some of the largest phosphate deposits in the world are found in Idaho.

Chapter 9

The Subjugation of the Plains Indians I: The Fetterman Massacre

In the early days the Indian peoples formed a barrier to American westward expansion, but it was hoped that when the Five Civilised Tribes[1] had been moved to Oklahoma and most of the other Eastern Indians had been settled across the Mississippi, the western plains might become Indian territory and the two races could live apart and in peace. Two factors prevented this concept of 'One Big Reservation' in the 'Great American Desert' from being carried out successfully. The territory east of the Rockies was not the infertile area that early explorers had thought. It was grassland and potential farming country, far too valuable to be handed over in perpetuity to large herds of buffalo preyed upon by a few Indians. Also, with the discovery of gold and silver in the West, prospectors travelling across the plains soon insisted that the US Government must keep the trails clear of aggressive Indians even though these trails, and the routes followed later by the railroads, cut across the Indians' best hunting country and threatened to destroy their traditional way of life by breaking up the herds of buffalo on which they depended. The Plains Indians ate buffalo meat, fresh and dried, and cracked the animal's bones for marrow. Buffalo skins, soft-tanned served as clothing and bedding. With the hair removed, the tanned skins were turned into *tipi* covers, clothing and moccasins; and raw hides made trunks and bags. Thick

[1] Cherokee, Creek, Chickasaw, Choctaw and Seminole, from the south-east.

neckskins cut in circular form provided war shields, and
stomach skins produced water-buckets. Buffalo hair could
be twisted into rope, or woven into bags, belts and saddle
girths. Buffalo horns were converted into spoons; slivers from
the animal's leg-bones made sewing awls and skin scrapers;
and its sinews produced thread. Buffalo droppings[2] were used
as fuel; and serviceable skin boats were produced by weaving
stretched hides on circular frames of willow poles. In fact,
although the Plains Indians ate the flesh and used the skins
of other animals, especially the antelope, and enjoyed edible
roots and berries when they could find them, the buffalo was
the foundation of their way of life.

There were seven principal tribes of Plains Indians. In the
south were the Cheyenne, Arapaho, Comanche, Kiowa and
Kiowa Apache; and in the north the Crows, and various
divisions of Dakotas (Sioux). The name Sioux given to the
Dakotas by white men was an abbreviation of the French-
Canadian term *Nadowessioux*, itself derived from *Nadowessi*
meaning a small snake or an enemy, a name the Chippewas
used. Siouan is also now the designation of a language group.
The Sioux moved on to the Plains from Minnesota. Their
most westerly group, the powerful Teton Dakotas, included
Sioux bands like the Oglala, Brule, Hunkpapa and Miniconjou, all of whom are mentioned later in this chapter.

Besides the Plains Indians proper there were tribes living
along the borders of the Plains who, although primarily
cultivators, fishermen or gatherers of roots, and although
dwelling in earth lodges, mat wigwams or grass houses instead
of portable skin *tipis*, nevertheless periodically indulged in
buffalo hunting. From the northern mountain areas came
those great horse-breeders the Nez Perce and their neighbours
the Shoshoni (Snake); from the central and southern mountain belts, the Ute and Apache; and from the eastern fringes
came the Mandan and Arikara who dwelt along the Missouri
and were traditionally the traders for the nomadic plainsmen.
The Pawnee from the Republican River, the Osage from
Kansas, and the Wichita from the Red River in the south,
also at times went buffalo hunting on the Plains.

[2] 'Buffalo Chips'.

The subjugation of the Western and Mountain Indians had been relatively simple, for being either pastoral or subsisting on fish, grubs, and roots, their way of life did not necessitate warlike habits and they were mostly peaceful. In the West, they generally co-operated with the whites, for example, some worked in the diggings; Colonel Mason's report[3] speaks of half the workers on Mother Lode being Indians. But any who resisted ceding land required by whites were ruthlessly driven from their settlements by force of arms, and a similar fate met the Shoshoni (Snake) and Bannock in Oregon and Idaho, and the Ute of Utah and Nevada. Intermittent warfare with the whites went on between 1850 and 1860; but frequent defeats combined with the incentive of monetary payments persuaded the Western Indians eventually to conform to the wishes of the Americans. In 1861, the Western Utes ceded most of the lands in Utah and accepted a small reservation south-east of the Great Salt Lake. In 1868, the Eastern Utes moved into a large reserve in the mountain region of Colorado. In the same year, the Bannock agreed to restrict themselves to a reserve about the Fort Hall, and the Shoshoni moved to one on the headwaters of the Big Horn. The Apache and Navaho of the south-west mountain country proved more troublesome. They were so menacing that prospectors feared to pass through their territory. In 1850 forts were established throughout the area, but this did not solve the problem, and there followed a bitter struggle which lasted several years in which Kit Carson, leading the 1st New Mexican Volunteer Cavalry, proved the outstanding American leader with a horrifying tally of hostile Indians destroyed. It was not until 1868 that the Navaho and Apache were at last persuaded to go into reservations and end their warlike habits. In that year the Navaho went to a reserve in the north-west corner of New Mexico, and in 1871 and on into 1874 bands of Apache moved into scattered reservations stretching across the southern parts of Arizona and New Mexico (see map 11).

The Plain Indians proper were more difficult to put under control even than the Navaho and Apache. Not one of the

[3] See page 183.

southern five tribes[4] was indigenous to the region. The Comanche were of Shoshonean stock and had once lived in southern Wyoming. Pressure from the Sioux and other tribes had caused them to drift southward. Early in the eighteenth century their home seems to have been in Kansas. During the next hundred years they ranged as far south as the Brazos River in Texas. Like other Plains tribes they were made up of a number of bands held together in loose confederation, which made negotiation with them difficult. They enjoyed a reputation for gallantry and had a high sense of honour, and considered themselves superior because their language was used universally on the Southern Plains.

The earliest traditions of the Kiowa placed them at the headwaters of the Missouri from whence they moved to their southern territory. About the year 1700 they formed an alliance with the Crows, who seem to have introduced them to the horse. Strays and runaways from the herds of the Spanish explorers found a natural home upon the Plains and multiplied there at an astonishing rate. The exact time at which the Southern Plains tribes recognised their value and acquired and mastered these animals is uncertain, but the Kiowa were mounted by the opening of the eighteenth century, and a horse culture with an attendant hunting culture aligned to the vast herds of buffalo had spread throughout the Plains area a few decades later. Pressure from the Cheyenne and Arapaho forced the Kiowa southward upon the Comanche with whom they waged war until 1795. Peace was then made and confederation followed.

The Kiowa-Apache were a small tribe which had been mistaken for an Apache band. They became associated early on with the Kiowa and moved southward with them. They were friendly toward the whites and were generally reluctant to take the warpath.

The Arapaho and Cheyenne were both of Algonquian stock and had apparently made their earliest home in Minnesota and Wisconsin. The Sioux uprooted them and drove them first to the Black Hills and then even farther westward, the Arapaho toward the headwater of the Yellowstone, and

[4] Comanche, Kiowa, Kiowa-Apache, Arapaho and Cheyenne.

the Cheyenne to the upper reaches of the Platte. Both tribes
later moved south to the area of the upper Arkansas River,
and engaged in a fierce struggle with the Comanche and
Kiowa. About this time the Cheyenne split into the North
Cheyenne and South Cheyenne. Five bands established themselves in the South Platte region and six went to live in the
north of New Mexico alongside the Kiowa. Meanwhile the
Arapaho settled between the two Cheyenne groups. The
Arapaho were the most peacefully disposed of the tribes of
the Southern Plains. They were much given to ceremony,
one of their principal observances being an annual sun dance.
Amiable and accommodating, and normally friendly to
whites, they exerted a moderating influence on the turbulent
Cheyenne.

The colonisation of Texas by Stephen F. Austin and the
other *empresarios* brought the Comanche into contact with
American settlers. The Comanche had been implacable
enemies of the Spaniards and the Mexicans, but were at first
disposed to be friendly to the Texans. For example, in the
spring of 1832 Austin and two companions were seized by a
band of fifty Comanche, but were released with their
belongings when they informed the Indians that they were
Americans. However, the great extent of the American intrusion soon caused the Comanche to change their attitude.
President Houston, during his first term from 1836–38,
adopted a conciliatory policy, but a series of Indian raids on
outlying settlements caused his successor to attempt to expel
the Comanche from the neighbourhood of white territory.
This resulted in a series of engagements[5] from 1838–40,
culminating in the Battle of Plum Creek, in which the
Comanche were worsted and driven away.

The annexation of Texas by the United States in 1845
transferred the problem of controlling the Comanche and
their Indian allies to the federal government. By this time
there was an organised department of state to carry out the
task. In 1789 the War Department had been assigned the
supervision of Indians, and in March 1824 a special office
for Indian affairs was established within the War Department.

[5] See page 144.

In 1832 a commission was appointed by the Secretary of War to manage Indian affairs, and in 1834 agents and interpreters were recruited. Later the staff of this office was to include frontiersmen like Kit Carson and Thomas Fitzpatrick. The former was renowned for his severity towards Indians, but there were also many agents who tried to do their best for their Indian clients, and who took their side against prospector and settler alike. In 1849 the office dealing with Indian affairs was transferred from the War Department to the Department of the Interior, and treaties were concluded with the Comanche and Kiowa which permitted the passage of American citizens across their territory, and under which the Indians specifically agreed to cease their depredations along the Santa Fé Trail. There was also an agreement whereby the two Southern Plains tribes kept the peace with the Five Civilised Tribes in Indian Territory (Oklahoma). In Texas the situation was not so satisfactory. In the spring of 1847 the federal Indian Agent attempted to establish reserves where his charges might settle, farm and live at peace with the whites; but the Texans were not willing to have Indians living among them and drove the red men away. The embittered tribes then began to raid Texan settlements from their new area, and the settlers demanded federal protection. Rather surprisingly, this brought a significant response from the authorities, and two lines of forts were constructed to guard Texas. The inner line ran from Fort Duncan on the Rio Grande, north of Austin to Fort Graham on the Colorado, and on to Fort Worth on the Trinity River. The outer line stretched from Fort Clark north of Fort Duncan to Forts Cooper and Chadbourne on either side of the Colorado, and on to Fort Belknap on the Brazos River. A band of some 200 miles separated the defence lines, which should have provided sufficient terrain for an elastic system of defence. Nevertheless, the swift-striking Indian war parties often managed to penetrate into the Texan settlements. The Comanche also raided in the opposite direction against the caravans on the Santa Fé Trail.

In 1853 an effort was made to ease both threats by peaceful means. On 27 July the Comanche, Kiowa and Kiowa-Apache were persuaded to sign a treaty under which they agreed to allow the construction of roads and military posts in their country and to stop raiding. In return they were promised government protection and $18,000 per annum for ten years. Under this treaty the Texas Legislature also agreed to provide some Indian reservations, and the Texas Indian Agent was at last permitted to survey two small sites. One known as the Brazos Agency and comprising 38,152 acres lay a few miles south of Fort Belknap; the other of 18,576 acres called the Comanche Reserve was on a tributary of the Brazos about forty-five miles to the west. By 1858 upward of eleven hundred of the smaller, peaceful tribes like the Delaware were settled in the Brazos Agency. and making good progress; but few Comanche showed much interest in their reserve, and after three years, less than four hundred had gone there. Comanche and Kiowa bands continued their depredations, and after a few years the Texans retaliated by attempting to drive out all Indians, peaceful and hostile alike. A threatened attack on the Comanche Reserve in May 1859 was thwarted by quick action by the Indian Agent who summoned federal cavalry from the nearby forts to protect his wards. Later, aided by four companies of troops, he moved his Indians some three hundred miles north to the vicinity of Fort Dobb near the Canadian River in Indian Territory (Oklahoma). By this time a generation of Texans had driven away most of the Indians from their territory and imbued them with a bitter hatred of Texas. In his report to the Commissioner of Indian Affairs, the Indian Agent of the Arkansas area wrote:

'The Kiowa and Comanche Indians have, for two years, appeared in full numbers and for long periods upon the Arkansas, and now permanently occupy the country between the Canadian and the Arkansas rivers. This is in consequence of the hostile front opposed to them in Texas by which they are forced towards the north. . . . A smothered passion for revenge agitates these Indians . . . fomented by failure of food, the encircling encroachments of the white population and the exasperating sense of impending extinction.'[6]

[6] Annual Report of Indian Affairs, 1859, p. 138.

The outbreak of the American Civil War in 1861 gave the hostile tribes an opportunity for revenge on the Texans. When Federal troops called to the war abandoned the two lines of forts guarding the north-west frontier, Texas, which joined the side of the south, was unable to man the defences adequately, so that war parties penetrated her territory and raided at will, pushing the line of resistance and control south-eastward. It was only when the war was over that the whites in Texas were able to expand again.

Meanwhile, the North Cheyenne, the Arapaho and South Cheyenne who had remained relatively peaceful in their new areas of settlement on the North Platte, South Platte and Arkansas respectively had already become unsettled. Traffic on the Oregon Trail kept on increasing, and during the California gold rush of 1849 it became a human tidal wave. In September 1851, in a bid to keep the Oregon Trail open, the government decided to negotiate with the tribes. The Treaty of Fort Laramie which emerged allotted them a large domain along the foothills of the Rockies between the North Platte and Arkansas. The tribes for their part agreed to the establishment of roads and military posts in their country in exchange for protection from white intrusion and an annual payment of $50,000 for fifty years. Unfortunately, the beneficial effects of the Treaty of Fort Laramie were short-lived. The discovery of gold in Colorado in 1858, and the mad rush to the Pike's Peak area that followed, brought in a mass of aggressive whites who occupied the area regardless of the Indians' rights so recently guaranteed. Indian resentment arose, and although major trouble was avoided for a few years by a new treaty giving the Indians protection in a reduced area, in 1864 an incident occurred that caused a bitter Indian war.

On the evening of 11 April a Colorado settler near Denver named Ripley reported that some of his stock had been stolen by Indians and was allowed the use of forty troopers of volunteer cavalry to go in pursuit of the thieves. After a few hours on the trail the posse came up with a band of Cheyenne herding horses, some of which Ripley claimed. The herd was stopped and a demand made for Ripley's animals to be handed over; when the Indians refused to do so a skirmish followed in which four troopers were badly wounded and the Indians and their stock made off unscathed.

When the incident was reported to Colonel John Chivington, who commanded the District of Colorado, he immediately sent out a larger force with orders to chastise any Indians they encountered. On 3 May an Indian village was attacked and many of its inhabitants were killed or wounded, and its lodges and property were put to the torch. This brought war, for the Cheyenne were quick to seek revenge. Aided by their allies the Arapaho, they disrupted mail deliveries, interfered with stage-coach services, and plundered several outlying settlements, killing fifty men and capturing a number of women and children.[7] Late in June, with the Indians beyond control, the Governor ordered all the South Cheyenne and Arapaho then under arms to assemble at Fort Lyon[8] or face a war of extermination. The Indians seemingly were slow to comply; but eventually a Cheyenne band under Black Kettle drifted towards Fort Lyon to parley. A ruling from the officer commanding the Department of Kansas that only unconditional surrender would be considered spoilt any chance of coming to terms, and the Cheyenne then moved off and set up a large camp at Sand Creek forty miles north-east of Fort Lyon. They seem to have believed that by visiting Fort Lyon they had complied with instructions sufficiently to avoid attack. At any rate they were quite unprepared when, without warning, Chivington loosed his troops on their camp. There followed a butchery unparalleled even in the bloody annals of Plains warfare. Although Black Kettle raised the white flag, Indian men, women and children were shot or sabred without mercy. Of the 700 encamped at Sand Creek some 250 were killed, 130 lodges were put to the torch and 500 horses and mules taken.

The result of the Sand Creek massacre was an Indian war

[7] Annual Report of Indian Affairs 1868, p. 36—the children were later handed back.

[8] On the upper Arkansas south of Denver; formerly Fort Wise, and before that Bent's Fort. Bent burned his fort in 1847 when the government refused to buy it.

of unprecedented violence. The survivors, among whom was Black Kettle, sought assistance from fellow Cheyenne to the north and neighbouring Arapaho, Comanche and Kiowa, and in combination these tribes set the Plains aflame, killing scores of whites and successfully resisting the troops sent against them. After a pause to get breath the army was just planning to start a new and extensive campaign when Congress halted hostilities so that new methods might be tried. Public indignation over the Chivington massacre had been such that there was a strong demand for a more humane approach to the Indian troubles. Of Chivington the Congressional Joint Committee on the Conduct of War had declared: 'He deliberately planned and executed a foul and dastardly massacre which would have disgraced the veriest savage among those who were the victims of his cruelty'.[9] With this verdict public opinion in the East agreed, and a more peaceful approach was demanded. This was materially assisted by similar overtures from the warring tribes who made known their wishes through Colonel Jesse Leavenworth, already a tireless worker for a peaceful solution. The result was a meeting at the mouth of the Little Arkansas River attended by sixteen chiefs of the Cheyenne, Arapaho, Kiowa-Apache, Comanche and Kiowa, at which a temporary cessation of hostilities was agreed on and arrangements made for a full-scale peace conference to be held on 4 October at Bluff Creek, forty miles below the mouth of the Little Arkansas.

At the appointed time a United States Commission—which included Leavenworth—arrived to negotiate with the assembled chiefs at Bluff Creek. The proceedings opened with apologies for, and repudiation of, Colonel Chivington's action, then came an offer of reparation. After this the Cheyenne and Arapaho were offered land in Indian Territory (Oklahoma) away from the main travel routes, though they would remain free to hunt in uninhabited portions of their old reserves east of the Rockies. After some hesitation, Black Kettle and Little Raven, speaking for the Cheyenne and Arapaho respectively, accepted the terms offered which

[9] Senate Report No. 142, 38th Congress, 2nd Series, Vol. 4 p.v. 1865 *Massacre of Cheyenne Indians.*

included annuities[10] for forty years, and affixed their marks to a treaty on 14 October 1865. On 17 October the Commission reached an agreement with the Kiowa-Apache whereby they would confederate with the Cheyenne and share in the fruits of the treaty. Next, on 18 October, the Comanche and Kiowa accepted with much grumbling a reservation occupying the 'Panhandle' of Texas and a small segment of Indian Territory south of the Wichita River. Their agreement was on similar terms to that of the Cheyenne and Arapaho, and included annuities. The treaties mentioned above, although not long lasting, brought a measure of peace to the South Plains.

In 1866, an attempt was made to guarantee the safety of travellers to the Montana goldfields,[11] and this provoked a conflict with the Arapaho, Northern Cheyenne, and Sioux[12] who resented intrusion of their hunting grounds. During the Civil War thousands of miners had travelled to the Montana diggings either up the Missouri River by way of Fort Benton or overland along the Oregon Trail, over South Pass and then northward via Fort Hall. These were roundabout routes requiring weeks of passage, and a demand for a better route had caused explorers in 1864 to establish two trails direct from Fort Laramie. Jim Bridger was aware of the Indians' determination to keep white men out of their hunting grounds east of the Big Horn Mountains, and so he avoided that area and blazed his trail west of the Big Horns. John Bozeman on the other hand ran his wagons through the heart of the sacred hunting country. Except for the menace of Indians who sometimes took their toll, the second route was preferable, and by 1865 several parties of prospectors had followed what became known as the Bozeman Trail.

In 1865 the Federal Government became interested in deciding on the best route to the new goldfields, and pro-

[10] $20 per capita until the tribes were in the new reserves: $40 thereafter.
[11] Discovered in 1862 during the Civil War.
[12] The Brule, Oglala and Miniconjou bands of Sioux.

tecting it. After four years of civil war the Treasury was empty and easily acquirable gold became highly desirable. With hopes of encouraging prospectors to go to Montana, a survey of the most direct route was set in motion. The survey train planned to start from Sioux City on the Missouri, follow the Niocabra River to Fort Laramie and then take the Bozeman Trail. The train consisted of 250 wagons and was led by Colonel James A. Sawyer. It included engineers and gold prospectors and was escorted by two companies of former Confederate soldiers who had sworn oaths of allegiance to secure release from military prison. Although Sawyer was attacked by Indians on several occasions he managed to reach the Montana goldfields safely, and his subsequent report, which received wide publicity, increased the pressure to turn the Bozeman Trail into the official route and make it safe for travellers.

The first attempt was made by General Connor, who sent three columns into Indian country east of the Big Horns. Two of Connor's detachments suffered severely from Indian attacks, losing many of their horses in night raids, but Connor's own column managed to destroy an Arapaho village and establish Fort Reno on the Powder River on the south section of the trail. Not long after Connor had withdrawn from the field, reports from Montana indicated that Indian attacks on the rest of the Bozeman Trail were as frequent as ever, so in the autumn of 1865 an attempt was made to come to terms with the Indians. Peace treaties were subsequently signed which guaranteed hunting rights within the area but insisted that in return the Indians must guarantee the safe passage of travellers on the Bozeman Trail. Next, when in spite of these treaties, Indians continued raiding, a body of infantry was dispatched to police the trail. The first order which set this action in motion on 10 March 1866 read:

> The 2nd Bn of the 18th U.S. Infantry will constitute the garrison of Fort Reno on Powder River and establish two new posts between that place and Virginia City in Montana[13]. . . .

[13] U.S. Congress, 50th, 1st sess. Senate executive document 33, p. 51.

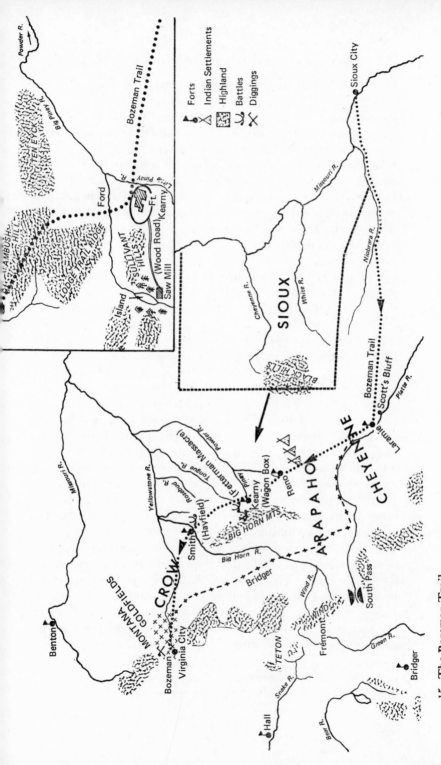

15. The Bozeman Trail

On 13 April further orders established a Montana District under Colonel Carrington which included the territory of Powder River, and placed him under the direct command of Brigadier General Philip St George Cooke[14] whose headquarters were at Omaha on the Missouri.

Carrington set forth from Fort Kearney[15] on 19 May 1866 with a small force consisting mainly of the 2nd Bn 18th Infantry. Following the wagons came a herd of cattle guarded by mounted men, and accompanying the expedition was Jim Bridger who knew Big Horn and Powder River country well, as he had been trapping, exploring and scouting in the area for forty years.

The journey up the Platte to Fort Laramie was relatively uneventful, though near Scotts Bluff, fifty miles from the fort, the steam sawmill taken along to saw the planks for the stockades crashed into a gully where it remained stuck for several weeks. At Fort Laramie, where peace talks with local Indian chiefs were in progress, Carrington was assured that all was going well, that most of the Oglala were represented by leaders who would sign, and that Spotted Tail, the influential leader of the Brule, had capitulated completely. Later, however, he was to learn that Red Cloud remained hostile, and would probably have to be defeated in battle if the Bozeman Trail was to be made secure. At Laramie they were not able to acquire all the replenishments they needed. They received only 1,000 rounds of ammunition instead of the 100,000 requisitioned, and no horses were available. On the other hand, twenty-six wagons loaded with provisions were acquired, and a number of mules.

It took the train five days to reach Fort Reno where Independence Day was celebrated appropriately by the firing of the fort's guns. This gunfire, however, did not stop the Indians from raiding that night and running off some horses. Before resuming the march Carrington relieved the two companies of volunteers manning the fort, and having sent them off home replaced them by a rifle company from his own

[14] Met with in the chapter on the conquest of New Mexico.
[15] Named after Gen. Stephen W. Kearny in spite of second 'e'; not to be confused with Fort Phil Kearny about to be built on Bozeman Trail.

force. After a rest of a fortnight at Fort Reno, the main body resumed the march along the Bozeman Trail until it reached the fork of Big Piney and Little Piney Creeks, headwater streams flowing north to join the Powder and Yellowstone. On a grassy shelf near the fork the column was halted and ordered to camp. Carrington had found the place he was seeking for the second of the posts on the trail north. And it was a good site with unimpaired all round observation and long fields of fire. But it had the disadvantage that the nearest stands of pine to provide wood for the fort's stockade and fuel for its fires lay five miles to the west.

Some of the junior officers suggested the new fort should be named Carrington, but Carrington knew that recent policy disapproved of the use of the names of serving officers for forts and would not countenance this. The matter was resolved, however, when mail arrived from Fort Reno containing an Army order which told Carrington 'to post two companies at Fort Reno on Powder River, and four companies about eighty miles nearly north of Reno on the new route to Virginia City, Montana,' and added, 'this second post will be known as Fort Philip Kearny.'[16]

Life at the fort to start with was promisingly smooth. Detachments of men with wagons went out daily unmolested to cut timber for the building of the post which was planned to consist of some thirty log huts surrounded by a strong palisade. The early period of calm ended just as the palisade was being completed, when the Sioux staged a night raid, ran off about two hundred mules and horses, and killed five of the soldiers sent to pursue them. After this there was incident after incident in quick succession. Whenever the Sioux saw a chance of a hit-and-run raid, they moved against parties moving to and from the saw mill, or attacked those minding stock near the fort and ran off animals. One member of the garrison after many spells of sentry duty described the night scene at Fort Phil Kearny as follows:

'The clear nights were beautiful with a sky full of huge glittering stars; and sometimes a moon bathing the snow-clad

[16] US Congress, 50th, 1st sess. Senate Executive document 33, p. 55.

Big Horns in magical silver. By moonlight the limitless
expanse of hills and mountains seemed empty, the silence
broken by a deep roar of Big Piney. Late in the month wolves
began gathering after dark around the slaughter-yard near
Little Piney, howling and snarling over the offal there, ending
the peaceful nights. For a time sentries were permitted to
fire at the wolves; but the firing disturbed the garrison more
than the howls, so Colonel Carrington forbade the practice
and ordered poison to be put out to kill them. The unseen
but watchful Indians noted the change, and one night a
warrior donned a wolfskin, crept up to the stockade and shot
dead a sentry on the step.'

Attacks were also made on parties on the trail from Fort
Reno and a heavy toll was taken of the wagon trains which
over-hopefully followed the army north towards Montana.
Carrington interviewed the leaders of some of the civilian
trains that had been attacked, and was disturbed by reported
treacherous action by the Sioux. In two instances the Indians
had approached trains, expressed friendship, and then after
shaking hands and accepting presents of tobacco had shot
their benefactors.

There was no longer any doubt in Carrington's mind that
Red Cloud had opened aggressive operations. But in spite of
the hostility all round, he dispatched two companies seventy
miles march northward to establish Fort Smith on the Big
Horn River. Beyond Fort Smith were still 280 miles of trail
before the Montana goldfields were reached, but this was
through Crow country, and the Crows were friendly. It was
reckoned that only the section from Fort Laramie to Fort
Phil Kearny and on to Fort Smith needed to be policed.
About this time the over-conscientious Carrington sent off
one of his many ponderous reports. These explained in great
length, not only the difficulties he had in carrying out the
task assigned to him, but also the full details of all the steps
he was taking. Such long-winded rationales not unnaturally
did nothing to endear him to General Cooke back at headquarters on the Missouri, who thought he should be spending
more time doing his job and less in writing about it. By the

first snowfalls, all three forts—Reno, Phil Kearny and Smith—had been established; but it was Phil Kearny which the Indians raided most constantly, striking at the woodcutting parties and cutting out cattle from the herds.

In November a reinforcement of a company of cavalry arrived, along with Captain William J. Fetterman of the 18th Infantry. Fetterman had fought in the Civil War and been made a brevet Lieutenant-Colonel for his services. It might have been thought he would be a useful addition to the garrison, but, in the event he only added to the many cares with which Carrington was beset. In the Civil War, while Fetterman had been fighting gallantly in the field, the solid, conscientious Carrington had been engaged in training troops, a task for which he was specially suited. Before leaving an Eastern assignment Fetterman had been told unofficially that in an impending reorganisation of the Army in the West he would probably be chosen to replace Carrington as commander of the Montana District, and he was eager for this advancement. He thoroughly despised Carrington because he had not seen active service, and from the first day of his arrival was critical of the fort commander's cautious policy towards the Indians. Fetterman won over to his view a number of old comrades among the officers of the garrison, including the quartermaster, who became his special friend, and the clique he led challenged Carrington to adopt more aggressive tactics. Fetterman's view was that a few bold sorties might very well drive away the hostiles for good. 'A single company of regulars could whip a thousand Indians,' was his boast. 'Give me eighty men and I will ride through the Sioux nation.'

The schism between Carrington and Fetterman reached its climax on 21 December 1866 when a message calling for help was received from the wood-train which had been attacked by Indians while out collecting the fuel for Xmas. Carrington immediately mustered a small force under Captain James Powell and sent it out to support the woodcutters down by the gorge near Piney Island (see map). Soon after Powell left, Fetterman approached Carrington and pressed to be allowed to take part in the rescue operation, and Carrington weakly agreed. Fetterman also demanded that he be given overall command of all the troops outside the stockade, and this the colonel allowed too. But Carrington was worried at what his hot-headed subordinate might get up to, and not only gave him written orders limiting the distance he might go from the compound, but also sent the adjutant down to the gate to repeat the orders before Fetterman left. These written instructions read: 'Support the wood-train. Relieve it and report to me. Do not engage or pursue Indians at its expense. Under no circumstances pursue over the ridge, that is, Lodge Trail Ridge.'

After Fetterman had left, Carrington went up to the main outlook-platform to view the scene, and saw that Fetterman was not taking the track to the saw mill which passed south of the Sullivant Hills, but was following a route north of the hills leading towards the ford on the Bozeman Trail. It seemed as if he might be trying to cut the escape route of the Indians attacking the wood party. Seeing some Indians crossing the Bozeman Trail ford ahead of Fetterman's column Carrington ordered his gunners at the fort to drop a few rounds among them. When the first exploded one Indian fell from his pony and the rest scattered, galloping over Lodge Trail Ridge. In fact they were trying to decoy Fetterman's men over Lodge Trail Ridge, but Carrington did not realise this at the time, and was confident that Fetterman would obey the strict orders he had given not to go beyond the ridge. Meanwhile, Captain Powell, having reached the woodcutters, and seeing that the hostile Indians had disappeared away to the north, decided the lumbermen were now safe. After following the fleeing Indians to the top of Lodge Trail Ridge, which his instructions like Fetterman's told him not to cross, he turned and led his men back to the fort.

Earlier when Fetterman's party was approaching Lodge Trail Ridge the decoy Indians started racing their ponies back and forth on the slopes taunting the soldiers to follow them. Fetterman responded by ordering his infantry to open fire at the Indians and his cavalry to gallop round their flanks. Just as he was issuing these orders, the warriors who had been originally attacking the wood party appeared, and although most of them made off over Lodge Trail Ridge and away up the Bozeman Trail to the north-west, a few stayed to support the decoys. It is possible that Fetterman planned to cross Lodge Trail Ridge, kill as many of the outnumbered decoys as possible, and then swing back down the Bozeman Trail to the fort. But if he had intended to turn back when he reached the Trail, he changed his mind. Tantalised by the decoys ahead which offered such good targets, he sent all his men along the Trail after them. Nor did he attempt to stop them until they had followed the Bozeman Trail away from the fort over what came to be called Ambush Hill and reached the flats of Peno Creek on the far side. In this way he did exactly what the Indians wanted and put his column right in the middle of the huge ring of warriors waiting to ambush him. Two thousand Sioux, Cheyenne and Arapaho were concealed in the high grass of the flats and behind boulders on either side of the Trail as it descended rocky Ambush Hill, ready to pounce on Fetterman's men. Among those present was Chief Crazy Horse, who won a great name for himself that day by his bravery. In old age Red Cloud claimed to have directed the fighting, but Indian testimony suggests that he was not present. Whether he was there or not, however, the ambush was the successful climax of his long campaign of harassment.

As the only survivors were the Indians, it is not easy to reconstruct the final stages of the encounter. It seems that directly the decoy Indians had crossed to the far side of Peno Creek, first the dismounted warriors and then mounted ones surged on the soldiers from both sides as they descended the Trail towards the flats. The troopers forming the point in advance of the column quickly dismounted and formed a defensive ring. This allowed Fetterman to pull back his infantry among the scattered boulders on either side of the trail. The rest of the cavalry, meanwhile, dismounted, led their horses back up the trail and having released them sought shelter among the boulders. The shower of arrows lessened while the Indians concentrated on capturing the abandoned horses, after which it intensified again. For a time the infantry sheltered by the rocks seem to have held off their attackers, and killed a great many of them. But when ammunition ran short, the Indians surged forward, and a series of hand-to-hand conflicts took place, bayonets, knives and weapon butts versus scalping-hatchets and clubs. As they had sworn to do rather than face capture and torture, Fetterman and his friend the quartermaster loaded their last revolver cartridges, and with the weapons pressed against each other's temple, counted quickly in unison to three and squeezed triggers. Just before the end, Indian scouts watching from the tops of neighbouring hills signalled that reinforcements were coming from the fort. Then the chiefs passed the word that all the soldiers must be killed as quickly as possible. When this had been done, the Indians made off in bands towards the north. All eighty-one of Fetterman's force died; and the most reliable information suggests that at least sixty Indians were killed on the field of battle and another hundred died of their wounds later.

The relief force of fifty-four men under Captain Ten Eyck followed the Bozeman Trail across the ford and then turned and took up a position on the ridge east of Ambush Hill. Ten Eyck could hear distinctly the sound of firing in the distance, and presently a few small bands of Indians came back down the Trail and began taunting his men to come down and fight. This Ten Eyck would not allow. He stayed on the ridge until the last band of Indians had cleared off and then descended and led his men up the Bozeman Trail towards the place from which the firing had first been heard. Having followed the Trail over Ambush Hill he came upon the battlefield. A horrible scene it was, with Fetterman and his men lying dead among the rocks on the hillside, stripped, scalped and mutilated. Ten Eyck had most of the bodies loaded on the wagons he had brought, but as night was approaching not all could be collected; and a second visit to the battlefield had to be made for the remainder. On 26 December the corpses were buried with full military honours at Fort Phil Kearny.

The massacre of Fetterman and his men had brought the number of fatal casualties suffered while guarding the Bozeman Trail to 145; and the distraught Carrington immediately sent off a messenger to ride through the snow[17] to Fort Reno to report the sad affair and ask for reinforcements. This preliminary notification was passed to General Cooke at Omaha by telegraph, and without waiting for a full report Cooke sent orders posting Carrington and his regiment to Fort Casper, and replacing him with Lieutenant-Colonel Wessells. Cooke, who was soon to share the blame for the disasters on the Bozeman Trail, held the view that Carrington did not have the confidence of his officers and had shown himself incapable of maintaining discipline at the post. Carrington reacted mildly to the news that his junior Wessells was replacing him, but was bitter over the way Cooke had deliberately worded the order to make it appear that the reason was the massacre. He may, however, have taken some satisfaction from the War Department's abrupt removal of General Cooke himself from the command of the Department of the Platte shortly afterwards.

Meanwhile, throughout the tail end of winter and on into the spring of 1867 Fort Phil Kearny and Fort Smith stayed virtually besieged. In July 1867 Red Cloud's hostiles began a new series of raids on the wood-trains, and to meet these Wessells assigned full companies to guard the woodcutters and built by the saw mill a defensive post so that they had protection away from the fort. This corral on an open patch near Piney Island was made of wagon boxes arranged in an oval shape. It was put to the test early on the morning of 2 August when Indians were seen on the Sullivant Hills to the north. In command was the Captain Powell who had been in the field during the Fetterman massacre. He had remained at the fort and joined the regiment that had replaced the 18th when Carrington left. Unlike Fetterman on his fateful day, Powell now had a prepared defensive position near at hand; he also had a second advantage in that his men were all armed with a new breech-loading Springfield rifle. As the Indians came nearer, the woodmen and their guards rushed to man the wagon-box corral. The Indians attacked mounted, first circling the position and then charging in. The continuous fire from the new rifles, however, proved devastating;

[17] The epic ride by John (Portuguee) Phillips.

down went ponies and braves before they reached the wagon-boxes. The survivors pulled back, dismounted, and attacked again, this time on foot. The result was the same. Terrific fire, accurately delivered, stopped them in their tracks, until eventually they broke and fled.

On the day preceding the Wagon-Box fight, a similar attack was made against soldiers and civilians working in a hayfield near Fort Smith. As at Fort Phil Kearny the men were prepared for the assault, having built a nearby barricade; and they too were armed with the new rifle. Three soldiers were killed and four were wounded in this so-called Hayfield Fight; but the result was the same as at the Wagon-Box Corral. The Indians were driven off with heavy losses.

These two victories revenged the Fetterman Massacre, and might well have made safe the Bozeman Trail for travellers and achieved the object of the Army's winter operations, if the authorities had not decided otherwise. In the event, the Government had been so shocked by the catastrophies on the Trail in 1866 and 1867—particularly the Fetterman Massacre—that by 1868 it was willing to consider making peace with the Indians. At Fort Laramie in May 1868 a conference was held with the chiefs of the hostile tribes, and eventually terms were agreed upon which were generally favourable to the red men. The hostile bands promised to cease hostilities if the three forts on the Montana road were abandoned, and this meant that Red Cloud had won the war to retain his traditional hunting country east of the Big Horns. On the other hand, although they had gained their point about the abandonment by the whites of the Bozeman Trail, the tribes agreed to move to permanent quarters in the large reservation in Dakota which stretched east from the Black Hills to the Missouri and only visit the Bozeman Trail area on hunting expeditions.

Chapter 10

The Subjugation of the Plains Indians II: Custer's Last Stand and Wounded Knee

In August 1868, anxious for revenge for what Colonel Chivington had done, Black Kettle, at the head of several Cheyenne and other bands, began pillaging and murdering whites in the river valleys of central Kansas. His raids inspired a more general Indian uprising, and soon roving bands which included Kiowa and Apache, Arapaho and Comanche, were laying waste whole tracts of Kansas and northern Texas. The senior officer in charge of the area was Major-General Philip Sheridan, the great Union cavalry leader of the Civil War. Sheridan considered that the 2,000 troops at his disposal were not yet sufficiently proficient to deal with such widespread trouble, so he wisely spent a few months in training them. By mid-November he was ready to start, and his first operation consisted of a drive eastward on Fort Cobb in the valley of the Washita where Black Kettle was then on the rampage at the head of several Cheyenne and Arapaho tribes. The first column moved east from Fort Bascom, the second went southeast from Fort Lyon, and the third, under Colonel George A. Custer, marched from Fort Hays to Camp Supply on the Canadian River and then turned east like the others on Fort Cobb.

Custer had passed out bottom of his class at West Point at the time of the Civil War; but he soon established a reputation as a dashing cavalry leader and was made a Major-General of Volunteers at the age of twenty-five. He had commanded a division under Sheridan in the Wilderness and Shenandoah campaigns, and, while still under Sheridan, received the flag of truce sent forward by General Lee at Appomattox Court House. Sheridan later gave him the flag as a memento. During the Civil War Custer adopted an extravagant form of dress; according to eye-witnesses he was wearing at Lee's surrender a white sombrero, a flowing scarf, gold sleeve galloons, and had his hair as long as a woman's. In the Indian campaigns that followed, however, he apparently had his hair cropped and dressed himself soberly in the brown doeskin of a frontiersman.

In the Washita valley short of Fort Cobb, Custer stumbled on a fresh trail in foot-deep snow, and throwing caution to the winds, started in pursuit without waiting for the other columns. On reaching the Indian camp, and having been told by scouts that Black Kettle and his warriors were present, Custer staged an immediate assault. Before dawn four separate detachments slipped cautiously through the trees fringing the river bank and surrounded the Indian position. At daybreak they attacked, taking the camp completely by surprise. In the few hours hand-to-hand fighting on the banks of the Washita which followed, the Indians were completely overwhelmed, 103 being killed, including Chief Black Kettle. After this successful operation Custer slipped back to Camp Supply before other Indian settlements in the valley could rally. His decisive victory had broken all resistance, and soon afterwards the other chiefs came in and signed treaties agreeing to move into reservations in Indian Territory (Oklahoma).

For a few years there was peace in the area, then another outbreak occurred with bands stealing cattle, raiding isolated homesteads and attacking overland freighters in the Panhandle of Texas. The even more distinguished Major-General W. T. Sherman had now replaced Sheridan in command in the West. Like his predecessor he consolidated his forces before mounting operations against the hostiles. In 1874, after an Indian attack had cost sixty Texans their lives, he assembled his troops, formed five formidable columns, and sent them in from all sides against bands operating in the

Red River area. The Red River War went on throughout the winter. There were fourteen pitched battles and innumerable skirmishes in all of which the Americans proved too strong for the hostiles. In June 1875 resistance ended, and, discouraged and worn out, the half-starved Indians straggled back disconsolately in submission to their Indian Territory reservations.

In the same year that the Red River War ended, a Sioux war began in the area of the Big Horn River. The Sioux had been allotted a large reservation in western Dakota, but although it included their favourite Black Hills, they were far from satisfied. They made endless complaints about the supplies of flour, beef and blankets meted out by the Department of the Interior, and expressed dissatisfaction when the Northern Pacific Railroad was seen approaching their domains. The railroad was not only bringing settlers to Dakota, but a horde of buffalo hunters who killed the animals for their skins, which were sold in the East. The extermination of the buffalo was bringing an end to the Plains Indians' way of life, for as has already been explained, the Indians relied on the buffalo for most of their needs. About the same time, thousands of prospectors were also pouring in, seeking to buy land in the Black Hills where precious metals had been discovered.

The first sign of trouble occurred when bands of young braves started to slip away from the reserves and join up with non-treaty Indians south of the Yellowstone. Fearing trouble, and regardless of treaties guaranteeing the Indians the right to hunt in the area east of the Big Horns, the authorities ordered the Sioux to return to their reserves in Dakota by 1 February 1876. Two Sioux leaders, Sitting Bull and Crazy Horse, not only refused to return, but started collecting supplies in the Little Big Horn River area, indicating they were preparing to settle permanently away from Dakota. Reluctantly, the Commissioner of the Indian Bureau now recommended that force should be used to compel the Sioux to return to their reservations.

The two commanders of the departments concerned were ordered to organise columns to converge on the area south of the Yellowstone where the hostile Indians were assembling. Brigadier-General Crook based on Omaha was instructed to send a column northward from Fort Fetterman; and Brigadier-General Terry based on St Paul was told to send one column from Fort Ellis in the west and another from Fort Abraham Lincoln in the east (see map 16).

The eastern column was at first entrusted to Colonel Custer, but Custer had offended President Grant by the nature of the evidence he gave at impeachment proceedings against the Secretary of War, and, in spite of his success in the Washita War, he was removed from command. He made frantic efforts for reinstatement and was eventually allowed to go with the eastern column as commander of the 7th US Cavalry, a regular regiment of renown, though with many recruits in its ranks.

This affair, combined with bad weather delayed General Terry's two operations, but in early March, in wintry conditions Crook's 800-strong column got going. In the van leading north from Fort Fetterman was Colonel J. J. Reynolds and six companies of the 3rd US Cavalry. The cavalry came upon an Indian camp by the Powder River, assaulted it successfully, and drove the occupying bands of Sioux and Cheyenne away. However, the Indians staged a counter-attack and Reynolds in his turn was thrown back. After he had rejoined the main column, Crook marched back to refit and try again. But Crook's second attempt proved even less successful. On 17 June 1876 his force collided near the source of the Rosebud with 1,000 braves under Crazy Horse who had been sent south from the main Indian camp to contest the soldiers' advance. After a severe action lasting most of the day, Crook gave the Indians best and once more withdrew to seek reinforcements. The Indians returned to their camp in triumph, but decided nevertheless to move westward to a more secure situation. They went across from Rosebud to the Little Big Horn and laid out a new camp-village stretching for three miles on the west of the stream. By their victory on the Rosebud the Indians had thrown back one of the three American columns. They were elated and full of confidence.

Terry had by this time set his two columns in motion, but

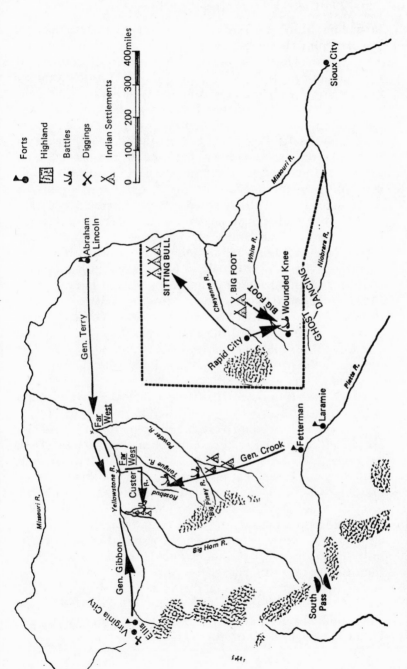

16. The Northern Plains

he had not heard of Crook's defeat. Gibbon's western column, starting from Fort Ellis, moved along the north bank of the Yellowstone. The main body which was mainly infantry did not contact any Indians, but the 2nd US Cavalry ranging south of the river beyond the Rosebud reported their presence in the valley of the Tongue. Terry's two columns were now approaching one another in the neighbourhood of the mouth of the Powder River where Terry set up his headquarters on the *Far West*, a river steamer chartered to transport supplies for the columns. Receiving the report of Gibbon's scouts concerning enemy presence on the Tongue, Terry sent forward Major Reno with his squadron from the eastern column to carry out a thorough reconnaissance. Reno's route took him to the Rosebud, and when he turned upstream he discovered the trail left by Crazy Horse's Sioux when returning from their victory over Crook's column. This trail, and other trails of Indians changing camp, led westward toward Little Big Horn. Satisfied that the new Indian camp-village lay in that direction, Reno retraced his steps to report to General Terry.

On the evening of 23 June 1876 General Terry had a conference with Gibbon and Custer in the cabin of the *Far West* moored to the bank of the Yellowstone near the mouth of the Rosebud. Terry said he estimated the Indian force as 1,000 warriors, and considered that unless they were surrounded and forced into battle they would flee to the western mountains as soon as they discovered the approach of the soldiers. He therefore ordered Gibbon and his infantry to move back to the mouth of the Big Horn to attack the Indian camp from the north. Estimating that Gibbon could not be in position before 26 June, he sent Custer and the 7th US Cavalry on a detour round to the south so that by the time they were in position to attack the camp from that direction, Gibbon would also be ready for a combined assault. Terry fully understood that the more forceful attack would come from Custer's cavalry, and offered him six of Gibbon's Crow scouts, hereditary enemies of the Sioux, to help him on his way. He also offered the squadrons[1] from the 2nd US Cavalry with Gibbon's force and two Gatlings. Custer gratefully

[1] More commonly called companies.

accepted the scouts, but declined the additional horsemen and the machine-guns. The latter he said, in truth, would slow his march; the 2nd US Cavalry he explained, less plausibly, were not necessary as his own men were enough for the task.

On the next morning, Terry gave Custer his orders in writing, stating that he must conform to them unless there was sufficient reason for not doing so. (In the event he did not conform, but whether sufficient reason existed has never been fully decided.) At noon, the 7th US Cavalry with Custer at their head rode past General Terry, and then began their march up the Rosebud. With scouts ahead they advanced steadily and cautiously, and that evening went into bivouac by the stream. At 9 p.m. the scouts came in and reported that a short distance ahead the Sioux trail discovered by Reno left the Rosebud and led across over the ridge between that stream and the Little Big Horn. Although it was now quite dark Custer ordered an immediate advance, stating that he wanted to reach the summit of the ridge, a distance of ten miles, before daylight. By advancing straight across to the Little Big Horn, and not making a detour to the south as Terry ordered, Custer had now lost all chance of co-operating with Gibbon's column in the north.

In the inky blackness progress was slow; but at 2 a.m. they came to Crow's Nest, a high point on the ridge from which there was a good view in every direction. As soon as it was light, some Indian scouts climbed to its summit from where their sharp eyes were able to pick out an immense herd fifteen miles ahead, undoubtedly close to the Sioux camp. Custer, who by now was experienced in this sort of fighting, believed the Indians would strike camp and escape directly they saw his troops approaching. He was sure that the only way to bring them to battle was to surprise them. He therefore decided to lie in concealment all next day, and then make a surprise night attack. Two circumstances, however, made him change his mind. During the march a pack fell off, and when a sergeant was sent back to recover it he found some Indian warriors examining it. On sighting the sergeant, the Indians rode off; but the Americans' approach had obviously been revealed. Also from the top of the Crow's Nest Sioux scouts were noticed moving away quickly towards the Indian camp. Because of these two incidents Custer realised that any attempt at surprise was useless. He decided to attack at once.

Custer divided his command into three. He sent Captain Benteen with 125 men on a detour over the bluffs to the south, telling him 'to pitch into anything' he might find; he ordered Major Reno to advance with his squadron along the south bank of the tributary running into the Little Big Horn; and he himself advanced at the head of the remainder of the regiment along the north bank. Following along opposite banks Custer and Reno advanced cautiously for about nine miles, their lines of march almost parallel, sometimes close together, sometimes as much as 300 yards apart. Shortly after 2 p.m. a lone *tipi* was sighted, and Custer immediately bore down on it. It proved to be the remnant of an Indian village, all the *tipis* having been removed except for this one which contained the body of a warrior. While the scouts were setting it on fire, an interpreter scanning the country ahead noticed a heavy dust cloud a few miles farther on, and between it and the *tipi* a party of Sioux in flight downstream. The man turned in his saddle and shouted excitedly, 'There, Colonel, are your Indians! Running like devils!' Instantly Custer ordered the Crows in pursuit, but they refused. Reno was just coming up at the head of his squadron, and Custer sent his adjutant across with a message. It told Reno to go forward as fast as he could, and charge the Indians when he caught them up, adding that he would be supported soon by the whole outfit.

When this order to attack was given, Sitting Bull's camp was not visible. Aside from this small party in flight there were no Indians in sight. The dust indicated a force on the move of considerable size, but Custer did not realise that 4,000 of the fiercest, bravest and most daring of warriors[2] were awaiting Reno in the valley of the Little Big Horn, warriors elated by their victory over Crook's column, and some of them armed with new Winchester repeating rifles.

[2] Sioux (Oglala and Hunkpapa bands) and Cheyennes.

Reno's squadron, accompanied by the adjutant, covered the three miles along the tributary (later to be named Reno Creek) to the Little Big Horn at a sharp trot. Sergeant Ryan later wrote, 'We arrived at the bank of the Little Big Horn and waded to the other side, and here there was a very strong current, and quicksand about three feet deep. On the other side of the river we made a short halt, dismounted, tightened our saddle girths, and then swung into our saddles.'

When the main body reached the far side, the scouts came galloping back to report that the Sioux camp was just ahead, and that the Indian party they were chasing had turned to attack them. The adjutant now retraced his steps to report to Custer, while Reno drew up his force in the fringe of some trees on the west bank in preparation for an attack. After a few moments spent in forming up, Reno led his squadron forward, two troops in line and one in reserve. In this formation they approached the camp, the first few *tipis* of which could now be seen through shifting clouds of dust two miles downstream. Reno called the reserve troop into line with the others, and taking up his position twenty yards in front gave the order for 'The Charge' to be sounded. Then he led his men forward at the gallop. A heavily timbered bend of the river jutted into the valley on the squadron's right, beyond which flowed the glistening river. To the front, between them and the nearest tipis of the camp a quarter of a mile away, were hundreds of yelling Indians. Some of these were already starting to ride round Reno's squadron's left flank, and many were already starting to shoot at the cavalrymen.

Reno was somewhat at a loss as he started forward into battle. Looking back he saw no sign of anyone coming to his support, and by now he had expected the aid of Custer's men, and perhaps of Benteen's squadron as well. Noticing the huge numbers of his opponents, and not wishing to sacrifice his command by leading them straight into the jaws of death, he speedily made a change of plan. Instead of continuing towards the camp, he led his men across into the trees on their right, and having ordered them to dismount, got them to take up a defensive position and send their horses back among the trees for protection. For something like half an hour there followed a battle in the wood while all the time the Indians moved round the troopers' left flank. At this stage Reno had only lost one man who was shot through the breast, but his ammunition was running low, and a quick survey of the situation convinced him that he must get out. He gave the order to mount, and then lined up his men in a clearing in the trees. Already beset by Indians who had rushed into the wood after them, they next formed an irregular column, and galloped out, pistols drawn, in a dash for the ford they had crossed earlier. Troopers and scouts were now falling: some died in the wood; others were killed as they emerged. The pressure of the masses of Indians blocking the escape route was too strong for the reduced force to break through, so Reno swerved to the left and led his men towards a place on the river bank more than a mile downstream from where they had first crossed. The head of the column reached the river in fair order, but hundreds of Indians closed in on their rear. Racing along, they pumped their new Winchesters as fast as they could load and fire, ducking behind the shoulders of their ponies whenever a trooper raised a pistol. At the river-bank a drop of six feet to the water below checked the horses, many of which refused at first to jump. The presssure of those behind forced them over the crumbling bank, and down they went, men and horses floundering together in the water. Meanwhile the pursuing Indians poured a steady rain of bullets into the jam of troopers; and 29 out of the 112 who reached the river were killed and scalped before the crossing was negotiated. On the far bank the land rose to a scarp towering above the stream, and up its slope the panting men and horses struggled. As they arrived, the discomfited scattered remnants of the force were gathered together and reformed on the summit, the uninjured being hastily posted to fend off the next Indian attack. Had many followed across the river, Reno's force might well have been wiped out. Those Indians, however, who did cross and were advancing up the slopes, had their attention diverted to another area where four miles to the north Custer's squadron was advancing upon them.

Meanwhile, Benteen's detachment, which had left the

route the rest were following, had travelled towards the bluffs to the south, and found no evidence of Indians. The ground was cut by gullies and ravines and consisted of bad lands of a rugged type not easily passable by anything but goats. After going about twelve miles Benteen felt satisfied that nothing was to be found, and turned back in the direction the regiment had taken when he left. After covering fifteen more miles, he reached the line of march near the burnt out remains of the *tipi* which had contained the dead warrior. Continuing to follow Custer's trail, he encountered first a sergeant sent back to hurry up the ammunition, and then an orderly who told him there was a big Indian camp ahead and that Custer wanted him to hurry and bring up the pack animals with the spare ammunition, still way back along the trail. Then, when Benteen's detachment came to a rise in the ground they saw the valley of the Little Big Horn to the front. There in the dust and smoke things were happening which must have dismayed them. An overwhelming force of yelling, painted Indians, sweeping and swooping from all directions were riding down and killing the rear members of a little band of soldiers who were trying first to reach the river, and then the safety of Reno's defence position on the scarp on the other side. These were the last of his men who had been unhorsed and left behind in the mad rush from the wood. Some of the pursuing Indians halted and opened fire from across the river upon Benteen's men as they appeared on the skyline, but the range was too great, and the shots fell harmlessly at their feet.

Drawing pistols, Benteen's men trotted forward towards Reno's improvised position on the hilltop. As they came up, Reno, his head bandaged with a handkerchief, ran forward to meet them exclaiming, 'For God's sake Benteen, halt your command and help me, for I have lost half my men.' Many of Reno's party, including Reno, were obviously overwrought. Some were firing their revolvers aimlessly at Indians out of range thousands of yards away. A subaltern of K Troop, however, seemed cool enough. 'I'm damned glad to see you, Benteen,' he said. 'We had a big fight in the valley and got whipped like hell.' Benteen was a man of great presence, and as brave as a lion. He quickly brought order out of confusion. He divided his party's ammunition with Reno's men who had almost exhausted theirs in the fight in the valley; he sent off a messenger to hurry up the ammunition-mules; and he set about reconstituting the defence around the top of the hill. For a time, however, they were not menaced by the Indians, most of whom had left to join the fight in the north from where battle noises could now be heard distinctly. As a series of distant volleys rang out clearer than before, Captain Weir of D Troop sprang to his feet and exclaimed, 'If that's Custer, we ought to go and help him.' He then asked Reno's permission for his unit to go to Custer's aid. When Reno demurred, he rode forward with his men without receiving it. Later Reno changed his mind and followed Weir with the whole of his command. Well in advance, Weir was the first to top the pinnacle (later called Weir Point) on the ridge ahead, and saw in the distance three miles away the smoke and dust of a battle. He was just ordering his men forward when hundreds of Indian warriors rode up the slope and drove them back. Soon the whole of Reno's command were in retreat. They were forced back to their old defence position on the hilltop where they were hemmed in by a ring of Indian braves. For three hours, until the light began to fail, the 350 troopers fought back against the Indians pressing in on them from all sides. Relief came with darkness when, their blood-lust seemingly satisfied for the moment, the Indians returned across the river to their camp for a great war dance illuminated by bonfires. When darkness set in the defenders of the hilltop improved their defences. Sergeant Ryan wrote: 'We went to work with what tools we had, consisting of two spades, our knives and tin cups . . . and using these and pieces of hard-tack boxes for spades, commenced throwing up temporary works. We also formed breastworks from boxes, sacks of bacon, corn and oats, blankets, in fact anything we could get hold of. During the night ammunition and rations reached us.'

At dawn a single rifle shot rang out followed at a short interval by another. It was the enemy's signal to renew the attack, and soon from all directions came the crashing fire of the

Sioux and Cheyenne. During the fiercest of the fighting bugle calls were heard and the hills were scanned for the signs of a relief column. But it was found to be a captured bugle blown as a ruse. The Indians worked ever closer, taking advantage of terrain and sage brush to escape being hit. They massed first in the south, and hurled themselves at Benteen's part of the line. Believing the best means of defence was to attack, Benteen called his men to their feet and led them in a counter-charge which threw back the Indians in confusion. Next Benteen went across to Reno's part of the perimeter and persuaded him to carry out a similar manoeuvre. This achieved equal success. Thirst became a torment for the defenders, especially among the wounded in the improvised hospital housed in a shallow depression in the centre of the position, but volunteers gallantly slipped down to the river and filled canteens which they brought back to afford some relief. For this feat nineteen men later received the Congressional Medal of Honour.

Early in the afternoon of the second day the siege relaxed, and by late afternoon only an occasional shot reminded the defenders to stay under cover. The Indians next fired the prairie grass around their camp village, and a thick wall of smoke hid their *tipis* from view. Soon, an immense procession of horsemen, women and children on foot, and loose ponies and dogs emerged from behind the smoke. The Indians were departing. The ordeal of Reno's and Benteen's men was over.

The Oglala Chief Low Dog and the Hunkpapa Chief Gall both took part in the battles against the 7th US Cavalry. From their accounts it seems that Custer, not realising the vast numbers in the village, thought that the Indians would escape him if he did not attack immediately. After following Reno's trail for a mile or two he turned north well short of the ford by which Reno's men crossed the Little Big Horn. No doubt he originally intended to reinforce Reno's attack, but on second thoughts decided to move round to the north and come in on the village from that direction at the same time as Reno's squadron was attacking it from the south. It is known that soon after turning off north Custer sent back a sergeant to hurry up the reserve ammunition, and later dispatched an orderly to bring Benteen's squadron to his support—not to support Reno which is what occurred. In the north Custer seems first to have led his men to attack the Indian camp down the ravine called Medicine Tail

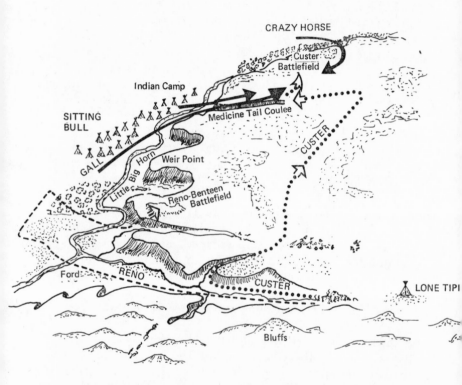

17. The three battlefields of Little Big Horn, 1876

Coulée. He was stopped by a horde of charging mounted Indians who forced him up again on to the top of the escarpment which flanks the river on the east. Afterwards, in his improvised defence position on the summit, he was attacked by vast bands of Indians moving in from all directions.

According to Chief Gall, Sitting Bull, who was the senior

Sioux chief present, did not lead his men in the battle. He remained in his *tipi* making medicine to propitiate the supernatural. The principal leaders were Gall who, after attacking Reno's squadron, charged up at the head of his warriors from the south, and Crazy Horse, General Crook's conqueror, who led his men right round the north of Custer's position and swept in at the rear. Other Indian bands crossed the river due west of Custer's position, pressed up the ravines and crashed into his flank. Caught in rough terrain unsuited to mounted action, and surrounded by overwhelming numbers of Sioux and Cheyenne warriors, Custer's squadron swiftly disintegrated. Judging by the position of the corpses, the troops seem to have made individual stands fighting on foot against waves of Indians that surged in from every direction. One troop covered the south of Custer's selected battleground, another the east, while on the west, two moved down into the head of a ravine to stop attacks from that direction. Yet another straddled the central ridge; and at the north end, where Crazy Horse's men blocked an escape route, a knot of fifty men gathered around Custer and his red and blue personal pennant, shot their horses for breastworks and fought to the last round and the last man. Inspired by their gallant leader they fought on for hours, but by 5 p.m. the only living member of Custer's command on the whole northern battlefield was an officer's horse named Comanche. Badly wounded this animal limped its way to safety. It was the sole survivor of Custer's last stand.

On Reno's hill during the last afternoon of the second day the men watched the Indians depart with relief tinged with a fear that they might return. During the following night the troopers buried their dead, still fearful that dawn might see a renewal of the attack. At daybreak, however, when they looked out down the valley they saw a comforting long blue column marching towards them. It was General Terry and the 2nd US Cavalry. When the relief party arrived, they reported the sad fate of Custer's squadron whose bodies a scouting party had discovered on the hill in the north. Most of them had been stripped, scalped and mutilated, but strangely, Custer's body had been left untouched. There he lay like a Saxon hero surrounded by the bodies of his men-at-arms. His expression was so peaceful that it seemed he had fallen asleep rather than met his death in the heat of battle.

The news of the slaughter of Custer's men stirred the feelings of the American people to such an extent that for a time the liberal views of the humanitarians of the East were no longer heard, and there was a demand that the Northern Plains Indians be subdued without delay. After the Battle at Little Big Horn the Sioux and Cheyenne bands involved had broken up and gone their separate ways. Soon they were to be pursued and engaged by powerful reconstituted columns of troops led by Crook and Terry. Although encounters with bands of any size were few, those there were resulted in defeat for the Indians, and by the autumn many of them had slipped back to their agencies to surrender. Next spring Crazy Horse gave in. Meanwhile Sitting Bull took part of his people over the border into Canada. He vowed he would never accept the restrictions of a reservation. Finally, however, disappointed with the food supplies available in Canada, he too surrendered. Thus the campaigns carried out by the United States Army during 1876–77 accomplished their objectives. The Sioux were compelled to abandon permanent residence on their hunting grounds south of the Yellowstone River, and were forced to accept Government control through its Indian Agents in their allotted reservations. What was more the frightened chiefs were forced to sell areas in the mineral-bearing Black Hills to prospectors.

The campaigns described above ended serious Indian resistance to American expansion and development in the West, though there was trouble with the Nez Perce in the northwest mountains in 1877, and an unhappy clash with the Teton Dakota (Sioux) at Wounded Knee in the Black Hills in 1890.

The Nez Perce and Cayuse were generally friendly to white intruders, though the Cayuse murdered Dr Whitman and his wife, and twelve men at the Whitman mission in 1847. These tribes, along with neighbouring Crow and Blackfoot, had accepted expulsion from parts of their traditional territories. But the discovery of gold on the Salmon River in western Idaho in 1877 led to the imposition of a more restricted reservation area for the Nez Perce, and although some chiefs agreed, others, including Chief Joseph, at first hesitated, and then refused to surrender their lands.

When pressure was applied, they made a historic fighting withdrawal of some 1,500 miles across the Bitterroot Mountains, through Yellowstone Park, past the Montana goldfields and on towards the Canadian frontier. They were pursued and harassed by columns under Brigadier-General Howard and Brigadier-General Miles, both experienced Indian fighters, and were finally forced to surrender just short of asylum in Canada on 5 October 1877; but Chief Joseph is generally considered to have conducted the retreat of his peoples with such tactical skill as to be classed as an Indian Napoleon. This and the noble words he was reported to have uttered when surrendering, 'Hear me, my chiefs, I am tired; my heart is sick and sad; from where the sun now stands, I will fight no more, for ever . . . .' aroused sympathy in the East. Nevertheless, the settlement that resulted was by no means generous. Only part of the Nez Perce were at first allowed to return to their ancestral lands; the bulk were moved unwillingly to Indian Territory (Oklahoma).

The Wounded Knee affair in 1890, another massacre, this time of Indians, resulted from the activities of a medicine man named Wovoka. At the time of an eclipse of the sun, Wovoka, suffering from high fever, believed he was transported to heaven and told that if the Indian people would indulge in certain ghost dances and incantations their shirts would be made immune to bullets and their dead would arise and help them drive the whites from their country. Wovoka's prognostications aroused great interest among the tribes of the Northern Plains. Several delegations were sent to confer with the prophet, and Sitting Bull, seeing another chance to hit back at the whites, gave his support. There followed extensive ghost dances held on the southern Badlands by Indians from the reservations east of the Black Hills. These dances made the congregated Sioux excited and potentially dangerous, and Indian Agents began to feel that control of their wards was slipping from their hands, and were soon demanding that troops should be sent to restore order. For example, one Dakota Agent wired: 'Indians are dancing in the snow on the Badlands and are wild and crazy . . . we need protection and need it now . . . the leaders should be arrested and confined in some military post.'

These calls for help from the Agents brought a quick response from President Harrison (1889–93). The army was ordered to take over from the Department of the Interior, and some three thousand soldiers were marched south-east from Rapid City towards the Badlands where the ghost dancing was in progress. The arrival of the military quickly quietened the scene. Ghost dancing in the Badlands almost stopped, but it was learned that Sitting Bull in the Standing Rock Reservation in the north was still fomenting violence, so Indian Reservation police, supported by two troops of cavalry, were sent to arrest him. Sitting Bull was found sleeping on the floor of his hut when the police broke in. At first he seemed to agree to go peacefully; but after being dragged out half-dressed, and taunted by his son for submitting so weakly, he changed his mind, and cried out: 'I am not going! I am not going!' This caused a fight between the Indian police and Sitting Bull's supporters, Indian versus Indian, shooting, clubbing, stabbing and choking one another. By the time the cavalry moved in, Sitting Bull, his son, and eight of his followers had been killed—and six Indian policemen.

There was not much reaction to the news of Sitting Bull's death, for the old medicine man had long lost favour with his people. But there was still another Sioux chief on the rampage. This was Big Foot from the central reserve lying between Sitting Bull's reserve in the north and the Badlands in the south. Big Foot was moving down to the ghost-dancing area just as the army was dispersing the earlier arrivals for the dancing, and driving them back to the reservations. As Big Foot's people made their way into the nightmarish terrain of the Badlands, seeking fellow Indians, but finding none, they bumped into a body of the 7th US Cavalry commanded by Major Whitside. Big Foot was down with pneu-

monia, and riding on a travois; but one of his followers raised
the white flag for him, and the band, having surrendered,
were conducted to a small nearby post named Wounded
Knee, and allowed to go into camp. Soon after this, Colonel
Forsyth arrived with the rest of the regiment and took over
command from Whitside. Forsyth had the soldiers tie up the
horses in lines, and set up an orderly tented camp alongside
the Indians; then, as a precaution, he placed his four Hotchkiss machine-guns in position on a nearby hill to command
the Indian camp.

The night passed without incident, and next day the
warriors were assembled in a circle, sitting on their blankets,
so that the disarmament of the band might be carried out.
Small groups of braves were sent back, one group at a time,
to collect weapons from the *tipis*; but when this search produced only a few unserviceable muskets the soldiers took over
themselves. They rooted round thoroughly, bringing forth
screams of protest from the squaws, and glowerings and
growls from the squatting warriors; but they only managed
to find some forty weapons, all of which were either old or
in bad repair. While the search was in progress, unbeknown
to the military, a medicine man was moving among the sitting braves exhorting them to strike the white man, and
telling them to wear their ghost shirts, so that bullets would
not harm them.

The search completed, the soldiers confronted the warriors
again, and one, seeing something suspicious, dropped on his
knees to look beneath the blanket of a squatting Indian. The
Indian immediately jumped to his feet, whipped out a rifle
from under the blanket, and fired. Instantly, as though they
had been awaiting a signal, the other warriors did the same.
Then, with rifles exploding right in the faces on both sides,
all hell was let loose. With magazines empty, they continued
the struggle using the butts of weapons, or clubs and knives.
The crews manning the machine-guns had by this time
sprung into action. Fearing to fire into the mêlée, they opened
on those fleeing the fight and entering the camp. They killed
a lot of warriors, but also a number of squaws and children,
and set most of the *tipis* on fire. The Indian loss was appalling,

some 170 including Big Foot; but 60 troopers also lay dead or wounded.

At Wounded Knee, that tragic field of melancholy name, there died the belief in the Ghost Dance as a panacea for Indian ills, for ghost shirts all too clearly failed to turn back bullets. There also died with Big Foot and his band the last spark of organised resistance in the Plains Indians.[3]

---

[3] When I was visiting the area in April 1973 there was trouble at Wounded Knee. Sheriffs and Sioux were shooting it out, with fatal casualties on both sides.

Chapter 11

Conclusion

After the subjugation of the Plains Indians the way was open
for a multitude of eager homesteaders to populate the area
much of which had earlier been known so erroneously as the
Great American Desert. The principal colonisers were the
railroad companies. They stood to benefit doubly from western
settlement, for newcomers would not only buy the large
areas beside their tracks which the government allowed
them to dispose of, but would also create a through traffic.
The companies set about the task of attracting pioneers in
a thorough-going way. They distributed a mass of literature
from their immigration bureaus, and advertised widely, not
only in centres of population in the East, but also in Britain,
Holland, Germany and Scandinavia. The results were reward-
ing. In the immediate post Civil War years, it is reckoned
that 14,000,000 people moved west; and between 1860 and
1930, some 30,000,000 immigrants arrived in America.

The central line pushing west beyond Omaha on the
Missouri brought the first significant influx. Then came the
Northern Pacific and Great Northern. These two lines were
extended across Dakota, which by 1873 boasted a population
of more than 20,000. In 1875 with the discovery of gold in
the Black Hills came a second Dakota boom, and there arrived
10,000 prospectors who created a new market for farm produce. Meanwhile, the Kansas Pacific and Santa Fé railroads
were helping to develop the territories of the south-west. The
soil of the Red River basin proved very fertile. First-comers
achieved such splendid yields that soon a large number of
hopeful homesteaders were heading in that direction, and by
1875 prosperous farms stretched for three hundred miles along
the valley.

Homesteading began to get underway in Dakota, Montana and Wyoming when it was realised that the eastern areas could nurture small-grain crops, and that the western plains which sustained such vast herds of buffalo could equally well support domestic stock like cattle. With settlement came demands for statehood. Dakota—where the Massacre of Wounded Knee took place—was organised as a Territory in 1861 with its capital at Yankton; but there followed such a long drawn-out political struggle as to which town should finally be the capital of the prospective State that in the end the north and south segments stayed separate. Thus, in 1889 North Dakota with Bismarck as its capital and South Dakota with Yankton were both admitted to the Union. Montana—which saw the battles of Little Big Horn and the long fighting march and surrender of the Nez Perce—received its first significant influx of immigrants in the early 1860s when gold was discovered, and mining camps were established at Gold Creek, Bannock, Helena and Virginia City. In May 1864 Montana was organised as a Territory with first Bannock, then Virginia City and finally Helena as its seat of government. In 1880 its first railroad was built, and in 1883 a transcontinental line was completed across its territory. Although founded on mining, Montana came later to depend mainly on agriculture. The major crop is hard winter wheat grown on the upland plateau and plains in the central and eastern areas. The valleys produce such diversified crops as sugar beet and beans. Corn and hay are also produced to feed the beef herds. The income from cattle and sheep raising is a major contribution to the economy, and a natural reserve of forest has led to a growing wood products industry. Montana became a State within the Union in 1889.

Wyoming—the scene of the Fetterman Massacre—began to be settled when the Union Pacific Railroad pushed across its southern plains in 1867–8. News of its valuable grazing soon spread and brought an influx of Texas cattlemen and their herds in the early 70s. The discovery of gold and coal was a further impetus to settlement. Wyoming was organised as a Territory in its own right in 1868. The very next year it granted equal suffrage to women—the first such act in

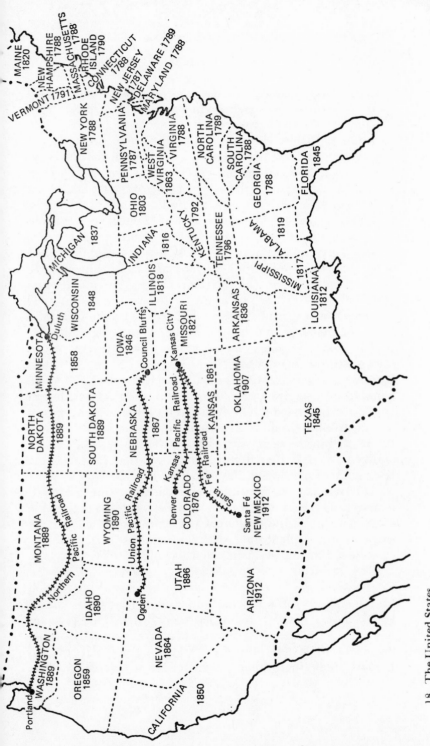

18. The United States

America. Admission to the Union as the 44th State came in 1890.

Kansas and Nebraska being nearer at hand were settled early on, and reached statehood in 1861 and 1867 respectively. Oklahoma, although equally convenient, was at first barred to white settlement because it was Indian territory; but it was eventually forced to open up a substantial portion of its lands through agitation and pressure by forceful private individuals. Officials of the railroad lines crossing Oklahoma petitioned Congress to open some Indian lands in 1874, but no action was taken. Then, a great deal of publicity was given to the fact that 2,000,000 acres of good land in the heart of Indian Territory had never been assigned to any of the tribes, and must therefore be available for white settlement. In 1879 a few bands of homesteaders drifted into the unalienated area, but were driven out again by federal troops. In 1880 an intrusion was made by David L. Payne at the head of a group of pioneers, and for the next few years he and other prospective Oklahoma homesteaders tried several times unsuccessfully to establish themselves in Indian Territory. Known as Boomers, they formed a society called the Oklahoma Colony to give an air of legality to their actions; but in 1884 attempts ended after Payne and his followers, now grown to some five hundred, were surrounded, arrested and removed. Payne died in the same year, after which his mantle descended on W. L. Couch. Couch sent several bands of Boomers into Indian Territory during the winter of 1884–5. Most of these were driven out, but four hundred men led by Couch himself managed to avoid the cordon of troops and established a settlement in Stillwater Creek. When surrounded, Couch threatened to fight it out. After his supplies ran short, however, he led his disconsolate followers out of Oklahoma again.

Next, the scene shifted to Washington where expansionist Congressmen put pressure on the authorities to extinguish Indian claims on the two main unoccupied portions, known as Oklahoma District and Cherokee Outlet. This pressure combined with more invasions by Boomers eventually turned the scales in favour of white settlement in Oklahoma. In January 1889 the Indians were forced to surrender their rights in the areas concerned in exchange for a cash award, and two months later President Harrison (1889–93) and Congress opened the districts to settlers under the Homestead Act.

In 1887 the Dawes General Allotment Act, initiated and supported by many people sympathetic to Indians, had been passed. This ended tribal relationships and gave a private plot to each Indian with the intention of turning him into an industrious farmer. The reserves were divided into family-sized farms of 160 acres for each adult in the family and 80 acres for each child. The allotted lands were held for a time in trust by the government, after which there was outright possession with rights of sale. Some tribes successfully resisted individual allotments, and in the south-west it was scarcely put into practice. Nowhere was it very successful. Many Indians were unable to adapt to European ways, and when permitted to do so leased or sold their lands to whites at bargain prices.

At first the Dawes Act did not apply to Indian Territory, but on 2 May 1890 a white-style organisation was set up there, and, during 1891, millions more acres were opened to white settlers in tribal lands, besides the two areas already alienated. Then, in 1905 the Indians of Oklahoma were persuaded to forgo tribal ways and accept allotment under the Dawes Act, which put them in line with the white homesteaders living among them. They then joined with the whites in preparing a constitution so that on 16 January 1907 Oklahoma was able to enter the union as a State.[1]

The end of the story of American expansion enfolds a flirtation with imperialism following the Spanish-American War of 1898. In 1895 the Cuban people revolted against their Spanish masters, and the battleship *Maine* was sent to protect American business interests. On the night of 15 February with the crew settling in their hammocks, the *Maine* was rocked by a tremendous explosion and sank in Havana harbour, carrying with her 260 members of the crew. This

[1] In 1924 the Dawes Act was superseded by the Indian Reorganisation Act which reintroduced some tribal government.

caused a wave of war-fever in the United States where the popular cry was, 'Remember the Maine! To Hell with Spain!' A full-scale war followed with American attacks in the West Indies and in the Pacific. In 1898, San Juan Hill at Santiago in the south-east of Cuba was spectacularly stormed by a force which included the Rough Riders (1st US Volunteer Cavalry) led by a distinguished pioneer and future President Theodore Roosevelt; and in the same year an American squadron under Admiral Dewey destroyed a Spanish fleet in Manila Bay in the Philippines. In 1899 the Filipino insurgents who had been fighting the Spaniards turned upon the American troops when it became clear they had come to stay. It was not until March 1901 that the principal insurgent leader Aquinaldo was captured and the war was over, though in 1898 the Philippines had already been ceded by Spain by the Treaty of Paris, 1898 to the United States. At the conclusion of hostilities with Spain, Puerto Rico and Guam also became possessions of the United States. But none of the above, nor the Panama Canal Zone ceded in 1903, were to become States within the Union. On the other hand Alaska, which had been purchased from Russia in 1867 for $7,200,000 in gold, reached statehood in 1959; and Hawaii, which had been dominated by American missionaries and traders since the 1820s was organised as a Territory in 1900 and became a State with the Union, also in 1959. The above States and the others which form the present United States are shown on map 18 together with the date of accession and the present population. This completes the story of the conquest of the West and of American expansion up to the present time (1974).

Indian Groupings by Language[1] of Tribes Mentioned, and their Locations

I

II Athapascan

Kiowa-Apache of Plains: Apache and Navaho of southwest.

III Algonquian

Delaware, in the Eastern Woodlands.
Sauk and Fox in the Midwest and around the Great Lakes, Chippewa, Arapaho, Atsina (Gros Ventres), Blackfoot, and Cheyenne, on the Plains.

IV Iroquois-Caddoan

A. Iroquois

Erie, Huron (Wyandot), Iroquois (Mohawk, Oneida, Onendaga, Cayuga, Senecal, Mingo, Tuscarora), Cherokee in the Eastern Woodlands of Canada and US.

B. Caddoan

Wichita bordering the Plains in the south-east–Red River area. Pawnee on the Eastern Plains–Revolution River area. Arikara on the Missouri.

Gulf

Chickasaw, Choctaw, Creek and Seminole, in the southeast; with the Cherokee, these formed the 'Five Civilised Tribes' who later were moved to Indian Territory (Oklahoma).

VI Siouan

Crow, Dakota Sioux (Teton Dakota-Oglala, Brulé, Hunkpapa and Miniconjou) Mandan, Osage on the Plains.

[1] After Harold E. Driver (Alvin M. Josephy Jr. pp. 15–22).

VII Utaztecan-Tanoan-Kiowan

A. Utaztecan

Bannock, Shoshoni and Ute, in the Great Basin and Rocky Mountains. Comanche on the Plains.

B. Tanoan

Taos Pueblos in New Mexico.

C. Kiowan

Kiowa on the Southern Plains.

VIII Mosan

A. Salishan

Flathead on the North-west Plateau.

IX C Klamath-Sahaptin

Cayuse and Nez Perce on the Columbia River Plateau.

Presidents of the USA 1789–1909

1	George Washington[a]	1789–93–97
2	John Adams	1797–1801
3	Thomas Jefferson	1801–05–09
4	James Madison	1809–13–17
5	James Monroe	1817–21–25
6	John Quincy Adams[e]	1825–29
7	Andrew Jackson[a]	1829–33–37
8	Martin Van Buren	1837–41
9	William Henry Harrison[ac]	1841
10	John Tyler[d]	1841–45
11	James Knox Polk	1845–49
12	Zachary Taylor[a]	1849–50
13	Millard Fillmore	1850–53
14	Franklin Pierce	1853–57
15	James Buchanan	1857–61
16	Abraham Lincoln[b]	1861–65, 1865
17	Andrew Johnson[d]	1865–69
18	Ulysses S. Grant[a]	1869–73–77
19	Rutherford B. Hayes	1877–81
20	James A. Garfield[b]	1881
21	Chester A. Arthur[d]	1881–85
22/24	Grover Cleveland	1885–89, 1893–97
23	Benjamin Harrison[f]	1889–93
25	William McKinley[b]	1897–1901
26	Theodore Roosevelt[d]	1901–05–09

a = ex-general
b = assassinated in office
c = died in office
d = vice-president when predecessor died
e = son of 2nd president
f = grandson of 9th president

Bibliography

ABERNATHY, T. P. *Western Lands in the American Revolution* (New York, 1937).

ABERT, J. W. *Journal of Lt. James W. Abert: from Bent's Fort to St Louis in 1845* (Senate Documents 438—Washington, 1846).

ADAMS, J. T. *Atlas of American History* (New York, 1943).

ALLEN, J. H. *History of the American Bison* (Washington, 1877).

ALTER, J. C. *Jim Bridger* (Columbus, 1951).

AMBLER, C. H. *George Washington and the West* (Chapel Hill, 1936).

ANDERSON, N. *The Desert Saints: The Mormon Frontier in Utah* (Los Angeles, 1972).

AUTOMOBILE CLUB OF SOUTHERN CALIFORNIA *Guide to the Mother Lode Country* (Los Angeles, 1972).

BAILEY, L. R. *The Long Walk: a History of the Navajo Wars 1846–68* (Los Angeles, 1964).

BAILEY, P. *The Ohio Company of Virginia and the Westward Movement 1748–1792* (Glendale, 1939).

BAKELESS, J. *Daniel Boone* (New York, 1939).

Background to Glory: The Life of George Rogers Clark (Philadelphia and New York, 1957).

BANCROFT, H. H. *History of the North Mexican States and Texas* 2 vols (San Francisco, 1884–89).

History of California 7 vols (San Francisco, 1884–1890).

History of Oregon 2 vols (San Francisco, 1886–88).

History of Nevada, Colorado and Wyoming (San Francisco, 1890).

BARKER, E. C. (ed.) *History of Texas* (Dallas, 1929).

BATES, C. F. *Custer's Indian Battles* (New York, 1936).

BERKLEY, W. C. *The Texas Revolution* (Baton Rouge, 1952).

BERTHRONG, D. J. *The Southern Cheyennes* (Norman, 1963).

BILLINGTON, R. A. *Westward Expansion* (New York, 1949).

The Far Western Frontier (New York, 1956).

BLEDSOE, A. J. *The Indian Wars of the Northwest* (San Francisco, 1885).

BOND, B. Jr. *The History of Ohio* (Columbus, 1941).

BRACKETT, A. G. *History of the US Cavalry* (New York, 1865).

BRIGGS, H. E. *Frontiers of the North-west: a History of the Upper Missouri Valley* (New York and London, 1940).

BRODIE, F. M. *No Man Knows My History: The Life of Joseph Smith* (New York, 1945).

BROSNAN, C. J. *Jason Lee, Prophet of New Oregon* (New York, 1932).

BROWN, D. *The Fetterman Massacre* (London, 1972).

BROWN, R. H. *Historical Geography of the United States* (New York, 1948).

BURNS, A. W. *Daniel Boone's Predecessor in Kentucky* (Frankfort, 1930).

CARRINGTON, J. B. 'Across the Plains with Bridger as Guide' (*Scribner's Magazine,* vol. 85, pp. 66–71, New York, 1929).

CASTANIDE, C. E. (trans. and ed.) D. R. M. CARO *et alia The Mexican Side of the Texas Revolution by the Chief Mexican Participants* (Dallas, 1936).

CATLIN, G. *North American Indians* 2 vols (Edinburgh, 1926).

CAUGHEY, J. W. *Gold is the Cornerstone* (Berkeley, 1948).

(ed.) *The Emigrants' Guide to California* (Princeton, 1932).

CHABOT, F. C. *The Alamo* (pamphlet San Antonio, 1936).

CLARK, T. D. *The Story of Westward Movement* (New York, 1959).

A History of Kentucky (New York, 1937).

CLARK, W. S. 'Pioneer Experience in Walla Walla' (*Washington Hist. Qly* vol 24, 1933).

CLARKE, D. L. *Stephen Watts Kearny* (Norman, 1961).

CLAYTON, W. *William Clayton's Journal* (Salt Lake City, 1921).

CLELAND, H. *George Washington in the Ohio Valley* (Pittsburgh, 1955).

CODY, W. F. *Adventures of Buffalo Bill* (New York, 1904).

COOKE, R. B. *Washington's Western Lands* (Strasburg, 1930).

COTTERILL, R. S. *History of Pioneer Kentucky* (Cincinnati, 1917).

COY, O. C. *The Great Trek* (Los Angeles, 1931).

CREER, L. H. *Utah and the Nation* (Seattle, 1929).

CREMONY, J. C. *Life Among the Apaches* (San Francisco, 1868).

CROOK, G. *Autobiography* (Norman, 1946).

CURTIS, E. S. *The North American Indian* 20 vols (Norwood, 1907–30).

CUSTER, E.   *Following the Guidon* (New York, 1890).
CUSTER, G. A.   *A Wild Life on the Plains* (St Louis, 1891).

DALE, L. (ed.)   *The West of William H. Ashley* (Denver, 1964).
DE VOTO, B.   *Across the Wide Missouri* (Boston, 1947).
DRIVER, H. E.   *Indians of North America* (Chicago, 1961).
DRURY, C. M.   *Marcus Whitman M.D. Pioneer and Martyr* (Caldwell, 1937).
DUNAWAY, F.   *A History of Pennsylvania* (New York, 1935).
DUNHAM, H. H.   *Governor Charles Bent* (Denver, 1951).
DUNN, J. P.   *Massacres of the Mountains—a History of the Indian Wars of the West 1815–75* (New York, 1886).

EMMETT, C.   *Fort Union and the Winning of the South-west* (Norman, 1965).
EVANS, H. C.   *Kansas: a Guide to the Sunflower State* (New York, 1939).

FLETCHER, F. N.   *Early Nevada* (Reno, 1929).
FOLWELL, W. W.   *A History of Minnesota* 2 vols (St Paul, 1956).
FORTESCUE, HON. J. W.   *A History of the British Army* vol. III (London, 1902).
FRANKS, J. M.   *Seventy Years in Texas* (Gatesville, 1924).
FRANZ, J. B. *et alia*   *Battles of Texas* (San Antonio, 1967).
FRAZER, R. W.   *Forts of the West* (Norman, 1965).
FREDERICK, J. V.   *Ben Holladay: the Stagecoach King* (Glendale, 1940).
FREEMAN, D. S.   *George Washington* 7 vols (New York, 1949).
FRITZ, P. S.   *Colorado the Centennial State* (New York, 1941).

GANOE, W. A.   *The History of the United States Army* (New York, 1924).
GITTINGER, R.   *The Formation of the State of Oklahoma* (Berkeley, 1917).
GOETZMANN, W. H.   *Army Exploration in the American West 1803–63* (New Haven and London, 1959).
GRAHAM, W. A.   *The Custer Myth* (Pennsylvania, 1953).
GRINNELL, G. B.   *The Cheyenne Indians* 2 vols (Newhaven, 1923).
GUDDE, E. C.   *Sutter's Own Story* (New York, 1936).

HAFEN, L. R.   *The Mountain Men and the Fur Trade of the Far West* 7 vols (Glendale, 1965).

HAFEN, L. R. AND A. W. (eds.)   *Powder River Campaign and Sawyer's Expedition of 1865* (Glendale, 1961).
   Relations with the Indians of the Plains 1857–61 (Glendale, 1959).

HAFEN, L. R. AND GHENT, W. J.   *Broken Hand—the Life Story of Thomas Fitzpatrick, Chief of the Mountain Men* (Denver, 1931).

HAFEN, L. R. AND YOUNG, F. M.   *Fort Laramie and the Pageant of the West* (Glendale, 1938).

HAINES, F.   *The Nez Percés* (Norman, 1955).
   Oregon in the USA (Seattle, 1954).
   The Appaloosa Horse (Livingston, 1950).
   The Story of Idaho (Boise, 1942).
   Red Eagles of the North-west (Portland, 1939).

HARMON, G. D.   *Sixty Years of Indian Affairs 1789–1850* (Chapel Hill, 1941).

HARRINGTON, M. R.   *Indians of the Plains* (Southwest Museum Leaflet 15 Los Angeles, undated).

HEBARD, G. R. AND BRINNISTOOL, E. A.   *The Bozeman Trail* 2 vols (Cleveland, 1922).

HILL, L. B.   *A History of the State of Oklahoma* (New York, 1908).

HINES, H. K.   *Missionary History of the Pacific North-west* (Portland, 1899).

HOIG, S.   *The Sand Creek Massacre* (Norman, 1963).

HOLMAN, F. V.   *Dr. John McLoughlin—the Father of Oregon* (Cleveland, 1907).

HOUSTON A. J.   *Texas Independence* (Houston, 1938).

HOWBERT, I.   *The Indians of Pike's Peak Region* (New York, 1914).

HULBERT, A. B.   *The Forty-Niners* (Boston, 1931).

HYDE, G. E.   *Spotted Tail's Folk—A History of the Brulé Sioux* (Norman, 1961).
   Red Cloud's Folk—A History of the Oglala Sioux Indians (Norman, 1937).

JACKSON, E. (ed.)   *Letters of the Lewis and Clark Expedition* (Urbana, 1962).

JACKSON, D. AND M. L. SPENCE (eds.)   *The Expeditions of John Charles Frémont* (University of Illinois, 1970).
   The Expeditions of John Charles Frémont Map Portfolio (University of Illinois, 1970).

JAMES, J. A. *George Rogers Clark Papers 1771–84* 2 vols (Springfield, 1922–26).
The Life of George Rogers Clark (Chicago, 1928).
JOSEPHY, ALVIN M. *The Indian Heritage of America* (London, 1972).

KAPPLER, C. J. (compiler) *Indian Affairs: Laws and Treaties* 2 vols (Washington, 1904).
KEIN, DE B. R. *Sheridan's Troopers on the Borders* (Philadelphia, 1885).
KERN PAPERS (Huntington Library San Marino California).
KING, C. *Campaigning with Crook* (Norman, 1964).
KLUCKHOHN, C. AND LEIGHTON, D. *The Navaho* (Cambridge, 1946).
KNOPF, R. C. (ed.) *Anthony Wayne's Correspondence* (Pittsburgh, 1960).
KORNS, J. R. 'West from Fort Bridger' (*Utah Hist. Qly.* Vol. 19, 1951).
KROEBER, A. L. *Handbook of Indians of California* (Bulletin 78, Washington, 1925).
Cultural and Natural Areas of Native North America (Berkeley, 1939).

LA FARGE, O. *The American Indian* (New York, 1956).
LECKIE, W. H. *The Military Conquest of the Southern Plains* (Norman, 1963).
LEUPP, F. E. *Indians of the South-west* (Philadelphia, 1897).
LOCKWOOD, F. C. *The Apache Indians* (New York, 1936).

MCFARLING, L. (ed.) *Exploring the Northern Plains 1804–76* (Caldwell, 1955).
MACLEOD, W. C. *The American Indian Frontier* (New York, 1928).
MADSON, B. D. *The Bannock of Idaho* (Caldwell, 1958).
MALIN, J. C. *Indian Policy and Westward Expansion* (Bulletin Univ. of Kansas Lawrence, 1921).
MARSHALL, S. L. A. *Crimsoned Prairie* (London, 1972).
MATTES, M. *The Great Platte River Road* (Lincoln, 1969).
Fort Laramie and the Forty-Niners (Estes Park, 1949).
MAYHALL, M. P. *The Kiowas* (Norman, 1962).
MILES, N. A. *Personal Recollections* (Chicago and New York, 1896).

MORGAN, D. L. *Jedediah Smith and the Opening of the West* (Indianapolis, 1958).

MORISON, S. E. *Oxford History of the American People* (Oxford University Press, London and New York, 1965).

NEFF, A. L. *History of Utah 1847–69* (Salt Lake City, 1940).

NEVINS, A. *Frémont* (New York, London and Toronto, 1955).

NIBLEY, P. *Brigham Young, the Man and his Work* (Salt Lake City, 1936).

NICOLLET, J. N. *Report on Upper Mississippi River* (Senate Report 237 Washington, 1843).

NATIONAL PARK SERVICE: HISTORICAL HANDBOOK SERIES *Custer Battlefield* (Washington, 1962 and various dates).
  Fort Laramie (Washington, 1962 and various dates).
  Fort Necessity (Washington 1962 and various dates).
  Fort Union (Washington, 1962 and various dates).
  King's Mountain (Washington, 1962 and various dates).

OEHLER, C. M. *The Great Sioux Uprising* (New York, 1959).

PARRISH, R. *The Great Plains* (Chicago, 1907).

PAUL, R. W. *California Gold* (Cambridge, 1947).

PAXSON, F. L. *The Last American Frontier* (New York, 1922).

PORTER, K. W. 'Roll of Overland Astorians 1810–12' (*Oregon Hist. Qly*, vol. 34, 1933).

PREUSS, C. (trans. and ed.) E. G. AND E. K. GUDDE *Exploring with Frémont* (Norman, 1958).

PRICE, G. F. *Across the Continent with Fifth Cavalry* (New York, 1883).

PRIEST, L. B. *The Reformation of US Indian Policy 1865–87* (New Brunswick, 1942).

PRUCHA, F. P. *Guide to the Military Posts of the United States* (Madison, 1964).

PUREY, W. A. *The Wilderness Road to Kentucky* (New York, 1921).

QUAIFE, M. M. (ed.) *Kit Carson's Autobiography* (Lincoln 1935).
  The Capture of Old Vincennes: Narratives of G. R. Clark and Gov. H. Hamilton (Indianapolis, 1927).

RANCK, W. *Boonesborough* (Louisville, 1901).

REEVES, J. S. *American Diplomacy under Tyler and Polk* (Baltimore, 1907).

RICH, E. E. (ed.) *The Letters of John McLouglin* (Toronto, 1941–44).

RICHARDSON, R. N. *Texas—The Lone Star State* (New York, 1943).
The Comanche Barrier to the South Plains Settlements (Glendale, 1933).

RIPLEY, R. S. *War with Mexico* 2 vols (London, 1850).

ROBINSON, D. *A History of the Dakota or Sioux Indians* (Minneapolis, 1956).

ROCKWELL, W. *The Utes—A Forgotten People* (Denver, 1956).

RODENBOUGH, T. F. *From Everglade to Canyon with the Second Dragoons* (New York, 1875).

ROOSEVELT, T. *The Winning of the West* (London, 1900).

ST CLAIR, A. Narrative (Philadelphia, 1812).

SABIN, E. L. *Building the Pacific Railway* (Philadelphia,1919).
Kit Carson Days 1809–68 2 vols (New York, 1935).

SCHMITT, M. F. AND BROWN, D. *Fighting Indians of the West* (New York, 1948).

SEGER, J. H. *Early Days among the Cheyenne and Arapaho Indians* (Norman, 1934).

SELBY, J. *US Cavalry* (booklet illustrated, Reading, 1972).
US Marine Corps (booklet illustrated, Reading, 1972).

SETTLE, R. W. (ed.) *The March of the Mounted Riflemen from Fort Leavenworth to Fort Vancouver* (Glendale, 1940).

SEYMOUR, F. W. *Indian Agents of the Old Frontier* (New York, 1941).

SHAW, L. *True History of Some of the Pioneers of Colorado* (Hotchkiss, 1909).

SHERIDAN, P. H. *Personal Memories* 2 vols (New York, 1888).

SHERMAN, W. T. *Memoirs* 2 vols. (New York, 1892).

SKINNER, B. C. L. *Pioneers of the Old South-west* (New Haven, 1919).

SMITH, E. T. *Magnificent Missourian—Life of Thomas Hart Benton* (Philadelphia, 1958).

SMITH, J. H. *The War with Mexico* 2 vols (New York, 1919).

SPAULDING, O. L. *The United States Army in War and Peace* (New York, 1937).

STEVENS, O. A. 'Nicollet's Expedition of 1839' (*N. Dakota Hist. Socy*, vol. 21, 1954).

SUTTER, J. A.   *The Diary of Johann Augustus Sutter* (San Francisco 1932).

TALBOT, T. (ed.) C. H. CAREY   *Journals* (Portland 1931).

TAYLOR, C.   'Charles Bent has Built a Fort' (*Bulletin of Missouri Hist. Socy*, vol. II, pp. 82–4, Oct. 1954).

THOMPSON, R.   *The Golden Door* (London, 1969).

THORNDIKE, R. S. (ed.)   *The Sherman Letters* (New York, 1894).

THWAITES, R. G. AND KELLOGG, L. P.   *Documentary History of Lord Dunmore's War* (Madison, 1905).

TONER, J. M. (ed.)   *Journal of Colonel George Washington* (Albany, 1893).

TWITCHELL, R. E.   *The Military Occupation of New Mexico 1846–51* (Denver, 1909).

US ARMY PUBLICATIONS   *Fort Leavenworth* (USA CGSC, 1957).

US CONGRESS   *Indian Hostilities* (40th 1st sess Executive Document 13 Washington, 1868).

Indian Operations on the Plains (50th 1st sess Senate Executive Document 33 Washington, 1888).

US INTERIOR DEPARTMENT   *Annual Report on Indian Affairs 138* (Washington, 1860).

Annual Report on Indian Affairs 36 (Washington, 1868).

UPTON, E.   *The Military Policy of the United States* (Washington, 1917).

UTLEY, R. M.   *Frontiersmen in Blue* (New York, 1967).

VESTAL, S.   *Sitting Bull, Champion of the Sioux* (Norman, 1957).

Warpath, The True Story of the Fighting Sioux (Boston, 1934).

WALKER, E. F.   *America's Indian Background* (Southwest Museum Leaflet 18 Los Angeles, undated).

WALLACE, E, AND E. A. HOEBEL   *The Comanches, Lords of the South Plains* (Norman, 1952).

WEBB, W. P.   *The Great Plains* (Boston, 1931).

The Texas Rangers (Boston, 1935).

WHARTON, C. R.   *History of Texas* (Dallas, 1935).

WHEELER, H. W.   *Buffalo Days* (New York, 1925).

WILLIAMS, S. C.   *Dawn of Tennessee Valley and Tennessee History* (Johnson City, 1937).

WISSLER, C.   *Indians of the United States* (New York, 1946).
North American Indians of the Plains (New York, 1912).
WORTHAM, L. J.   *A History of Texas* 5 vols (Fort Worth, 1924).

YOAKUM, H.   *History of Texas* 2 vols (New York, 1856).
YOUNG, O. E.   *The West of Philip St George Cooke 1809–1895* (Glendale, 1955).

ZOLLINGER, J. P.   *Sutter, The Man and his Empire* (New York, 1939).

Index

Adams, President John 63
Adams, President John Quincy 83
Alabama 78, 80n, 81, 90
Alamo 125n; the fall of 128–137
Alaska 246
Albuquerque 174
Allegheny Mts 19, 32, 53, 160
Allegheny River 21, 23, 24, 27, 32
Almonte, Col. 133, 136, 142
Alligator, Chief 88
American Fur Company 97–99, 102–104, 157
American River 165n, 166, 180–183
Apache 146, 156, 175, 176, 187, 200–202, 221
Apalachiocola River 82
Appalachians 17, 35n, 42, 90
Appaloosa 99
Appomattox C. H. 222
Anahuac 126
Angel's Camp 191,192
Arapahos 100, 200–209, 221
Arikara 200
Arizona 175–177, 186, 201
Arkansas 90, 99
Arkansas River 85, 86, 104, 148, 157, 161, 167, 168, 172, 203–208
Armijò, Gov. M 145, 173
Ashley, William Henry 96, 97
Astor, J. J. 91, 92, 94, 97, 103
Astoria 91, 92, 94
Auburn 181, 182
Austin, Moses 123, 124
Austin, Stephen F. 124–145, 203

Bad River 90
Baltimore 31
Bannock 242
Bannocks 72n, 201
Barbe- Marlouis 63
Bascombe, Fort 221
Bear Flag 171, 172, 176
Bear Lake 97, 98n

Bear River 114, 157, 184
Becknell, William 149, 150
Bedford, Fort 32, 33
Belknap, Fort 204, 205
Bent, Charles 157, 161; Gov. New Mexico 174
Bent, George 167
Bent's Fort 104, 149, 157, 161, 167, 168, 172, 173
Benteen, Capt. 228–236
Benton, Fort 209
Benton, Senator T. H. 158, 168
Big Foot, Chief 238–240
Big Horn Mts. 209, 210, 220, 223
Big Horn Rivers 96–98, 201, 212, 223–236
Bird, Fort 32
Bismarck 242
Blackfoot 73, 92, 94, 100–105, 157, 159, 236
Black Hawk, Chief 84
Black Hills 202, 220, 223, 236–240
Black Kettle, Chief 207–209, 221, death 222
Blue Mts. 93
Blue Ridge 42, 48
Boise, Fort 157
Boise River 163
Bonham, James Buller 138n
Bonneville, Capt. B. L. E. 97–104, 168
Bonneville, Fort 97
Boomers 244
Boone, Daniel founds settlement in Kentucky 36–42; 70, 172
Boonesborough 40–42
Boston 73, 91, 99
Bouquet, Col. 33–35
Bowie, James 127, 132; his knife 132n; in Alamo 133–137
Bozeman Trail 209–220
Boulder 197
Braddock, Gen. 31, 56

Bradstreet, Maj. 34
Brandywine 49, 58
Brannan, Samuel 114, 180, 183
Brazos 124, 130, 141, 142, 202–205
Bridger, James 97–115, 157, 159, 109, 212
Bridger, Fort 114, 120, 186
Brigham 118
British North-West Company 91–94, 154
Broad River 49
Brock, Maj.-Gen., Isaac 76
Brown, Aaron V. 186
Brown's Hole 97
Brule 200
Buchanan, President James 119, 120, 187
Buenavista 172n
Burgoyne, Gen. 42
Burleson, Col. 128, 140
Burnet, D. G. 140–142
Bushy Run 33, 34
Butterfield, John 186–190

Cahokia 42, 47
California 98, 112, 114, 118, 119, 146–198
Campbell, William 48–50
Camden 48
Camp Supply 221, 222
Canada 21, 26, 33, 34, 62, 236, 237
Canadian Rangers 60n
Canadian River 205, 221
Carolina, N. 36–40, 49–53
Carolina, S. 48–50, 82
Carrington, Col. 212–220
Carson, Kit joins Young's expedition to West Coast 151–156; 157; joins Frémont's expeditions 158–177; 201, 204
Carson City 118
Carthage 112
Castro, Gen. 169, 171
Cayuse 92n, 93, 94, 163n. 236
Cedar City 118

Central City 197
Cerré Mts. 97
Central Pacific Railroad 190
Champlain, Lake 17
Charleston 48
Charlotina Colony 19
Charlotte 48
Chattanooga 52
Cherokee 38, 40, 48, 52, 84, 85, 131, 144, 199n
Cheyenne 86, 159, 200–209, 221–236
Chickamauga 51, 52
Chickasaw 56, 74, 84, 85, 199n
Chile 181
China 181
Chippewa 76n, 89, 90, 200
Chivington, Col. John initiates massacre of Cheyenne 207, 208; 221
Chotaw 84, 85. 199n
Clark, Fort 204
Clarke, George Rogers founds settlement Illinois 42–48, 51, 58, 70
Clarke, Capt. William 58–60; crosses to W. Coast with Lewis 70–74; 91, 92, 197
Clatsop, Fort 73, 91
Clearwater 94, 105
Clinch, Gen. D. L. 87
Clinch, River 36, 38
Coast Range 103, 165
Cobb, Fort 221, 222
Cody, William 188
Coeur d'Alenes 198
Coloma 178–183
Colorado 100, 188, 197; 206–208
Colorado River (Texas) 124, 140, 141, 154–163, 175, 204
Columbia River 73, 91–97, 98n, 170, 193
Colvile, Fort 193
Comanche 72n, 85, 146–149, 187, 200–206, 221
Comstock T. P. 194–196

Comstock Lode 196
Connecticut 34, 55
Connor, Gen. 210
Cooke, Philip St. George 85, 173, 175, 212, 214, 219
Coosa River 80
Cornstalk, Chief 39
Cornwallis, Gen. 48, 50n, 53
Couch, W. L. 244
Council Bluffs 184, 190
Cowpens 49
Cos, Gen. 127–131
Crazy Horse, Chief 217–220, 223–236
Creek 48, 52, 58, 78–84, 132, 199n
Crockett, Davy 80; in Alamo 132–140; 172
Crook, Brig.-Gen. 224–236
Crows 92, 200, 202, 214, 228, 236
Cruger, Col. 48
Cuba 245, 246
Cumberland, Fort 23, 31, 32
Cumberland Gap 31
Cumberland Mts. 36
Cumberland River 17, 40, 51–53, 84, 104
Cumorah Hill 106–108
Cummings, Alfred 120n
Custer, Col. George A. routs Indians on Washita 221–223; at Little Big Horn 223–236

Dade, Maj. 87, 88
Dakota 105, 220, 223, 236–242
Dallas 144, 163
Dalles 93
Davis, Jefferson 85
Dawes Act 245
Defiance, Fort 59, 61
Delawares 19, 34, 35, 84, 98, 168, 205
Denver 159n, 188, 197, 206
Des Moines, Fort 86
Deseret 116
Detroit 32–34, 46, 76

Dewey, Adm. 246
De Witt, 125, 127
Dickinson, Mrs. 137, 140
Dinwiddie, Lt.-Gov. Robert 20–28
Dobb, Fort 205
Dodge, Col. 85–87
Dolores Mine 146
Donelson, John 51, 52
Dripps, Capt. 158
Drips, Andrew 99, 102
Dry Diggings 181, 182
Duncan, Fort 204
Dunmore, Lord 39
Duquesne, Marquis 21
Duquesne, Fort 28, 31

Echo Canyon 114n
Edwards, Hayden 125
El Paso 146, 186
Ellis, Fort 224–226
Erie 17
Erie Lake 19, 21, 32, 34, 59, 77, 84
Everglades 87–89

Fallen Timbers, battle of 60, 61, 70, 76
Fannin, Col. J. W. 137–140
Fargo, W. G. (Wells Fargo) 187–190
Feather River 181, 182, 191
Ferguson, Maj. on King's Mountain 48–50
Fetterman, Fort 224
Fetterman Massacre 119–220
Fetterman, Capt. William J. 215
Field, Col. 39
Finny, James 194–196
First Dragoons 85–87, 150, 172, 175
First New Mexico Volunteer Cavalry 201
Fitzpatrick, Thomas 97, 99, 102, 157–162, 204
Five Civilized Tribes 84n, 199, 204
Flatheads 93, 101, 105
Florida 63–67, 74, 78, 80–83, 87–90

Floyd, John 36
Fontenelle, Lucien 98–100
Forbes, Gen. 31–33
Forsyth, Col. 239, 240
Forty-Eighters 182–184
Forty-Niners 184–186, 190–192
Fox, 76n, 84
Franklin 149n
Franklin, Benjamin 19
Fraser River 193
Frazier, John 21, 23, 32
Fredonian Revolt 125
Frémont, John C. 112, 156n, his
   expedition to W. Coast 158–177
Fry, Joshua 28, 29

Gadsen, James 177
Gadsden Purchase 177n
Gains, Gen. 87
Gall, Chief 233
Galveston Island 142
Garden Grove 113
Gates, Gen. 48
George II 20
George III 35n
Georgia 58, 68, 74, 80, 82, 138
Gibbon, Brig.-Gen. 226–236
Gibson, Fort 85, 86
Gila River 151, 156, 175, 177n, 186
Gillespie, Lt. 170–177
Gist, Christopher 21–30
Gladwyn, Capt. 32
Golden Gate named by Frémont 171
Golden 197
Goliad 123, 128, 131, 137, 140, 143
Gonzales 127, 135, 138, 140
Graham, Fort 204
Grand Canyon 154
Grant, President 197, 224
Gray, Capt. 73, 91
Great Kanawha River 20, 36, 39;
   battle of 40
Great Lakes 19
Great Meadows 24, 29, 30
Great Northern Railroad 241

Great Salt Lake 103, 112, 114, 115,
   162, 167, 168, 186, 190, 201
Great Smoky Mts. 48
Green River 97–99, 104, 105, 114,
   157–168, 184
Greenbrier Company 19
Greenbrier River 19
Greene, Nathanael 58
Greenville, Fort 58, 59
Greenville, Treaty of 61
Gregory, John H. 197
Gros Ventres 100
Guadalupe River 127
Guadalupe Hildalgo, Treaty of 174,
   177
Guam 246

Hall, Fort 104, 157, 162, 163, 201,
   209
Hamilton, Fort 55
Harrisburg 141, 142
Harrison, Gen. W. H. 74–77, 238,
   245
Harte, Bret 191, 192
Hastings Cut-off 168, 186
Hastings, Lansford W. 112, 168n
Havana 245
Hawaii 166, 181, 246
Hayfield Fight 220
Hays, Fort 221
Helena 242
Helm, Capt. 44, 46
Henderson, Richard 40, 42, 53
Henry's Fork 97
Henry, Gov. Patrick 42
Hillsborough 50
Holladay, Ben 188–190
Holston River 36n, 38
Holston 40, 43, 53
Homestead Act 245
Honolulu 166, 170, 181
Horse Creek 97, 99

Houston, Sam 131–40, leads ' Runaway Scrape' 140–142, wins battle of San Jacinto 142–144, 145
Howard, Brig.-Gen. 237
Hudson's Bay Company 91n, 93, 94, 104, 154, 157, 162–166, 181
Hull, Brig.-Gen. William 76
Humboldt River 103, 168, 184, 186
Hunkpapa 200
Huntington, Collis P. 190, 191
Huron 17
Huron Lake 32

Idaho 105, 197, 198, 201
Illinois, 19, 42, 43, 48, 51–53, 58–61, 73, 74, 84, 110, 111
Independence 109
Indiana 61, 74
Iowa 90, 112
Iroquois 17, 34, 45, 60n

Jackson, Gen. Andrew 80–83, 132, 133
Jackson's Hole 97
Jaredites 108
Jay, Chief Justice John 62
Jay's Treaty 62
Jefferson, President Thomas 63–74
Jefferson, Fort 56, 57
Jesup, Gen. Thomas S. 87, 88
Joncaire, Capt. 25
Johnston, Col. A. S. 119, 120
Joseph, Old Chief 94, 237
Joseph, Young Chief 94n
Judah, Theodore D. 190

Kanaka 166
Kane, Thomas L. 120
Kansa 149, 150
Kansas 84, 159, 200, 202, 207, 221, 244
Kansas City 149n, 158
Kansas Pacific Railway 241
Kaskaskia 42–47

Kearney, Fort 212
Kearny, Fort Philip (Phil) 212n, 213–220
Kearny, Col. Stephen Watts, 86, 87; conquers New Mexico 172–177, 188
Kentucky 17, 36, 40–43, 48, 53, 59, 61, 64, 70, 74, 77, 151
Kern, Edward M. 168
King, Fort 87
King's Mountain, battle of 49–51
King William's American Regiment 49
Kiowa 86, 200–206, 221
Kiowa Apache 200–206
Kirtland 109, 113, 119
Klamath 164, 170
Knoxville 74

Lacy, Edward 49
Lamanites 108
Lamar, M. B. 144, 145
La Pointe 90
Lapwai 94
Laramie River 98
Laramie, Fort 104, 114, 117, 157–159, 206, 210, 212, 220
Larkin, Thomas O. 169, 182, 183, 191
Las Vegas 118
Leavenworth, Fort 113n, 149n, 172, 184, 188
Leavenworth, Gen. 85, 86
Leavenworth, Col. Jesse 208
Le Boeuf, Fort 21–33
Lee, Rev. Jason 93
Lehi, Prophet 108
Lewis, Gen. 39
Lewis, Meriwether 59n; crosses to W. Coast with Clark 70–74, 91, 92, 197
Ligonier, Fort 32, 33
Lincoln, Abraham 84
Lincoln, Fort Abraham 224
Little Raven, Chief 208, 209

Livingston, Robert R. 63–69
Logstown 21, 24, 26, 30
Long, Maj. S. H. 159
Los Angeles 118, 154–156, 175, 176, 180, 186
Louis XVI 43n
Louisville 43n
Louisiana 74, 78, 85, 90, 147
Louisiana Purchase 62–69, 83, 91
Lyon, Fort (Bent's) 207, 221

McAfees 36
McDowell, Joseph 48–50
Mackenzie, Donald 92
McLaughton, Patrick 194–196
McLoughlin, Dr. John 93, 94, 154, 163
Madrid 62
Magoffin, James W. 173
Malden, Fort 76, 77
Manchester N.Y. 106, 107
Mandan 70–74, 200
Manila Bay 246
Mansker, Kasper 51
Marengo 63
Marin, Gen. de 24, 25
Marshall, James Wilson finds gold at Coloma 178–180; 183
Maryland 54, 55
Mason, Col. 176, 182, 183, 191, 201
Massachusetts 34, 54
Matamoros 137
Maumee 58, 59, 60, 61, 76
Mazatán 170
Meigs, Fort 78, 80
Memphis 186
Merritt, Ezekiel 171
Mexico 91, 123, 144–149, 169–177, 181, 186
Mexico City 87, 124, 145, 170, 172n, 173
Miami 35, 55–61, 99
Michigan Lake 32
Michigan State 61
Michilimackinac, Fort 32–34

Milam, Ben 125, 128–30
Miles, Brig.-Gen. 237
Mims, Fort 78, 80
Mims, Samuel 78, 80
Mingoes 21
Miniconjou 200
Minnesota 90, 147, 200
Mississippi Company 20
Mobile 78, 80
Mohave 154
Mohawk 17
Mokelumne River 191
Monongahela 21, 24, 29, 30
Monroe, President James 63–69, 83
Montana 105, 209–220, 237, 242
Monterey 103, 169–172, 176, 180
Monterrey 172n
Mormons (Latter-Day Saints) 105–122, 178–182, 186, 191, 194, 198
Moroni 106–108
Mother Lode 181–186, 191–193, 201
Muscle Shoals (Tennessee River) 52

Nacogdoches 123, 125, 128, 142
Napoleon 63–69
Nashville 52, 53, 74
Natchez 52, 52n, 53
Nauvoo 110, 112, 119, 120
Navaho 147, 151, 201
Nebraska 84, 105, 113, 159, 244
Necessity, Fort 30
Neches River 144
Neill, Col. 132
Nephites 108
Nevada 116, 164, 166, 201
New Hampshire 34
New Helvetia 172
New Jersey 19
New Jersey Volunteers 49
New Mexico 122, 146–177, 186, 201
New Orleans 19, 62, 63–69, 78n, 87, 127
New Orleans Grays 127–130
New Wales Colony 19

New York 17, 19, 34, 54, 62, 109, 165, 186
Nez Perces 92–94, 99, 105, 163, 200; surrender of Chief Joseph 236; 237
Niagara 33
Nicollet, J. N. 158, 161
Niocabra River 210
Nolichucky River 36n
North Pacific Railroad 223, 241

Ogden, 118, 180
Ogden, P. S. 154, 163n
Oglala 200
Ohio 17–61, 62, 74, 109, 112
Ohio Company 19–23
Okeechobee, Lake 88, 89
Oklahoma (Indian Territory) 87, 159, 199, 204–208, 222, 223, 237, 244, 245
Old Spanish Trail 166
Omaha 113, 212, 219, 224, 241
Oneida 17
Onendaga 17, 19
Oregon 91, 94, 104, 105, 112, 114, 158, 159, 162, 165
Oregon Trail 87, 93, 96, 98, 161, 167, 184, 186, 206, 209
O'Riley, Peter 194–196
Osage 84, 86, 100, 148–150
Osceola, Chief 87, 88

Pacific Fur Company 91
Palmyra 106
Panama 184, 186, 191, 246
Pawnee 148, 150, 200
Payne, David L. 244
Pennsylvania 19, 21, 31–34, 38, 43
Pensacola, Fort 81, 83
Perry, Cdr. 77
Peters Colony 144
Peyster, Capt. de 50
Philippines 246
Phillips, John (Portugueese) 219n
Pico, Gov. Pio 169

Pierre's Hole 97–102
Pike's Peak 157, 161, 167, 197, 206
Pike's Peak Express 188
Pike, Z. M. 147–149
Pinckney, Thomas 62, 63
Pitt, Fort (Pittsburg) 31–34, 43, 55, 58
Pittsylvania Colony 19
Placerville 181
Platte 98, 104, 113, 114, 157–160, 197, 203, 206, 212, 219
Plum Creek 144, 203
Polk, President James Knox 104, 145, 167–170, 173, 176
Pontiac, Chief 31–35
Pony Express 187, 188
Popo Agie 97
Portland 94n
Potomac 23
Pottowattamies 148
Powder River 210–213, 226
Powell, Capt. James 215–220
Powell Mts. 36
Powell River 36
Powell River 36
Presque Isle, Fort 21, 32
Preuss, C. 160, 161
Price, Col. Sterling 174
Procter, Col. 76, 77
Promontory Point 190
Prophet, Chief 74, 75
Provo 118
Pueblo 122, 146, 167, 174
Pyramid Lake 164, 168

Quebec 26, 31
Queen's Rangers 49

Rangers 85, 150
Rapid City 238
Recovery, Fort 58–61
Red Cloud, Chief initiates Fetterman Massacre 212–220
Red Eagle, Chief 78–81
Red River 123, 200, 223, 241

Redstone Creek 21, 29–32
Reno, Fort 210–220
Reno, Maj. 226–236
Republican River 200
Reynolds, Col. J. J. 224
Rhode Island 34
Riley, Capt. 150
Rio Grande 131, 137, 145–147, 170, 172, 175, 204
Robertson, James 51–53
Rock River 84
Rocky Mountain Fur Company 97–103, 157, 158
Rogers, Maj. 31
Roosevelt, President Theodore 246
Rose, Moses account of flight from Alamo 135–136
Rosebud River 224, 226–236
Royal American Regiment (60th) 32
Russell, Majors and Waddell 187–190
Russell, William Green 197
Rush, J. J. 141
Russia 246

Sacramento 154, 155, 164–170, 176, 187, 188
St. Charles 70
St. Clair, Gen. 55–59
St. Joseph 32, 184, 187, 188
St. Lawrence 19
St. Louis 70, 74, 85, 93, 99, 117, 147, 157, 186
St. Paul 224
St. Pierre, Capt. 26, 27
St. Vrain, A. 157, 159
St. Vrain, W. 157
St. Vrain's Fort 157–161
Salmon River 105, 198, 237
Salt 151
Salt Lake City 110; setting out of 115; 118, 120, 121, 181, 186, 188
Sandusky, Fort 32, 34, 61
San Antonio 123, 126–145
San Bernardino 118

San Diego 175–177
San Domingo 64, 65
San Felipe de Austin 126, 131, 141, 142
San Fernando 154
San Francisco 103, 154, 155, 166, 169, 171, 180–186, 190
San Gabriel 146, 154, 156
San Gabriel Mts. 154
San Jacinto 141
San Joaquin 103, 154, 166, 168
San José 103
San Lorenzo, Treaty of 63
San Rafael
Sand Creek Massacre 207–209
Santa Anna leads expedition against Texas 126–144
Santa Fé 144–151, 156, 165, 172–175
Santa Fé Railroad 241
Santa Fé Trail 97, 149, 172, 186, 204
Santa Rita Mines 146, 156, 175
Santiago 246
Saratoga 42, 48
Sauk 76, 84
Sawyer, Col. James A. 210
Scott, Gen. 59–60
Scott, John 110
Scott, Gen. Winfield 84, 87, 172
Seminole 78–83, 87–89, 199n
Seneca 17, 19, 25, 34
Sesma, Gen. 140, 142
Sevier, John 48–50
Shawnee 19, 34–39, 60n, 74–78, 84, 99
Shelby, Isaac 48–50
Shenandoah 222
Sheridan, Maj.-Gen. Philip 221, 222
Sherman, W. T. 140, 222
Shoshoni 72, 92, 93, 105, 162, 200–202
Sierra Nevada 103, 118, 154, 157, 164, 168, 181, 184, 190–193

Silver City 146

Sioux 74, 76n, 84, 86, 87, 105, 159, 200–240

Sioux City 210

Sitting Bull makes medicine at Little Big Horn 223–236; killed at time of Wounded Knee 236–240

Six Nations 17, 19, 27, 34

Smith, Fort 214–220

Smith, Henry 132

Smith, Hyrum 112

Smith, Jedediah S. 96, 97

Smith, Joseph has visitation and collects plates from Mt. Cumorah 106–108; founds Church of Latter-Day Saints 109; 110, 111; killed at Carthage 112

Snake River 94n, 96–98, 104, 105, 160–163, 198

Snakes 72n, 200

Sonoma 171, 172, 176

Sonora 181

South Pass 87, 96–98, 114, 158–168, 184, 209

Spain 62–64, 70, 83, 123

Spalding, Solomon 109

Stanilaus River 181, 182, 191, 192

Stockton, Commodore 176

Strother, Fort 80

Sublette, Bill 97–102

Sublette, Cut-off 184

Superior, Lake 90

Sutter, Capt. A. 165–178, 183

Suwanee River 83

Sweetwater 98, 114

Tallapoosa River 81

Tallega 80, 81

Talleyrand 63–67

Tampa Bay 87, 88

Tanachariston, Half-King 19, 24–30

Taos 99, 122, 147, 151, 154, 157, 174

Tarleton, Col. 50

Taylor, Gen. Zachary 88–89; crosses Rio Grande 172

Techumseh, Chief 74–78

Ten Eyck, Capt. 218, 219

Tennessee 38, 43, 48–53, 64, 74, 83, 84, 104, 131, 132

Terry, Brig.-Gen. 224–236

Texas 123–146, 167, 186, 202–208, 221, 222, 242

Thames River 77, 78

Three Tetons 160

Tierney, J. H. 197

Tippecanoe Creek 75, 76

Tome, Col. 171

Tongue River 226

Toussaint de l'Ouverture 64

Transylvania Colony 42, 53

Travis, W. B. 126; his appeal from and death in, Alamo 132–137

Trent, William 21, 24, 28

Trinity River 128, 204

Truckee River (Salmon Trout) 164

Tubac 176

Tucson 176

Tulare Lake 168

Turtle Creek 21, 24

Tuscany, Duchy of 63

Twain, Mark 191, 192

Tyler, President John 145, 167

Uinta Mts. 167, 186

Union, Fort 96, 98

Union Pacific Railroad 242

U.S. Cavalry, 2nd 226–236

U.S. Cavalry, 3rd 224

U.S. Cavalry, 7th 224–240

U.S. Cavalry, 1st Volunteer (Rough Riders) 246

Urrea, Gen. 139, 140

Utah 97, 106, 116–121, 166, 194, 201

Utes 200, 201

Vancouver, Fort 93, 94, 98n, 163, 166
Vancouver Island 165
Vanderburgh, William H. 99, 102
Vargas, Don Diego de 147
Venango, Fort 21, 25, 26, 32, 33
Vera Cruz 170, 172n
Verde 154
Vermont 62
Vincennes 42–47, 55, 75n
Virginia 20–54, 69, 131
Virginia City Nevada 196
Virginia City Montana 210–213, 242

Wabash 19, 35, 42, 46, 55, 58, 75n
Wagon-Box Fight 219, 220
Waiilatpu 94, 163
Walker, J. R. 97, 103, 168
Walla Walla 92–94, 163
Wasatch Mts. 112, 114, 120, 162, 167, 186
Washington 105, 193
Washington-on-the-Brazos 140
Washington, Fort 55–59
Washington, Augustine 20
Washington, George visits French posts on Ohio 20–31; 56, 56n, 63
Washington, Lawrence 20
Washita 221, 224
Washoe 164, 193–196
Ward, Edward 28
Warner, Lake 164
Watauga River 36n, 38
Wayne, Gen. Anthony 58–61, 70
Wayne, Fort 61
Weber, Charles M. 181, 183
Wessells, Lt.-Col. 219
West Point 221
Westport 149n, 158, 161, 184
Wheeler, Rev. L. H. 90

Wheeling, Fort 58
Whitman, Rev. Marcus 94, 96, 161, 163, 236
Whitside, Maj. 238–240
Wichita 200, 208
Wilderness 221
Wilderness Trail 31, 40
Wilkes, Lt. Charles 161
Williamette River 94, 96, 181
Williamsburg 27, 42
Wills Creek 21–32
Wind River Mts. 97, 160
Wind River 160
Winnebago 76n
Winter Quarters 113, 117, 118
Wisconsin 61, 84, 90
Wolfe, Gen. 71
Worth, Gen. William J. 89
Worth, Fort 204
Wounded Knee 236–240, 242
Wovoka 237–240
Wyandots 61, 76n, 84
Wyeth, Nathaniel 99–101

Yankton 242
Yuma, Fort 186
Yuba River 181–183, 191
Yerba Buena 172
Yellowstone 73, 74, 96–98, 160, 202, 213, 223–237
Yorktown 53
Youghiogheny River 21–29
Young, Brigham leads Mormons to West 109–115; founds Salt Lake City and establishes Mormon State 115–122
Young, Ewing 151–156

Zendel, Louis 161
Zion 109